Henry Thoreau

Henry Thoreau

BACHELOR OF NATURE

by Léon Bazalgette

Translated by
Van Wyck Brooks

"My friend will be bold to conjecture.
He will guess bravely at the signifi-
cance of my words."

—*Autumn*

KENNIKAT PRESS
Port Washington, N. Y./London

HENRY THOREAU

Copyright 1925 by Harcourt, Brace and World, Inc.
Copyright 1953 by Van Wyck Brooks
Reissued in 1969 by Kennikat Press by arrangement with
Harcourt, Brace and World, Inc.
Library of Congress Catalog Card No: 74-85984
SBN 8046-0600-5

Manufactured by Taylor Publishing Company   Dallas, Texas

AUTHOR'S NOTE

ABUNDANTLY as Henry Thoreau informs us about himself in his Journal, his correspondence and his writings, his story, owing to the extreme reticence of his nature, would obviously be incomplete if it were reduced to these elements alone. To finish it remained the task of certain of his contemporaries, members of his circle. What the following pages owe to their invaluable testimony is so evident that it has not been thought necessary to emphasize this indebtedness by crowding the book with notes, as if it laid any claim to erudition. Nevertheless, this absence of references, ill-judged as it may be, must not be taken to imply that this portrait-study has been inspired by any desire less exacting than their own for the pure and simple truth. It merely means that behind this truth there was perhaps another, less often sought for, but no less moving after these vanished years.

HENRY THOREAU

BACHELOR OF NATURE

I

SOMEONE has died in the village: the man who bought the house on the square a year ago—the retired seaman.

A new face that has soon disappeared. Perhaps he had his reasons in choosing for his retreat this straggling village, twenty miles from the city from which he came. Or perhaps it had been enough for him to chance upon it one day, a city-dweller in search of a resting-place, to be won by the fine elms and maples that sheltered a gracious village, nestling among the low hills and deep woods and named after the slow-moving river that watered the broad meadows: Concord.

For a man who had lived in the bustle of a port after a life of adventure, everything there breathed a blessed peace. Nor was the silence of the fields too sedative for one who had come from a capital. Concord smiled in the agreeable spectacle of its thousand inhabitants, farmers, workmen, tradespeople, village officials, and formed a stopping-place for the stage-coach, the travellers, the carters who passed through it on their way to the high pastoral regions of New Hampshire. There was an inn, there were taverns where they served you a stiff glass of liquor, several stores, the Town Hall. There was the wooden church, too, and a fine stone jail that sheltered the county criminals. They even hanged people there now and then. A man who was accustomed to the world would not feel too remote from civilization.

I

Perhaps, too, the renown of a spot where the country-folk had offered a bold and decisive resistance to the troops of His Britannic Majesty, at the dawn of the Revolution, had affected his choice. But this memory of twenty-five years ago was of far less importance than the promise of the forests of pines and oaks and the fields and the footpaths along the slopes for a man who knew he was ill and was looking for a retreat where he could recover the strength of his lungs. . . In the pine-scented air of Concord floated the hope of a cure. And here he had indeed found himself at rest, forever. The pure air of the valley had not been able to restore the consumptive to health, no, nor the whey he used to take at the houses of his friends on the days when they made cheese, nor the simples from which he had made a syrup for his evil cough. A man of moderate height, but broad-backed, who would once have seized a barrel of molasses and carried it on his head. An old seaman, in short, dying now of consumption, at the age of forty-seven, in the year one of the nineteenth century, in the house on the square that he had just bought the year before, and going to his rest in the cemetery of a New England village, twenty miles from the ocean that he had put between himself and his kindred, the Thoreaus of Saint-Helier.

For he was a lad from the Old World who had set out to seek his fortune in the colonies, leaving behind him at nineteen a little green island in order to attempt a great continent of mystery and chance. In Jersey, where he was born, his family lived in comfort as people of sub-stance, of good Norman stock, speaking the old *langue d'oïl*. How would the old family name sound in another tongue? The mother was a certain Marie le Galais, who had had nine children and was in her seventy-ninth year at the moment when her John, over there, had just been laid, without her knowledge, in the Concord cemetery, laid there by the children he had left behind him. The late Philippe Thoreau, her husband, had taken over the business of his father, a wine merchant, with a branch in London, where two of their daughters had married extremely well. They belonged to the solid bourgeoisie, these Norman Thoreaus.

The younger son of a numerous family, John had not waited for his twentieth year before yielding to the invitation of a sailing vessel that plied between Boston and Saint-Helier, and he had set out, leaving his family to their casks on the little Channel island. John had gone to sea. On his first long voyage he was shipwrecked and suffered much. At Boston, along the docks, he found employment with various ship-chandlers. Then the war broke out; no more work. The Harbour was blockaded by the British fleet. He dug in the trenches round the town, under the fire of the guns. Then he shipped on a privateer that set out in pursuit of English vessels: for a Jerseyman, this was to follow one of the hardiest traditions of his race. At the end of the war his share of the prizes enabled him to open a shop on Long Wharf, where, with one partner, he carried on business for twenty years. John had not discredited his family; in the sale of molasses and other substantial products, he had resumed the family path of business and sound principles.

At twenty-seven he married Jane Burns, the child of a Scottish emigrant to Massachusetts and of the daughter of a Quaker who was a sailor too. When she died, after fifteen years, he owned, aside from the proceeds of his prosperous trade, the town-house which Jane had inherited from her grandfather David, the Quaker: a fine house worth all of $10,000. A widower, forty years old, with a houseful of children—the eldest, eight years

old, still a little girl—John Thoreau, the merchant of
Long Wharf, took for his second wife a certain Widow
Kettell. Shortly after this, finding his health affected,
he sold out his business and retired to the country to
live on his income.

And now the house he had bought on the square at
Concord, thanks to the handsome fortune amassed in
these twenty years of trade, sheltered a woman widowed
anew and the little children of whom the oldest boy,
John, second of the name, was fourteen at the death of
his father—and four others bearing in their breast a
heritage that weighed more heavily than the few thousand dollars that were to come to each of them. . . .

A child was born on the Minot farm, on the Eastern
edge of the village, by that road down there, a little to
one side, which they called, no one knew why, the
Virginia Road. Perhaps because it dived down into
a vague country, in the other direction from the road
that led to the market-place.

But there was no need to take the child to the market-
place. The father with his wife and his two chicks,
Helen, not yet five, and John, who was three, found
themselves there, for want of anything better, because
his mother-in-law Minot, left a widow for the second
time, had given him a chance to turn his ability to
account on the farm. This agriculturist by accident
was the eldest son of the old sailor who had come to
Concord to die: John Thoreau II, now thirty years old
and a man upon whom fortune, far from smiling, had
turned its bare teeth.

No luck yet for good little John. Nevertheless, the
paternal shade had guided him along the right path: he
should undoubtedly have been a merchant, like his
father, like the Thoreaus of Saint-Helier. Good blood

4

would tell. After a year of school to complete his primary studies begun in Boston, he had lost no time in apprenticing himself to their neighbour, who kept a store and added to the dignity of a merchant that of parish Deacon. Thus the potent sisters Grocery and Piety took the little store-clerk by the hand. Then he enlarged his experience of the world and affairs at a small dry-goods store in the little town of Salem. The kindly epoch still existed when people were not afraid of humanising trade by offering you a glass of liquor over the counter, when you had made a sizable purchase.

At twenty-one, rich in practical knowledge acquired elsewhere and with a few bank-notes borrowed from his good step-mother, John had returned to Concord to open a store. The beginning was most promising, but he took a partner with whom he had a misunderstanding—the result was a law-suit, which he won. Meanwhile the store had failed. He had to begin all over again. Elizabeth, his older sister, had married and gone to live in Maine. John followed and joined them, establishing himself at Bangor with his brother-in-law, on the edge of the wilderness, where the Indians were their best customers. Was John homesick, or was the trade insufficient to maintain two managers? However it was, Concord soon saw him back again, and at twenty-five, like a wise little man, he married there.

This charming, sprightly Cynthia certainly brought our brave John the greatest happiness of his life. But she brought him nothing else; so the two of them set out together to try their fortune in Boston, the great city. Who could tell, if one had had no luck thus far in villages and small towns, perhaps one was cut out for success in a capital. Not in this case, not this time. The solidest wealth they acquired was a new baby, John, third of the name, following Helen, born the

same year as their marriage. And then they returned
to Concord, to the house of Cynthia's mother, the farm
where Cynthia herself had been living at the time of
her marriage. Home enough for a young family without
any definite situation; before tempting chance elsewhere, a little farming, to help the mother-in-law,
would serve in the interval. And then the maternal
presence would not be unprofitable for Cynthia, during
her imminent confinement.

Little chick, born by chance on an out-of-the-way
farm, when your grandfather died in a big house on the
town square, are you as poor as all that at the moment
when you are cast upon this earth where he, the old
privateer, has been resting for sixteen years? In your
veins the calm blood of the Thoreaus is united with the
impetuous blood of the Dunbars; from this mixture you
will be able to make something perhaps, if you have a
touch of fancy. Your father is a fine, sturdy fellow,
serious and kind-hearted, who is doing his best to make
his way with his three little children. If he has not
developed into a great commercial strategist, fate has
made up for it by giving him a superior wife. A very
good thing, for your arrival in the world has not im-
proved their fortune.

No more than her husband was Cynthia a child of
Concord. They were of the same age. Just as he had
come as a boy, with his people, so she had come as a
little girl, with her mother, from New Hampshire,
where the father whom she had never known, Asa
Dunbar, had died. Cynthia was the daughter of a
minister, a minister who had been at the same time a
counsellor-at-law and a zealous freemason. On the
maternal side, the great crisis of the Revolution, which
had given the first John Thoreau an opportunity to
amass a handsome capital, had ruined the family, who

had once been important and influential gentlefolk. Colonel Jones, her grandfather, who, with his eight sons, had taken the side of the Crown, had shared the lot of the vanquished: confiscation of their land, imprisonment, banishment. The chivalrous and adventurous race of the Joneses had left their mark upon Cynthia in traits as pronounced as the obscurity of her husband's character: a taste for elegance, a gift of eloquence. She knew how to talk, and there was as much conviction in her words as in his silence. She loved to set the lively tone of a bow of ribbon singing on a piece of cloth, like a declaration of independence. She was not afraid to startle people by a freedom of speech that was sharp enough to be malicious. It was a handsome girl with dark eyes that John had taken for his wife, with the calm assurance of these little serious, sedate men. Her charming voice, when she sang, the animation of her talk, the vividness of her replies had made up for his abysses of silence and self-effacement. Happiest of harmonies, secured by an unassuming man whose wife talks and is cheerful and has enough wit for two. John and Cynthia formed one of those happy unions to which one brings genius, the other his lack of genius, and both have courage enough to meet the ups and downs of existence.

Cynthia, the youngest of her family, had two sisters, Sophia and Louisa. She had the luck to possess a brother also, the gem of the Dunbars, the rare flower of generations that had multiplied their branches to blossom at last in the alliance of a minister with the daughter of a gentleman-farmer. Charles Dunbar had taken the sunny side of life. He had not asked it to make dollars grow on the counter of a shop or in the furrows of husbandry where a man strains his back, greatly to the detriment of his good-humour; he had let it go its own way, since it was full of amusing things and he himself was a strong man, capable of mastering it. Not stupid enough to settle down, he rambled from village to village, an eternal apprentice whose apprenticeship pursued its course especially in taverns. A splendid voice, bursting from his athletic frame, was enough to assure him success among his jolly comrades. But Uncle Charles was also an incomparable wag. It is not enough to draw the long bow and talk well in a tavern to put the company in a cheerful mood: you must show what you are. Then you do astonishing tricks with cards, toss your hat into the air and catch it again on the top of your head, swallow your nose, or juggle away the knives, forks and plates on the table, refusing to restore them until the landlord agrees not to charge you for your meal. And as if this were not enough, you seize a ten-foot ladder, stand it upright without any support, clamber up to the last rung and descend on the other side, pushing it back with your foot. Yes, and handsomely. Would any of these gentlemen like to have a try? . . . But old Charles's great feat was wrestling. With him wrestling was a primal, necessary function, like eating and drinking. In the most natural way in the world, he would walk into your house with the flattering remark, "Come along, I'm going to throw you. Out with you." And you had to go out, spread some straw in the yard and place yourself in position. Of course he did throw you. And then he was as pleased as if you had invited him to the best of dinners at your house. This passion for wrestling seized him suddenly as sensual desire seizes people who are badly brought up. And you never had to be afraid that he would break your ribs: an accomplished wrestler, he would displant you neatly, like an artist and a gentleman. In this vocation he had lost all his teeth at the

8

age of twenty-one, which did not prevent him from having every blessed one of them later on. Perhaps they had grown again—you never can tell with these fire-eaters.

To judge him from this unconventional manner of living, anyone might suppose that Charles would have been the victim of bad habits. A great mistake. He did not gamble, he drank only in reason, he did not smoke—at most, for the sake of politeness, he would take a pinch of snuff if you offered it to him. His dress was always correct and his language free from coarseness. Among his rare privileges Charles possessed that of suddenly falling asleep in the very midst of whatever he happened to be doing. Sometimes, with his razor in his hand, before his mirror, without any reason he would succumb to sleep; and in order to conform to the strict observance of the Sabbath which, as we know, prohibits sleep, he found it necessary to devote himself on that day to some absorbing occupation, such as sprouting potatoes. In pursuing these artistic hobbies one does not gather very much of this world's goods, but he had found more enviable advantages: a reputation solidly established in various public places and the promise of restoring to the Lord a soul as fresh as on the day when it had been confided to his care. Charles Dunbar, you are the salt of your family. Your kindred should bless you. And as for this baby nephew who is just born, to have an uncle who can hold himself in equilibrium on the top of an unsupported ladder and possesses that formidable voice which, from the strand, hails a ship at sea—what self-command this will give him later, and what carrying-power for anything he may have to say or proclaim. . . If he is seized with a desire to leap over some obstacle, his legs will remember you who, while leading your oxen, sprang over the

yoke with your feet together, once, twice, a mere nothing to amuse the lads of the saw-mill whose eyes popped
out of their heads at this phenomenon.

When she was eight years old, Cynthia had set out by
sea on a ramshackle boat, with her mother and her two
sisters, to see her Jones uncles, the refugees in Maine
and Canada. It was shortly after this rather risky
voyage that the mother and the daughter had come to
Concord, where the former had remarried and the
latter, fifteen years later, had fixed her destiny, sought
her fortune, by uniting her poverty with John's.

To their possessions had now been added this youngster born on the farm. The 12th of July, 1817, was
inscribed on the tablets of the household. Also the date
of baptism, three months later, when, stoically, uttering
no shrill cries, Henry David (this latter name in memory
of Uncle David, who had just died) entered upon the
Christian life. One enters as one can. But whatever
might be the virtue of the baptismal water and the
minister of the parish, Dr. Ripley, would it prevail
against the farm and the old deserted road on the edge
of which the child had been born? Glance at this farm:
it is an ancient two-storied dwelling, with plank walls
discoloured with age, a setting as appropriate for the
birth of a god as for the coming of this poor little soul.
It stands on a knoll where the grass grows at will. No
fence. In front, a running brook. Around it, meadows
and orchards, where you smell the good soil and the
turf. The nearest neighbour is a long way off. The old
winding road leads to no point whither the interests
of the villagers call them; and left to itself, it smiles at
its turnings, its ruts, at all the weeds on its banks,
inviting the fields it passes to share its delightful futility.
The family occupies one wing of the dwelling, the other
half being inhabited by some people who also have a

little boy, in whose company John, with the authority
of his three years, drives the turkeys to pasture.

For the rest, the revenues of the farm were so small
that the mother-in-law had barely enough to live on.
Eight months after Henry's birth, the household went
to rejoin her in the red house where she lived at the end
of the village. The head of a family whose peregrina-
tions had not yet brought him wealth tried to think of
some better means of providing bread for these three
little importunate beaks. One must manage somehow.
What remained of the paternal heritage was scarcely
worth talking about: the numerous minors having once
grown up, the lawyers and the trustees had left it nothing
but a pale memory. At the death of the Widow Kettell,
each of the children of the old sailor had pocketed a few
crumbs, and that was the end of it. And John's share
of the Boston house was already mortgaged. He had to
put his wits together. John had an idea. A vocation is
not so easily renounced, especially when it is confirmed
by the voice of one's ancestors. Suppose they were
to try Chelmsford over there, ten miles away, and take
a store. Cynthia could wait on the customers, while
John, who was very fertile in manual resources in spite
of his modest air, would try to find work outside. He
could paint signs and do odd jobs, and they would get
on somehow.

Henry's Aunt Sarah had already taught him to walk
when, at sixteen months, he took part in the exodus to
Chelmsford. They remained there two years and a
half, keeping a grocery with a bar, near the church.
They sold spirits. They were honest and upright. But
it's always the same story: fortune, which so joyously
allows herself to be captured by dare-devils, has not
even the shadow of a smile for these honest and reserved
little Johns, even when they offer it a glass over the

counter. A pity, but there was no need to be discouraged because a fourth child had been born. This one was a daughter; she was going to bring them happiness and they would call her Sophia. Once more they set out to try the capital, where people were rolling in money and might be willing to let a few crumbs drop into the till of an honest man. They found a perch in the southern part of Boston, calling on the way at Concord. During this journey a pair of infant eyes that were hardly open as yet to the images of the world were impressed by the glimpse of a wild pond in the setting of an immemorial forest. The gaze of a tender little creature, who knew nothing about the gold they had set out to win among the rich, secretly absorbed the lustre of this pearl.

In two years of the great city they had three abodes. The town offered every facility for sending to school a little boy of five, but there was no great harvest for his parents to reap there. They were obliged to give it up as hopeless. These removals had brought the young household no success.

There was nothing to do but to return to the fold, to the house on the square in which Thoreau the father had died, the father upon whom fortune had smiled, and where John's two sisters lived. It was the last resource. John had been an apprentice in the village, he knew everybody there, and there the little ones had been born. After all, it might be better to live in poverty in Concord than to tempt chance elsewhere. Off for old Concord. An honest little man, pursued by ill fortune, with four chicks and their mother, was to seek his destiny henceforth in the shadow of the great elms.

You will soon be six years old. Your parents have toiled and tried every expedient to make ends meet, but

for you who do not enter into these domestic consider-
ations life is a long holiday. All Concord is spread out
on your lap, like a great book full of pictures and songs.

You go forth and meet the adventures the roads offer.
A dog passes, a man, a cart. The great elms sigh. A
cock calls in the distance of the grey-white village. Two
neighbours are soberly gossiping. The first beautiful
drops of a shower drum on the leaves and the wooden
sidewalk. You have no desire to turn back. The little
girl ahead of you is hurrying to the store. All these and
how many other marvels, from morning to bedtime, the
long stretch of unmeasured hours, are all for you, you
who are not a king's son, but the little Henry of the
man who lives on the village square, in the centre of a
bustling, confused, spangled universe, striped with sun-
rays and surprises.

You are growing, and about you as you grow the
world takes form. When you are big and able to stand
firmly on your feet, people depend on you and entrust
you with important commissions: leading the cow to
pasture, running on errands in the village. When you
are very big you are allowed to do everything; and if
you have a brother who is much bigger than you there
are no limits to the conquests you can make together.
You are bound only by the four points of the compass.
The country about the village stretches away to the
impossible. You have a knife in your pocket, with
which you can whittle anything you please, a whistle,
a weapon, a slingshot, a wagon. You make a trap.
You rove on wild adventures through the sunny meadows, gorge yourself with huckleberries, run about,
playing Indian, dig a cave, build a hut and store it with
provisions. At twelve you go hunting with your
brother. To feel the fowling-piece hanging from your
shoulder, to be the crafty master of the life and death

of the creatures who have no suspicion of your overwhelming power, to lie in wait for them, press the gun
to your shoulder, take aim, see the animal roll or tumble
over: fearful joys.   There will be others later, but will
they have the pure taste of these?   When you penetrate
into these deep woods, a swarming world opens before
you that probably has no end.   No village, no houses,
no parents, no fences any more; nothing but the great
pines and the solemn oaks, assembled like conspirators
to hold counsel far from listening ears.   You are alone
and very small under those heads touching one another
up there, but you feel no fear.   You are armed, and,
besides, your big brother is with you.   In the middle of
the woods there is a pond towards which the arches of
foliage bend amid their garlands of wild vines.   You
come there to fish for pouts and breams.   You have
brought your lunch to spend the whole day there, as if
you were on a desert island, on the edge of this smooth
water that mirrors the patriarchal trees.   Night has
fallen; you have made a fire on the stones and before
going away you seize the red brands and shake them,
describing fiery circles in the air, then throw them into
the water where they hiss and go out.   Then, when the
flames are dead, you find yourself once more in the
dense night, in a darkness thick enough to cut, and groping your way you return to the village with your fish—
two Concord boys, who scour the earth barefoot the
better to possess it.

To be a Concord boy is to be intoxicated with the
joy of the river, the two rivers that unite here, the
sluggish one and the lively one, and pull as well together
as John and Cynthia.   It is to swim by the hour in the
cove with your comrades, under the arbour of pine
branches that shelters your duck-like sports.   In the
spring the overflowing river floods the meadows—an

immense sheet of water from which the trees emerge: it is no longer fifty yards from bank to bank but half a mile wide and more, like a great lake with gulls flying over it. There is hay-time and the cranberry season; there are the Cliffs from which you descry the faraway peaks where you have never gone, where perhaps the world ends—since over there is the empire of the setting sun. You sail a boat with a paddle or a mast, drink in the fragrance of the banks, the waterplants, the crumpled mint-leaves, or you carry your line with you and are engrossed for hours, dividing your attention between the mystery of the depths that spread quivering up to your float and the squadrons of clouds that cleave the great sky spread out over the meadows. At these times you encounter now and then an old fisherman, leathery and taciturn, who blends into the bank of the river, his ancient cloak having taken its colour with time, and returns at evening with slow steps to his little shanty on the edge of the village. When he is fishing you have no desire to disturb him; he looks so grave. He is not amusing himself, he is conducting a rite—the rite of the compleat angler. No one pays any attention to the old chap: but Henry knows him well and is attracted by his silence. Perhaps he has been there since the time of the Indians; he is ageless. This must be old Father Musketaquid, who is on the most intimate terms with all the fishes.

And then the immense charm of the passage of an occasional barge on the river, come who knows whence? —the rivers, whence come they? whither do they go?— floating soundlessly towards nowhere. One day you see that barge moored at the edge of a meadow; the following day it has disappeared. To what race do these men on board belong? What language do they speak? They have come from the world outside and yet they know the river so well. . . When will they pass again? On these boats are piled hogsheads full of lime or bricks or iron-ore, with wheel-barrows. How do they manage not to sink under this formidable weight? And yet, when you climb up there, it is firm, it does not give. Strange. And these men who, they say, sleep in their boats and live there as Henry lives in a house on the village square. . . How he would love to sleep in a boat too, eat there, light a fire, spend the whole night on the water! There are people who insist that these boats have sails like the boats that go on the ocean; they have seen them. How can you believe that? They pass like the birds, conjuring up other lands and a whole unknown world to which the river may lead, a world that is certainly impenetrable. Henry dashes off with his brother to feast on this marvel. But he has still more beautiful sensations. Once a year a group of men with reddish brown faces, altogether different from the men of the village, come and camp under a tent in the meadows. They make baskets and offer you collars of glass beads. Among themselves they speak the language of sorcerers. They have a canoe which they manage in the strangest fashion. The big people tell you that they were once the masters of the country, in the days of old Tahataivan, before such a place as Concord ever existed. If you had a canoe and were one of the Redskins, you would not make baskets; you would spend your time hunting and fishing and making expeditions; you would be one of the kings of the country.

There is, of course, a school to which they send you, for it is a fine thing to know how to read straight off, like your father, who reads the newspaper. But the class is only an interlude between two sessions of school out of doors. The river, the ponds are hard and smooth as steel; it is the season for skating and sleighing-parties on the snow. What does it matter that your sled has no iron runners and the other boys make fun of it? You love it just the same because it is your own, and nothing in the world could induce you to give it up. When you know how to read, write and cipher, you still have a great many things to learn, for your family dreams of a more brilliant future for you than that of a storekeeper. So you enter the Academy founded by the well-to-do for boys who want to become learned men. You must master Greek, Latin, French, plunge into the classics, and grind away till you are sixteen.

To follow the course at the Concord Academy and become better educated than your parents is all very fine, for Concord has so many ways of compensating you. But afterwards? These ambitious parents have conceived the bold project of sending their younger boy to college to learn what the Concord Academy cannot teach him. To leave Concord. . . Ah, how desolate the Greek, the Latin, the French, this stupendous human learning looks at the thought of all you must leave behind in order to fathom its mysteries! . . . How heavy your heart is, at sixteen, Henry, with these early tender affections to which you are to bid an abrupt farewell as you set out for Harvard. . . you, the son of the little store-keeper, to serve your time in a department store of learning.

II

At the age of twenty the student Henry Thoreau left the university with his bachelor's degree. This was the recompense for four years passed away from Concord, four years save for the vacations and the time he had returned to spend with his family because of ill-health. As for this title, he may have given it its due—he was certainly not inclined to over-value it.

Upon entering college, he had left a village environment where equality was not a joke but a daily observance—left this environment to find himself, the child of small folk, suddenly thrown among the offspring of the fortunate ones of this world. In spite of the part-scholarship which they had obtained for him, his parents, his sister Helen, his aunts, in order to provide for the cost of his studies, had been obliged to deprive themselves. At college also, to be sure, a kind of equality prevailed among the students; but there it was an equality with a difference. He was a country boy among these wide-awake young men in whose eyes he was from the village indeed. Since his parents, his sister, had been obliged to scant themselves to purchase his right to a share of learning, he was inclined to feel certain things a little differently from the way he would have felt them if he had been the son of a senator.

He was assigned to a little room on a top floor of the hive. This was natural enough. Natural too that the young men in the neighbouring rooms liked to kick up a shindy when he wanted to work. But it only made him react the more strongly, and he dreamed.

This environment exhaled an odour that rather annoyed him, not so much because it had nothing in common with that of the new-mown hay of the Concord meadows but because it was the odour of an exclusive humanity, comfortably quartered in first-class state-rooms while the common passengers made shift as they could between decks. No doubt there were some charming fellows among these young men, and most of them were generous enough to treat a poor comrade as if he were one of themselves. And was it their fault, these college boys, if their papas travelled in the first class and the atmosphere that surrounded them was a first-cabin atmosphere? Among these sons of the well-to-do, future lawyers, future ministers, future diplomats, captains of industry, pillars of society, Henry felt out of his element. He was anything but in tune with them. With a secret pride in his plebeian hands, he exaggerated his reserve, his remoteness, his stiffness in the presence of these boys who knew so little of the world of toil. The hand he held out to them was nerveless. He was a Henry always absorbed in his own thoughts, with his eyes on the ground as if he were seeking something that did not grow there. He was, indeed, somewhere else. If he had hardly any real comrades, it was because he had no desire to make them. These well-dressed, jovial souls, with their special recreations, their fine parties, their student manners, left him surprisingly cold. Their sisters, their mothers had not had to deprive themselves to pay for their studies. He was the son of a little village shop-keeper, with a soul that already aspired very much higher than the great stores where they were to lord it.

Besides, he was decidedly rustic in his appearance, this oddly dressed scholarship-holder. He should have been dressed in black; it was the rule of the institution. The colleges see the world in black and he was here to adapt himself to their vision. But the only suit Henry had was a green one which his father had had made for him at great expense, and he was obliged to put it on every morning. There were evenings when, as he undressed, he wished that its greenness were still greener so as to be even more conspicuous among all these black backs. A good olive green is less shabby-looking than a black coat that is always threatening to let you see the thread. You must never let the thread be seen in this fine black-coated world.

And then in his secret soul homesickness tormented him. Everything he loved was out there, and it left a great void in his eighteen-year-old heart. When he heard the thrush singing in the college yard, Harvard ceased to exist, the library, the examinations he was preparing for. . . Nothing remained but a dejected prisoner in his prison. Sometimes, as he bent over a textbook, the meaning of the words he read was lost in the sound of the wind that came to him in gusts from the woods of Concord, and with a wild bound the fancy of the exile leaped over the wall and sprang towards those dear haunted spots. It required a great effort to recall the heart-sick fugitive and set himself to work again in the cell of that austere building. At such moments as these, when he compared the quality of what he had left behind him and the cost of what he was acquiring, how could he help feeling in his bitterness that what he was missing was beyond price? The only remedy was to bury himself in study. All his free time Henry passed in the library, in the company of the classics or the old English poets, from Chaucer to the Elizabethans, who spoke to his solitary heart, a habit that rendered him still more unsociable and so isolated him that he felt, in this buzzing community, as if he were doing penance in the desert. That natural gravity, which had caused him to be nicknamed "the Judge" by his little playfellows of the village sleighing-parties, had not been softened by solitary study, his impressions as a college boy, his loneliness—far from it. The already taciturn child, who had given himself up to play passionately but with an utter seriousness, ultra-sensitive to everything that pricked his self-esteem, became still more self-absorbed the more he grew during these lean years. The hedgehog remained rolled up. It was as if he had something as precious as his life to safeguard and was protecting it fiercely. This student in his little room on the top floor was not one of those creatures that people tame.

Henry was not conspicuous for his success. He had made a good record in his studies, working hard to please himself. But in the examinations he had not shone. It was even remarked, not without surprise, among his professors, that this studious, gifted boy took no particular pains to distinguish himself; in the holder of a scholarship this was almost an offense and they had made him feel it. Thanks to the benefactors of the college his studies were partly paid for by the revenues of an old farm which he had to go and collect himself, braving the watch-dogs and the ill-humour of the unwilling farmer. In any case, it was a favour. A beneficiary should show his gratitude by exerting himself to the utmost and carrying off all the honours. When you are poor, you are expected to make up for this fault by your vigorous performances in composition.

He had read enormously aside from the curriculum and his preparation for examinations. And he had learned how to express himself. His early prose exhibits that firmness which is only acquired through a certain quality of mind after much thought and the assiduous following of the old masters. In some of his compositions and letters he reveals a surprising independence, that of a boy who sturdily believes in another civilization than that of the "civilized" and turns aside from the beaten roads to follow a road of his own where his instinct directs him better than the guide-posts. Hear this: "Our Indian is more of a man than the inhabitant of a city. He lives as a man, he thinks as a man, he dies as a man. The latter, it is true, is learned. Learning is Art's creature, but it is not essential to the perfect man; it cannot educate. . ." Words of a solitary in the midst of the crowd, written in a temple of knowledge with the accent of faith and the pungency of revolt. At eighteen, he does not fear to make an apology for extremism, denouncing half-way solutions, the herd-spirit, the fear of being singular, the cowardice that follows the fashion and makes men "mere tools in the hands of others." Henry wearing his green coat among the black costumes, far from apologizing for this incongruity, vigorously translates it into a rule of conduct. "We are a nation of speculators, stockholders and money-changers," he writes before his nineteenth year, hinting at a native literature still to be born in the New World, "the establishment of a pure and nervous language." And at the moment when he leaves Harvard, he attacks in his Commencement oration the spirit of lucre, the cur-spirit, with a vivacity, a conviction that slightly oversteps the tone of university controversy: "Could one examine this beehive of ours from an observatory among the stars, he would perceive an unwonted degree of bustle in these later ages. . . Where he found one man to admire with him his fair dwelling-place, the ninety and nine would be scraping together a little of the gilded dust upon its surface. . . This curious world which we inhabit is more wonderful than it is convenient; more beautiful than it is useful; it is more to be admired and enjoyed than used. The order of things should be somewhat reversed: the seventh should be man's day of toil, wherein to earn his living by the sweat of his brow; and the other six his Sabbath of the affections and the soul. . ."

He had emerged from the factory, but it had not succeeded in casting him in its mould. On the contrary, "the Judge" had judged it. It formed one of the wheels of a society which he was beginning to understand. Between mathematics, literature, the classics, the dead languages, some living truths had crept in, upon which Henry had seized, and he brought the latter home rolled up in his diploma like some happy find. With that society there, as it appeared to him, he could have very little to do. It was a machine of which the fly-wheels, the chains, the pinions were all too apparent to him. From the whole apparatus falsehood leaked like a sickening oil. Look sharp, my boy: if you do not, you will be snapped up.

All this knowledge which he had acquired in his four years of probation in the factory he measured with a lucid glance. An untutored fellow with the right quality could put in its place all the science of the colleges. A flash of the most everyday reality was enough to expose the poverty of a culture that formed such ignorant beings, such paupers in the face of life: little gentlemen with white hands who came there to be confirmed in the pale tradition of their class, "to study chemistry and not learn how [one's bread] is made. . ."

At the same time he had undergone victoriously the ordeal of this famous culture. It had done him no harm. He regretted nothing: everything he had acquired, scanty as its weight might be in the destiny of a man, he would be able to put to his own use, employ for his own ends. He was going to dispose of knowledge; knowl-

edge was not to have the best of him. It was a very
good thing to possess, as an additional qualification,
like a garment you put on when you need it and hang up
again later when it burdens you. Others might take
home from Harvard the beautiful uniform that people
don for a lifetime. Henry had returned with his old
green jacket.

Since he had come back, his family had observed a
certain change in his replies, his attitude, his judgments.
This decisive tone of their Henry and his radical views
on the world were a little disturbing to those good
people who had scraped together their dollars to send
him off to college but had never possessed themselves
an ounce of rebelliousness. So that was what they
taught at Harvard? Insubordination? His aunts
could hardly believe their ears; their nephew, expressing
himself in this condemnatory fashion? His sister Helen
who loved him dearly and firmly believed in him, Helen
who, from her salary as a teacher, had contributed to
pay Henry's college expenses, even mildly urged him to
moderate his expressions a little. The good girl had
her illusions about the fond authority of an older sister:
with his uncompromising sincerity he ceased for a while
to write to her. She had not suspected that her brother
would come home from Harvard with other resources
besides "the old joke of a diploma." She had remained
the same Helen as ever, and he, after these years, had
become a Henry multiplied by four.

In this month of August, 1837, a boy of twenty
returned home who had mastered everything that
college had to offer, in the books and outside the books.
No need to press on to an A.M.; he knew quite enough.
In this respect, if not in others, the years at Harvard
were certainly worth the sacrifices that Helen and the
father and the good aunts had made. The certitudes he

had brought back were even worth the sacrifice the college boy had made of his free years of adolescence.

And now the problem was to earn his bread. The "old joke of a diploma" might help him just the same in finding a livelihood.

Since his final return to Concord, his father had undertaken a new business. He was manufacturing pencils. After the grocery and the odd-jobbing, this was a step up: a manufacturer, the creator of that beautiful thing, the hard casing with its marrowy flesh that a pencil is, destined to the noblest uses—reckoning up accounts, taking notes, drawing. For twenty years a pencil factory had existed at Concord when John Thoreau cleverly bethought himself of setting up in competition. It was rather bold for a little man who had been so unlucky hitherto and had such slender resources.

Before his college years and during his long vacations, Henry had lent a hand in the paternal workshop. It was their means of livelihood and the aid of the two boys was necessary. They worked together under the name of "John Thoreau and Son." At the end of the summer of 1836, when a serious illness had obliged him to return home for several months, Henry had even accompanied his father to New York, whither they went to put their merchandise on the market. It was his first visit to the great metropolis, this visit as a commercial traveller who had come to offer the city folk an article that had issued from his village hands. The people of the metropolis obtained the softest and most perfect pencils directly from Europe; would they have any use for his stuff? Wait, you people of the metropolis, you spoiled folk who are so hard to please, one of these days we are going to show you something just as perfect, something better than your beautiful pencils from abroad.

But this was no sort of destiny for a college boy. Not for the sake of manufacturing pencils had he spent four years in college at the expense of his family. It would be disloyal to defeat their hopes, and circumstances at home were in rather a bad way. Now that he had his degree he would have to try something else. His Aunt Louisa was a schoolmistress, and so was Helen; John was very clever at teaching. They set him his example. Why should not he attempt the same thing? Why not, indeed? This was the first experiment to be tried with the armament of the "old joke."

As a matter of fact, he had already had some experience in teaching. During his long college vacations, to assist his family in paying the other half of his expenses, he had followed the custom of students who are not born with a silver spoon in their mouths, and taught a little, as an assistant master, in the neighbouring villages; visiting in this way at Canton, just outside Boston, he had even learned a little German from the minister with whom he had stayed. This had brought him in a few dollars, and he had studied himself while he was teaching others. And now the time had come to find employment as a schoolmaster. To find such a position at Concord itself would be ideal, and it so happened that there was a vacancy in the Town School and he was accepted. In September, the month after his return, he was established there.

So there he was, one of the wheels of the machine. The respectable citizens had confided their children to him to teach them, not simply the three R's, but sound principles as well. It was the immemorial Christian custom to inculcate sound principles upon the young by means of the rod. Henry, however, was not the flogging kind. He was going to talk to the young hopefuls as young hopefuls, appealing to their feelings as good boys. Everything went well or seemed to be going well; but there were eyes on the watch. These eyes saw what this innovation was leading to, the ruin of the moral foundations upon which Concord and the world rested. The master, this enemy of rods, had to reckon with the committee in charge of the school, one of whom was a certain Deacon—that same worthy man perhaps who also kept a store and with whom, not long before, the elder Thoreau had served his commercial apprenticeship. He or his like, it matters little: a guardian of the sound traditions. Whereupon His Morality the Deacon represented to the young master that his method was a menace to the discipline of the school. It was inadmissible. Henry had been appointed to a function that included the ritual distribution of the rod to scholars who deserved it. There were always in a class scholars who deserved the rod. He did not see them. He was not carrying out his function.

Very well. Since flogging formed a part of the work ordained in exchange for a salary, that very day the master took at random and punished conscientiously six boys of whom one at least was never to know what had suddenly seized this gentle master and was to cherish a bitter memory of him. . . So there, Henry has earned his money. And now, good-bye, Deacon, good-bye, all of you. Go and find another master who will flog your school for you. . . Henry had been a teacher for fifteen days. The wheel had hardly been put in place before it had sprung off.

Too bad, but he could go back to pencil-making. It was not exactly the thing he had dreamed of, but it was free work into which the Deacons did not thrust their pious noses. If he was obliged to ply the ferule to earn his living, he would go and pick huckleberries and sell them in the market. Or fish for pike and peddle them in the village, or take up any sort of work that wouldn't oblige him to report to committeemen.

In spite of all this, he still wanted a school. He had the ability and it meant independence. Working with his father, he was a help, but he was dependent on his family, and they found it hard enough to make ends meet. The fall, the winter passed. How much he would have liked to go out and snatch a little air! There were moments like that. The surroundings of his childhood had been so dear to him that, stoical as he was by nature, the tears came to his eyes at the thought that some day he might have to leave them. But people had affronted him; he loathed his fellow-villagers. He wanted to push out into the world. But he wanted to go with John. To set out without John would be to sacrifice the best part of himself. For John was much more than his brother, he was the cream of all possible brothers. John the third was a delightful being who made him think that his grandfather, John the first, had crossed the ocean simply to prepare for his coming and make Concord an inestimable gift. John was a true Thoreau like Helen but with an exquisite charm, a flavour that belonged to him alone. Gifted as he was, none of his other gifts was equal to this faculty of making himself loved. He was a warm presence like a ray of sunlight and the freest-hearted companion to work with or to go off with, hunting, exploring—the two of them, Indian chiefs, older brother, younger brother, similar in their tastes, the gaiety of the one multiplied by the happiness of the other. Everything became possible, easy, everything brightened up, when John was with you. Would Concord have been Concord if Henry had not explored it and made it his own, dur-

ing the whole of his childhood, with this perfect play-
fellow?

Spring broke. Helen and Sophia would soon be
leaving to take up their teaching at Roxbury. John was
at present a schoolmaster at Taunton. Henry wrote to
him. A friend of the family, settled in the West, assured
him that they could have a fine situation if they were to
go out there and open a school. What if they were to
set off together? . . . What do you say, brother? If
we were to go out there and set up a *real* cabin, far
away from these deacons and respectable numskulls,
in some raw, half-built town or out on the open prairie?
We could borrow money for the expenses of the journey,
and as for the rest we have workingman's hands, we are
not afraid of adventure, we could pull through. What
couldn't we do, the two of us together? . . . Henry
was pressing. Stagnation weighed on him; on the river
the ice was breaking. He longed to undertake something. It was high time to begin. And if his brother
was willing. . . A few weeks later he heard of a school
that was going to be opened in Virginia. He was certainly going down there if they wanted him. . . And
soon after the question of another school came up, in
Maine, where his cousins were. He went up there and
came back the same hungry Henry as before, in spite of
the brilliant certificate he was able to show, signed
with fine names, among them R. W. Emerson.

Well, then, if they didn't want him and his diploma
anywhere he would change his plans. That was settled.
His father and mother lived in a house in the centre of
the village: it was big enough for them to open a private
school there. John and Henry would teach at home,
free from all prying committees. They counted on
finding pupils.

They did not count in vain. They had four already,

and the promise of a fifth. Henry, urged to begin in
June, had not waited for his brother's arrival. As soon
as the latter came he took over the direction of the
school. Henry took charge of the Latin, Greek, French,
physics and mathematics. They were so successful that
they were obliged to think of moving the school for the
following year: their father's house was no longer big
enough to hold it. Just then the building of the Academy, where Henry had been prepared for college, became
vacant, and they took up quarters there. It looked as
if the Thoreau school was going to become the Academy.
But not to underrate its masters, when had the latter
ever had such a director? A John, with this art of teaching children and understanding a school as John understood it?

Very strange, the method of the two brothers. They
obtained discipline without punishment or threats.
How did they manage this? All the deacons in New
England might well ask. They interested their pupils,
won them, attached them to themselves by a living
bond, that between the man-child and the child-man.
Study ceased to be a mere heaping up of ennui and
constraint; it was a conversation between brothers.
With the money which the rod would have cost they
had bought a little common sense and good will; and
though the pedants could not pardon these two presumptuous souls, the pupils worked, the pupils stayed.
Boys of ten to fifteen came to listen to the two young
masters, the elder of whom had made them promise,
when they entered, to do their best, and the boys kept
their promise because they were listening to a master
who was their friend. If they missed now and then,
the punishment was to remind them that they had not
kept their word. No one dreamed of playing pranks,
yawning with misery or pulling wings off flies when

the master told stories or prolonged the recess playing with the boys himself. The delightful invitations of the out-of-doors were less tantalizing in a class where penal tasks were unknown. Outside the lessons there was an attachment between the young master and the pupils created by a thousand little subtle bonds such as ordinary pedagogues, with their crass ignorance and their ferules, cannot imagine.

You arrived at school in the morning and, opening your desk, you found a beautiful slice of melon there. You thought it was a joke that one of the boys was playing on you. Not at all: John, your teacher, knowing that you had a sweet tooth, was unostentatiously offering you a taste of the melons from his garden; he was proud of them, for he and his brother raised them, and this year they had a wonderful crop. A slice of melon adds to study a taste which the poor imagination of the pedants knows nothing of. It is refreshing, delectable, and the flavour lingers in the lesson you are reciting. Especially the kind of melons that John and Henry raised—those succulent citron-melons.

Besides, the school did not consist entirely in the lectures, the lessons and the compositions. It spread out to include the more familiar concerns before, after class, during recess, in the street. If you came across John outside school, you ran to meet him of your own accord, joined him and went part of the way with him. He was grown up, your professor, but you were not afraid of him, for his friendliness effaced these distances. Henry, who taught the big boys, had a colder, soberer air; when you saw him going by, you had no desire to joke with this personage who knew Greek and Latin. But you had only to wait till you became his pupil. When you knew him better, how much you wanted to overtake him too in the street after class and walk along

with him, hand in hand, and how much you were re-
warded by the ſtories and the amusing things he told
you! Henry was as much your friend as John.

At school they also ſtudied surveying—a beautiful
chance to go out for a walk and have lessons in the
open country. Henry was the one who showed the
boys how to draw up a plan. And one afternoon each
week they had school in the open air; the whole crew,
maſters and pupils, poured out into the woods, plunged
into the meadow grass, for the moſt enlightening of
object-lessons. Then which of them all was more of
a boy than Henry? Which was the faſtest runner?
The moſt indefatigable gatherer of huckleberries? The
moſt enraptured of them all? Anyone who saw him
exulting with this troop of schoolchildren would have
said that it was he who poured this childlike zeſt into
the others, as if he possessed an inexhauſtible ſtore.
You, teacher of Greek and Latin, will never be, under
your grave airs, anything but a youngſter. They are not
miſtaken, the good people who say this, smiling dis-
dainfully as they see you pass. For they are men,
auſtere, dignified men, weighed down by cares, exhaling
an odour of old prayer-books and warranty deeds.

Sometimes Henry carried off a pupil for a swim in a
pond or a boating party on the river; they made discoveries; they landed on unknown shores. All this was
part of the school and helped to keep up the spirit of
comradeship. One day young Edmund Sewall took
his place in the boat—Edmund, who was so like his
big siſter Ellen of whom John and Henry were particularly fond. Ellen was the daughter of the miniſter of
Scituate. Her grandmother and her aunt, old friends
of the family, boarded with the Thoreaus; and when
the girl came to Concord to see them, gay parties were
organised and they had beautiful evenings at home.

Ellen's fresh seventeen years had made an impression on the two brothers. But it was the lovable John especially who made an impression on her. Presently he had in his class this young Edmund, whose charm haunted him and to whom he was devoted because behind the child's face rose that of the big sister, his play-fellow, the thought of whom sometimes made him dream and gave him the desire to say to the pupil tender things that might have been addressed equally well to her.

At home they met again, for the Thoreaus boarded and lodged those youngsters whose parents did not live in the village. They sat at the same table, masters, pupils, boarders, old friends, and the vivacity of the mother presided over the family meal. It was no banquet, for they had neglected to be rich, but the bread tasted better than elsewhere, and the vegetables came from the garden. The school was only a step from the house. They carried the homelike atmosphere over with them. Is that why the memory of these years— years in which two brothers, in a village, taught them what they knew—was to flavour the whole lives of those who had passed through the Thoreau school? You worked well there, better than anywhere else, and the study left no musty taste behind it. What was John and Henry's secret? They were no lesson-mongers. And so when the parents of a pupil who interested them found it difficult to pay for his studies they asked the parents to let them keep him for nothing. Let him come and work with the others; time enough to talk about money later.

Nor did the pupils take up all their time. The day is long when you are twenty-five; it knows how wonderful it is and turns slowly, slowly, so as to give you the leisure to admire all its aspects. The hours of school left a beautiful margin of independence: the morning, the very early morning, the glorious late afternoons in summer, and the Sundays, and the vacations! When Henry had finished in the garden, put to rights this or that little matter in the house, off he went! All the surroundings of Concord awaited him. The woods were waiting for him, the fish in the river, those luxuriant plants, swollen with sap, which nobody ever looked at, on the edge of the marsh. He had to go and get the latest news of them. So Henry seized his gun and set off on a stroll through the woods. Perhaps today he would bring back some rare bird to study, for he had a true passion for the birds, the plants, and all the creatures of the open air. In any case, he would undoubtedly bring back something, if only the certainty of his own happiness in the woods. This man who was setting out, with his gun on his shoulder, for the fields, was no common huntsman in quest of game; he might not take a single shot with his gun, but he would not return with an empty bag. There are different kinds of good hunting. The discoveries, the surprises, the confirmations, an attention awakened by a certain phenomenon do not fill your game-bag, but fur and feathers would not satisfy you half so much. Henry would pick up an Indian arrow-head to add to his collection. His brother and he were immensely interested in these finds. One day, as a token of their respect for the red aborigines who had once been the kings of the country, they raised a cenotaph to the memory of a sachem on Fairhaven Hill, where they had often come as boys to watch the sunrise. They were fond of the names the former rulers had left everywhere, full of the calls of animals, twittering birds, murmuring winds, gliding waters, roaring cataracts.

Henry took his fishing-rod and set out through the

fields in search of a good nook on the river. He might perhaps bring back some fish. But to catch fish, when he went fishing, was not, after all, the finest part of the adventure. The river had many other presents to make him besides its fish. He even had fishing-parties when the fish were only an unimportant incident, as, for example, on a calm, warm evening, when he set off with an eel-spear, at the break of spring, before the fish had begun to hide among the tall reeds or in the deep water. He fastened a grating to the bow of his boat, a yard above the water, where he burned resinous roots. From a distance it looked like a will-o'-the-wisp in the meadows. For himself, in the boat, armed with his long harpoon, it was like sailing in the midst of enchantment. The water was so violently illumined over a large space all round the bow that he could stare down many feet into the depths and surprise the fish in the inmost recesses of their hiding-places. Strange sojourners, some of whom seemed to be asleep or dreaming, others very wide-awake, the latter ferocious in their aspect, the former on their backs as if they were floating. . . They had so little fear of the monster who brandished the iron and the fire over their abodes that he could have caught them with a fork, as you spear a potato in the pot, or could even seize the sleepers with his hand. But as he was not a mere brute, the most thrilling thing was not the basket of fish he might have brought home but the spectacle itself, the supernatural beauty of the reflexions of the flames in the water, on the willows and the pines on the bank. Surprised by this brutal dawn, a song-sparrow wakened and began to sing as if it were morning—singing for Henry who, in this raw glow that cut the shadows, rowed along in silence, groping his way, listening, meditating. . . .

35

Most radiant of all were the times when he left gun, fishing-rod, boat and harpoon behind for a simple ramble on foot when the earth seemed to respond to the pressure of his soles and his being dilated as if all the good news carried through space were addressed especially to him. This is what Henry felt every time he explored the country of his childhood, in hours of liberty, finding once more the old confidences and secret favours in those nooks he had left behind in the days of his homesickness.

Invariably the schoolmaster's day closed with another escape. Every evening, before going to bed, he gathered together, worked over, expressed with the greatest exactness to a sure and discreet confidant the most secret impressions of the day. Since his return from Harvard he had formed the habit of this daily rendezvous with this other self who never betrayed him and would never bore him with complaints and expostulations but accepted everything. Later on, this was going to be an unexceptionable witness when, published to the world, it would reply to those who questioned it. The solitude of the college years had developed in him a natural tendency to examine himself—the taste for the inner dialogue. All the knowledge we acquire through study or the society of others will never compensate for our indifference where our own souls are concerned. This is a subject for study that is worth all the pains you devote to it—a book that is of more importance for you to read than those that lie on your shelf. And this over and above the fact that when you have read it you will be prepared to understand other books and other men. Henry was anxious to know where he stood in relation to himself. An orderly man does not go to bed without making up his accounts.

Henry confided to his Journal his intimate thoughts, his discoveries of the day. He reckoned up his stock.

HENRY THOREAU

To what end? He would see later on. In the meantime, a man who was aware of what he possessed
slipped, with his spirit at peace, into sheets that were
as white as the page of to-morrow.

To have the good luck to be born on the brink of two
rivers, to be twenty years, twenty-five years old, to
have a hearty, open-air appetite, and not to have a
boat, is a flaw in the happiness of a man. Fishing or
swimming, loafing about the banks or skating on its
firm back, you have never known the joy of the river if
it has not taken you and rocked you, led you, carried
you off, made you dance at its own will and pleasure.
If you were to build a boat? . . . You can find the
timber, you have a few tools and fingers that know how
to handle a piece of wood. A real boat. Not a mere
dugout such as Henry had made when he was nineteen,
a dugout that looked like an oblong trough, though even
that was better than a tub in which you drift with the
current; it was delightful; it did not move swiftly, but
with patience and skill you could risk yourself in it for
a quarter of an hour's adventure. No, a real boat this
time, a boat that really travels over the water. If you
bought one, or had it built by a boat-builder, you would
spend a lot of money and have nothing but the joy of
the boat itself; whereas if you made it with your own
hands you would also have the joy of building it.
To assemble your materials for building a boat in the
open air, in the first days of spring, is a very different
pleasure from expounding the Odyssey; you feel as if
you were living like a man of Homer's day, you inhale
in advance the scent of discovery. To wield the saw
and the hammer, take your careful measurements, fit
together the pieces of the body, see the work taking
form, to be two brothers under the sky, busy in your

37

dock-yard, among your tools, your timber, striking with precision, trimming neatly, responsible to nobody—schoolmaster as you are, the gods that roam New England on their tour of inspection might envy you, those gods who have never had the joy of building a boat themselves. John and Henry's hearts are in their work. At the end of one week the masterpiece is finished. It is a dory, heavy and strongly built, with a sharp bow, such as fishermen use; it is fifteen feet long by three and a half in breadth at the middle. A real craft: you can move about in it, sail it, stow away a little cargo in it. A good coat of paint will protect it and give it a tidier appearance. As it is destined to take part in open-air holidays on the water, it must be painted green with a blue border. The painting is done in a jiffy, and then comes the glorious moment when with a final glance the creators survey their creation, weaned at last from themselves and ready to face the broad daylight of the world. . . For legs the dory has wheels that will enable it to be rolled around falls.

Nothing remains now but to equip it. It must have two sets of oars, poles, two masts; you must foresee everything when you have these vast projects in your head. As the boat is going to carry you a long way and you are going to camp out under the stars, the tent is indispensable. Then there is no limit to your dreams. With a boat and a tent you can sail round a continent, coast along all the shores, disembark on an island, set up your tent there, light a fire and survey the landscape with that knowing air: It's I, exactly. Do you recognize me? . . . Yes, you can do unbelievable things with this boat. You can begin to enjoy the world, measure the amplitude of the earth. You can carry Concord with you to all sorts of strange countries, scour the land, found colonies.

Meanwhile, you begin experimenting with it, you lose no time, you are prouder of being a good mariner than a good schoolmaster and you invite the boys on board to teach them things that are not to be found in the books. New aspects of the world are revealed, you make important discoveries, for you are the man who has a boat.

To think there were so many unknown things around you: brooks, mountains, buildings, men, flocks of ducks, and all the people on the banks—unsuspected neighbours! If it were not for the school, you would like to follow the watery road as far as ever it could lead you. Concord widens into a vast province, as if newly peopled with animals and landscapes and surprises. In the succession of the springs and the summers, this spring of the year 1839 will aways bear for you the colours of the boat — green and blue, will bear a sail swelling against a mast, which two brothers have planed with their own hands in an open-air dock-yard.

When you really know your boat you are ready for the decisive adventures for which it has been fitted out. The long vacation has come. Your departure is fixed for Saturday, the last day of August. This is to be no mere airing before supper: it is the great embarkation for a week or two weeks, for good and all—who knows? —for the fabulous regions where men speak another language.

John and Henry have made plans to go all the way to the White Mountains by water, from little Concord, their village, to big Concord, the capital of New Hampshire. It is a plan that requires some reflexion. They have thought it over and made up their minds, and they are to set out to-morrow. Preparations, the cargo. First the tent and a buffalo-skin; then a few tools, some utensils for their cooking; as provisions in reserve some potatoes and melons from their own patch. Do not laugh, you sceptics. You don't know what it is to have at hand, under all circumstances, a fruit whose virtues are perfectly known to you. And isn't it like having on board a friendly presence, a remembrance of the garden, that will bring the pilgrims good luck on their perilous voyage? Like the boat itself, the melons are the fruit of their own labour, and thus, without borrowing anything from anyone, they set forth, side by side, for the conquest of the world.

At last, the thrilling moment. Vain for you your Harvard diploma, vain your teaching of Greek and Latin this August afternoon, when you finally jump into the boat that awaits you, all provisioned, and gently gives under your feet. What are your learning and your evening dreams beside the certitude that floods you with happiness like a child, beside the glamour of this dazzling day and this running water that is going to carry you to the beyond? . . . Books? The most beautiful of them all is a thousand times less beautiful to you than that which this rude dory under your oars and your sail is eager to bring you. Wisdom? Listen to that rippling along the bank; the river whispers to you as it passes that she herself is wisdom—and how your soul responds to the invitation of the voyage!

It has rained in the morning, as if the gods of the Concord had wished to thwart the plans of two good boys who are setting out in search of them; but this only makes the smile of the afternoon more calm. Come along, off we go! Good-bye, friends. A cup of air to your health! A little further on, as a final farewell from the navigators, a salvo of joy which the forest echoes after noting it on its leaves. The sounds of the village are stilled, you sink into a deep dream, rhythmical with the gliding of the oars. You slip along this road that runs, buoyant, fresh, through the recesses of the landscape. You surprise it, as it were, gently, in its privacy, not seizing it by the throat as you do on those beastly, dusty roads where the world leaves its dung and the imprint of its iron feet. The watery way flows on and carries you past the willows, the water-plants with their white and rose-coloured flowers, the meadow grass with the faded tints of the closing summer. A bittern sails away, a tortoise drops into the water. From afar the familiar heights salute you courteously. Farewell, village, farewell, last fisherman with your motionless line and your dog.

We are rowing towards fresh promises: see how the river widens out. We pull straight ahead, in cadence, not like apprentices. The evening draws in; it makes good rowing, and what good haying it ought to be at this hour for those reapers over there, almost lost in the grass of the meadows, where every blade they cut seems to exhale a sigh of gladness and commit it to the breeze, the courier of the evening. It is time to look for a good place for the night. We are seven miles from Concord. Billerica already. . . It is astonishing what this name stands for when you have been rowing for hours and are ready to pitch your tent on *terra firma!* And here are some ripe huckleberries for dessert. The fire crackles. A good cup of cocoa, some bread. And sunset to finish the meal. Before you, as far as the horizon, nothing but a solitary farmhouse, far away, lost in the glorious wilderness, amid the clumps of pines, the hills, the rocks, all the squatting people of the brush. Fireflies in the grass. The good night awaits the two of you under the cotton tent that is fastened to one of the masts. But the hour is so captivating, this August evening is so charged with messages in the depths of the silence, that you have no desire to go to sleep at once. Neighbours betray their presence. A fox makes his rounds; some creature fumbles among the potatoes and melons in the boat, disappearing into the water when you go to see what it is. On the horizon a great blaze from a fire over in Lowell; the fire-alarm reaches you in snatches, mingled with the barking of the watch-dogs from invisible farms. Two lads who have rowed with a will roll themselves up in the buffalo-skin and close their eyes on the thought of the boat moored by the clump of alders for the next day. Good night, brother. Good night, Henry. How about the school? . . . And the eight, ten, twelve, fifteen days like this one to look forward to? Blow out the lantern.

Sunday morning. You come out of your tent into the mist of the dawn and light the fire for breakfast. Then, like the pagan you are, oblivious of the fall of man, fold up the tent and embark with your Sunday soul in the rising sun that disperses the fog. You give names to the spots along the way, the hills, cliffs, woods, as fresh as if no human eye had ever touched them. The river is a mirror: it is Sunday on the water, too, and you hesitate to disturb it with a stroke of your oar. A skiff passes with two men, gliding so lightly that it seems almost unreal among the reflexions of the foliage in the water. The meditation of the frogs, motionless on the reeds, contemplating the day of the Lord's rest, is tinged with the grave Sabbath beauty.

Just above the Billerica Falls they take the canal through the woods, and one of the two mariners pulls the dory with the rope along the tow-path as far as the dam. The people are coming out of church in the village and the good folk look down from the height of the bridge upon these two good-for-nothings who are voyaging along, just as if the Lord's day were not made

to cement the nothingness of the week that has passed
with the nothingness of that which is dawning. But
the lock-keeper is more liberal-minded: he knows two
merry souls, out for adventure, when he sees them, and
he opens the locks for them, in spite of the Sunday rule.
The lock-keepers of this world are broad enough to
redeem its narrowness.

And now they find themselves on the Merrimac, the
great river. The dory is a mere insect striking out on this
sheet of water, one hundred, two, four hundred yards
wide, over which every sound glances and comes to
you with a marvellous clearness. Those children repeating their catechism in a cottage are a good third of a
mile away from you who catch the murmur of their
voices; or is it that the words of the catechism have a
miraculous carrying-power? The cows in the meadow
do not know their catechism; they are content to be
beautiful in silence and enrich the look of those villages
with their tiny harbours and their fairylike setting. The
boat has burst into a new part of the world; this is
the valley that leads up into the heart of New Hampshire
by a succession of natural dams, with a rapid, leaping
current of yellowish water cut by falls. When you
have rowed since morning against the current, your
nooning is very precious in the shade of an apple-tree.
It is Chelmsford here, the village where your parents
came once to seek their fortune. The hour is so beautiful
under this apple-tree that you would like to read a
poem as ample as the landscape of the valley; when
Sunday chimes within you and as far as the horizon,
you would like all this music to be crowned in that of a
poem.

See those islets. High up on one of them are perched
two men who hail the little craft, asking to be taken
off. But there are the melons, the tent, a whole outfit

on board, and with this cargo the dory already has enough trouble making headway against the stream. Can't be done, boys; you will have to make *terra firma* and Nashua on foot. Good luck! Further on, what is this enormous fish whose back rises and sinks in mid-stream? A sturgeon? A monster? Look out there: with a blow of that assuredly formidable tail it could send to the bottom two brothers and their fortune. But no, this old fraud that is going to capsize us is nothing but a wooden spar fixed there as a buoy to warn sailors of sunken rocks. . . .

The sun sets, twilight creeps in; shall we think of resting, like the fish who, save for a few that prowl all night, are preparing themselves for sleep? You have stretched out the most beautiful of Sundays as long as you could between the two shores and rowing hard against this strong current. You have well earned the favourable spot for pitching your tent and tasting the sleep of adventurers.

The earth is firm and sweet under your feet when you trample it after a whole day tossing about in a walnut-shell. You unload the provisions, like con-quistadors who have reached a far country after count-less perils, arrived at a shore where you will make your-self understood by signs to the natives, if any appear. Once the lantern is hung to the tent-pole, the fire ready, the kettle on the fire, you are at home; nothing is missing to make life solid and satisfying. After closing the tent, Henry scribbles a few notes in the glimmering light of the lantern: the shore journal of the navigators. And after a little chat they go to sleep in the buffalo-skin. On the opposite bank, some Irish labourers on the railroad are celebrating the Sabbath with wild shouts, whirling up and down the track. But their brawling is not loud enough to disturb the sleep of the two oarsmen who soon forget where they are. The two lads are dead to the world among all the sleeping creatures who, like them, have drained the happiness of Sunday on the banks. Alone, the river, eager to reach its end, pursues all night its course to the sea; its adventure will brook no delay.

But why does this evil beast traverse in a dream the sleep of a happy man, torturing him after a blissful day? . . . Happily, in the same buffalo-skin sleeps his good genius, with a sleep that is peaceful and unbroken all night long. The phantoms of agonizing dreams are dispersed by the brotherly voice sounding under the tent in the early day. And listen now to this little world of oak-leaves, under which you have slept, saying their morning prayers in the breeze.

It is enough to hear the rippling of the river, when you emerge from your tent, and to see once more the boat that is calmly waiting for you, to feel a hunger for adventure. So off you start again through the fog to devour the beautiful week that lies before you, round and new; you have not yet broken the loaf, you have merely nibbled a few crumbs; the country you have passed is only a tiny morsel of the territories you plan to annex.

Occasionally, when you have watched the banks gliding by for a long time, the desire seizes you to draw nearer and explore a little the hinterland of the country you are skirting. Nothing easier for you who are at once the commanding officer, the crew and the passengers. One of the two coxswains runs along the shore, while the other continues to row and a little further on picks up the explorer and hears him recount his discoveries. There have been surprises. By good luck the rover has happened into a cottage, and because he looks well and it is a summer morning when hearts are softened with generosity, the farmer's wife has offered him a bowl of milk which he has tossed off, while the children have watched the stranger amorously plunging his big nozzle into the little bowl. During this excursion the other one on board, if he is thirsty, halves a melon and dispatches it, drawing up under the bows on the bank, where he waits for the explorer. In the heat of the day, a New England lad whose muscles are hard enough to manage the oars feels himself invaded by an Oriental indolence, with a great pity for the vague humanity toiling and moiling down there in the world. Amid the delights of the siesta, with a succulent slice of melon in a boat in the shadow of a willow, he can find some apology for pleasure-lovers, even for smokers of opium.

The river seems to flow solely for the joy of these two comrades who have set out one fine Saturday for the conquest of the world. Just this side of Nashua a fleet of great canal-boats appears, with sails set and high bulwarks, like junks. Have you really been asleep on the stream and actually reached the Orient? Let's make the most of it. The rowers will enjoy a little idling. From the dory they throw a rope and get themselves towed a bit of the way like pashas; it has grown so hot that two schoolmasters, who are not of the soft kind, can allow themselves to be towed by a great merchantman. They toss into the water some of the melons that remain on board; they have seen enough of them, and the fish may like them. These jovial boatmen with whom they chat do not break the beautiful harmony of the landscape; they belong in it, and their language has the flavour of the river-grass. When they have passed and you find yourselves alone again in your dory, oars in hand, the solitude has almost a new taste.

Noon suggests a swim and a siesta under a tree. Suddenly a boatman's horn, echoing from bank to bank, rouses the sleepers, and they set out again. The linden trees on the shore are a revelation. Nashua drops behind, the bridge, the junction of the rivers, the mills; they are in the woods again, and the evening clouds are reflected in the water like a warning. This evening the gods have planned for the encampment a beautiful, solitary spot on the border of a pine-wood, under the rocky walls of a deep ravine. The gods that voyage along these shores know how soft is the carpet the pine-needles make and what a fragrance they will add to the fire and the smoke. The song of the kettle, like an incantation, calls up this evening the friends they have left in the village; their images prowl and linger about the tent, bending over the shoulders of these two companions on the edge of the forest who are trying to discover on the map in the centre of what universe they are this evening and what country they will annex to-morrow. If you are awakened to-night by the shrill grating of a cricket, or the rambling of a spider over the peaks and passes of your face, the brook that flows at the bottom of the ravine has a cradle-song that will lull you to sleep again. Later, through a restless night at home, you will think of the quality of this sleep close to the earth after a day on the water.

Far away in the night someone is beating a drum—some tyro preparing for a country muster—and this trivial rat-a-tat-tat, ennobled by the distance and the darkness, seems, in the warmth of heroism that pours through the buffalo-skin, strangely to arm you for the most extravagant deeds. What will the coming dawn suggest, the Deliverance of the Holy Sepulchre or the Quest of the Golden Fleece? And has this high wind that shakes the tent a mission to inform the sleepers and publish the great news along the banks and under the pines? In any case, you are awake before dawn to be ready to welcome the great day, whatever it may be. Hand me the hatchet, I am off for fuel. The birds are still on their roosts and the kettle is already singing like a nurse. They haul the boat up on land, upset it and empty it and give it a good rinsing. At three o'clock everything is reshipped, stowed away, ready for departure, with the tent spread over the bow, for it is drenched with dew. The heavy morning fog, the curtain that had fallen to conceal the surprises to come, promises a glorious day.

As the banks are cleared of their velvety coverlet, sparkling with dew under the first rays, and the pines on the shore reveal their outlines, the river appears as large as an arm of the sea. The day of glory announced by the drum rises between the high slopes of the river: not a village in sight; you might think you were in the days of the Redskins, in the midst of a primitive country. You row with a will. Drummer of the night, the meaning of your rat-a-tat-tat becomes clear. We are going to review landscapes and men.

First, at Cromwell's Falls, the lock-keeper, with whom the boys exchange some wholesome gossip. Several canal-boats are waiting to pass. On such a morning, if you encountered humanity in the form of some fellow with affected manners, a crabbed face and the look of a deacon, you would bless anyone who would force his respectable head under the water. But as for these shapely, strapping boatmen, in their shirt-sleeves, bareheaded, slouching or leaning on a pole, they have a sort of accent that heightens the meaning of the proud word on your own lips, fellow-creature. See that flaxenhaired brother there, with his skin tanned by wind and sun, young or old, you could never say which, but rugged and beautiful as a tree. Don't put yourself out to be polite; it doesn't go with these fellows. A few words of the language of men and everything is understood. The banter you shout back to them as you pull away is as cordial as a farewell. With all the boatmen you meet you exchange a friendly greeting.

Happy souls. . . . To be the two men on board these canal-boats, pushing with the pole when you are going up the stream, steering with the aid of an oar at each end when you are in mid-stream, hoisting the sail if the wind is favourable, transporting wood or bricks and bringing back odd freight: what could be jollier on a rustling September morning like this on the water? You contrive a little shelter under the cargo, where you may retire from the rain. As you sail your boat along in this way you do not seem to be toiling for wages or an employer; it is as if you were playing some very ancient game. The day's work ended, you get your supper and lodging at some house or other by the waterside, breakfast in the morning with the lock-man, load your boat, travel all day, unload, receive your pay, take a drink at the inn, where you hear the news of the world, and then off again. A fine life, blooming with songs that sound over the river.

These were the people the marvelling eyes of a child had seen now and then, when a canal-boat passed the village. Their fabulous race, as he has come to know it better, has lost none of its glamour in the eyes of the man. Sometimes when the high road approaches within a few hundred yards of the shore, what a sorry, absurd figure the parti-coloured stage cuts beside these barges, as it sweeps past in a cloud of dust! Good luck to you, my fine fellows, who are in such a hurry to get there, piled in together, busy, with your worries and your trunks heaped up on the rack behind. . . . No doubt you are making good time, but you have not the least notion of the sights we are passing, that cottage bathed in a patriarchal atmosphere, with the well and the barn, and the old grandfather sitting on a bench; and those shagbark trees, unlike anything to be seen in Concord or where you live, in all probability, and those magnificent maples. See that scow there turned up on the bank, which those carpenter boys are mending. The joyous ring of the great strokes of their hammers, echoing from shore to shore, and the glittering of their tools in the sun, are not for townspeople who take the stage. These things that make work as beautiful as a festival, the work that nourishes the soul and the muscles of a man . . . repairing a boat, building a hayrick, woodcutting in the forest, setting up the frame of a house under the benediction of the open air . . . what have they in common with your infernal routine, you passengers of the stage?

The burning sun plumbs the landscape. That large island with the shade and the cattle, at the mouth of a river, is too inviting to be ignored. They put into port, and as the flesh is weak they no longer resist the temptation of those pigeons that have also stopped there, during the heat of the day, and are innocently cooing among the branches, heedless of the two savages that approach with their engines of death. One of the pigeons has fallen. You savages, wash in the river the hands that have killed in cold blood one of these beautiful pigeons that had also set out on a journey; do penance, eaters of innocent flesh, who have already brought down some squirrels for your supper, and now, in sheer wantonness, replace them with a pigeon: boil a bowl of rice. After the feast, recite some poetry, since you have no music, and yield in your satiety to idleness in the shade of this island where you have been behaving like abject creatures of civilisation.

But it is time to re-embark. They raise the sail to take advantage of the breeze. From the top of a hill forming the bank, some lumberers are rolling down timber that falls into the water with a thundering roar; their axes and levers glitter in the sun. That cottage, with its dooryard bossoming with sunflowers and poppies, smiles with such confidence that they skirt the bank to see it better. This is a wild region that makes them want to explore it a little. Those old oaks welcome them as friends who do not often receive visits. A lonely horse in a pasture, then some cows grazing in the shade, after the warm day, and some wild apple trees with the sourish fruit that Henry knows so well and likes. That ruined mill shrouded in creepers, which the pedestrian discovers while following a torrent through the woods, sets him thinking when he regains the boat of the life and the dreams of the old settler who lived there once and the taste that his flour must have had.

At Coos Falls, in a solitary part of the river, some stone-masons are repairing the locks. They stop for a chat. One of them, a young man, questions the voyagers about their adventures, examines the little craft and its outfit with a confession in his eye. If he only could set off with these two fellows to explore the world! What a trio they would make, a mason and two schoolmasters, who are not more than twenty-five. . . . A wild desire seizes him to throw away the chisel and mallet, leap into the boat and say to them: "Take me! I have had enough of stone-cutting. Now I want to cut into the stuff of the vast world. . . ." But the stones remain, little mason, weights heavier than your vision, which soon disappears with the two explorers, leaving you pensive at your work.

As they continue to ascend, the watery landscape becomes more rugged, interspersed with rapids, rocks, falls. On the fifth day they are between Manchester and Bedford. There are many locks to pass through, and sometimes no lock-keeper is at hand. Then they have the fun of manipulating the lock themselves, no easy task but so amusing. . . . They are at once the passengers and the all-powerful being who locks the boat through.

Contemplating the cottages of these lock-keepers, gloriously lost before a vast stretch of whirling waters, roaring, foaming, you are filled with envy at the thought of the good soul who lives his life there as a lockman, almost as solitary as a lighthouse-keeper, and the desire seizes you to go in, just to ask for a glass of water and hear the sound of a human voice as a contrast to that of the river. This one seems to be asleep on the earth under the benediction of the summer sun, like an infant in the warmth of its mother's breast. Henry crosses the little garden and knocks at the door. A woman opens it: he can't have such a shaggy face, after all, in spite of five nomadic days, or she would not invite him in so prettily. The freshly scoured floor has a fragrant odour; the visitor is afraid of soiling it with his big boots. He takes a glass from the dresser, then goes to the well where he catches a glimpse of his hairy face, the face of a voyager who has not had the leisure to shave himself like a true Christian. The lockman's wife offers him a little molasses and ginger to temper this hard water, for the day is warm. Nearby her brother, the sailor, who seems a little out of his element among these freshwater folk, dandles the family cat; with his sea-dog's eye, filled with the horizon, he scrutinizes the visitor curiously, sympathetically. Oh, these lockmen's cottages, with their fireplaces and their door-yards, in this solitude! . . . What honey one could make here, a wild and exquisite honey, with that lingering suggestion of bitterness in the taste which is so grateful to healthy palates.

The oarsman is a happy man who turns his back on his discoveries, lets them come, and only enjoys them after they have well passed. This wooded island is the largest they have encountered thus far. It seems to say: I have been here since the beginning of things, waiting for the day when you would plant your tent-pole for the night in the shelter of my great elms. Who knows but I shall yield myself to you with such trust that you may decide to conclude your adventure and set up your hearthstone here? Between the world and myself there is nothing but a strip of water: would not that protect you from it and connect you with it sufficiently? . . . But as it is still morning, they leave behind them the great island and the great dream, to resume the course of the big wonders that are offered two poor devils who scan the world from a little boat of their own making.

After Amoskeag Falls, as steep as a staircase where they are in danger of capsizing every minute and have to jump into the water to right the boat, the river opens out into a lake. They make fast under a grove of alders for their lunch and siesta. A good breeze blows up. Boats pass, with their sails set, great, heavy, one-winged birds advancing with a stately solemnity. The boats pass which they saw before lunch and the last of which offered to take the two navigators and their traps on board and carry them the rest of the way; when the brothers are resting in the shade, the wag at the helm calls out a proposal to take them in tow. Many thanks, my boy, not just now; it is too good under these trees. When lunch is finished, John and Henry also raise their sail and, rowing vigorously, catch up with the big canal-boat which has hardly advanced at all, the breeze having fallen. Now then, my barge-boy, would you like us to take you in tow? Here's a piece of rope if we can oblige you. The little dory you laughed at a while ago has the laugh on you. And one by one the oarsmen overtake the other monsters that are painfully dragging their bellies in a file along the watery road.

They have become once more the sovereigns of the river; but this does not make it less necessary for them to look for provisions before night. Their stock is low. John jumps ashore and sets off to find a farmhouse where they can revictual, while Henry explores the other bank for a suitable haven for the night. Again the canal-boats loom behind them, advancing with much effort, for the breeze has quite died away. John comes back with a loaf of bread and some melons, accompanied by a little flaxen-haired boy who wants to have a close view of the boat of these people who have set out for adventure on the water and have brought nothing to eat. He too, like the little mason, would love to go with them; who would not love to go with John? They would be happy to take him on board, this lively boy with the sparkling blue eyes, who would not weigh very much among the cargo; but his father will not allow it. But he is a very good-natured father, just the same, and he invites the travellers to come and visit his farm the next day. With pleasure. Are they not colleagues? Who knows more about raising melons than they? They might even be able to recommend some seeds. They taste his products, one of which, set in the water to cool while they are pitching the tent, has taken it into its head to go off with the current, like a melon on vacation that has been seized with a desire for the sea; they have to jump into the boat to capture it, for it is already far away. They taste his melons, sitting on the bank, facing the glow of the sunset in which the river wishes to share, to light its depths on its evening journey. The song over there, close by, is that of the brook at the mouth of which they have pitched their camp, and which hastens to confide to the great confused current a few secrets it has brought from afar.

That night Henry's dreams under the tent file past amid the babble of this neighbour and disappear as he awakens at the soft tapping of drops of rain on the cotton roof. A sparrow trills cheerily in the morning: a good omen. They set out with this promise. More locks. And then the last one: nothing beyond but impassable rapids. A pity, for the navigators, who have set out from Concord, Massachusetts, want to push on by boat to Concord, New Hampshire. It would be more of an adventure but it can't be done. Since their goal is the White Mountains, they will leave the boat here and continue along the shore on foot. Before they became great navigators, they had been great walkers.

So they cut a pair of sticks and set out like pilgrims in the mist and rain. If they are to have no more the joy of the river and the boat, they will have the pleasure of the hard earth under the freedom of their big boots. The earth and the watery meadows have a sweet smell. All the frogs in Christendom are sounding the hymn of deliverance and the toadstools smile with joy in the starch of their little collars. The travellers resolutely drench themselves. Are you afraid of a little wetting? Then stay shut up at home; stay where it's dry, dry souls. You are not cut out for sitting in the rain, on the side of a brush-covered hill, happy even if your clothes are soaking. Perhaps it will clear in the afternoon; but what if it doesn't clear?

A good welcome to big Concord. To save time they take the stage (yes, like those other idiots) as far as Plymouth, where a friend lives with whom they want to shake hands; then they resume the staff and the road. They come to a little sylvan inn where, in the evening, the people of the neighbourhood gather to discuss their business and hear the news over a glass of whisky. They wonder where in the world these people have come from when all day they have not caught even a glimpse of a roof. On the inn-table lies an old newspaper. At home Henry has little use for this kind of literature; he leaves the paper to his father who enjoys it so much. But in this poor, solitary inn, when you have tramped all day through the woods, it is astonishing what savour an old newspaper that gives you the stale news of the world acquires, a newspaper that has been rumpled by all sorts of rough hands, astonishing how your eyes fasten on a paragraph and you are led to believe in the virtues of the soap recommended in the advertisements.

And then, in this lost country, you have surprising encounters. Along a path in the woods a young soldier advances in full regimentals, going to muster no doubt with his musket on his shoulder; he marches with military step, with an air of being very sure of the importance of his mission. He must carry himself well, you see, before these civilians, and safeguard in the depths of the forest the prestige of his military apparel. Poor little soul! As he passes close to John and Henry his martial mask falls, he becomes a little boy again in his absurd harness in the presence of these trees that are judging him, and, crestfallen under his warrior helmet, he steals away unheroically, embarrassed by the greaves that chafe his legs. Honest little lad, we wish you well! They can send you off and dress and drill you in the barracks or get you killed for no reason at all. Your ingenuousness consents to it all in advance.

As they leave Sanbornton the mountains appear. They spend several days exploring them. It is a great revelation. The culminating point of the journey is at an altitude of 6288 feet, that of Mount Washington, which the two comrades climb. On the twelfth day they are back again at the place where they left their boat. Everything is in good condition, and the tent, the blankets, left in charge of the melon-grower, are quite dry. This lovable man expects his friends to carry off an immense melon to ballast the little boat: see, this one, which he long ago gave his flaxen-headed heir permission to dispose of as he chose. John carries it off, to the satisfaction of the owner, for he is the friend to whom you give whatever is dearest to you.

They are not homesick in the least, but they must return southwards to their own anchorage. The return is beautiful too. They set off spinning like an arrow, with the current, as far as the confluence of the Concord. The departure is at noon, this very Thursday. The river smiles under the fresh mid-September wind; they raise the sail, they can rest on their oars occasionally without loss of time. And everything drifts past them again, in the other direction. As they see the funny little dory repassing with its two savages on board, the people recognize them and give them a friendly halloo. To watch the sail, the lumbermen, rolling their timber down with an immense splash into the water, pause for a moment. From their boat the two adventurers salute every nook of the landscape, banks, islands, mouths of rivers, like old acquaintances. They must set up their tent once more, at least: it shall be opposite the large island of the slaughtered pigeons where they took their siesta on the way up. The boat is drawn up on the sand. Not a sail in sight; nothing but the spiders of the grassy jungle which come out curiously at the light of the lantern, and explore the mystery of the buffalo-skin spread out on the ground.

It is fragrant this evening, and every blade of grass, damp with dew, seems to be on its doorstep taking the air. They have journeyed far to-day and are tired; and after dipping their slices of bread in a cup of cocoa and scribbling the main things down in their journals, they blow out the lantern and bid farewell to Thursday. A high wind in the night flaps the curtains of the tent. In the morning, the heavy fog rolls away over the water, uncovering a landscape suddenly tinged with autumn. In the flitting clouds, in the look of the cottages, in the lowing of the cattle in the meadows, in the flying troops of flickers, the death of summer is confirmed. And when they set foot on earth and clamber up the bank to cast an eye over the countryside, they catch almost everywhere the prevailing yellow note of the asters, coreopses, tansies, golden-rod, little flowers of autumn already burning with the flames of the declining summer's sun—the little candles left lighted all day long for the pilgrims in the church of the meadows.

But they carry on at a good pace, with sail stretched, one steering with an oar in the stern, the other rowing. The boat, seized by the autumnal ferment, speeds along; in the rippling of the water before them they seem to hear it laughing to itself at the promise of the splendour the season is preparing to bring forth. They are invigorated by this brisk wind that obliges them to sit muffled in their cloaks. See how they bound along; they are almost home again already. Here is the beginning of Massachusetts. They pass—rare spectacle—a pleasure-boat with a young man and a girl, and a dory, a commoner sight, with some people who are gathering driftwood for the winter. As they sail, they munch an apple-pie they have bought at a farm; it is rather tart. Driven by this famous breeze that bends the trees on the bank, they scud merrily along, with a devil-may-care look in their faces, at a speed that astonishes the men on some scows which they pass. Already the locks of the canal through the woods that gives access to the Concord. Yes, here we are, dear old Musketaquid! We shall have to row hard, against the current, and try to arrive this evening.

The sun reappears to make Chelmsford and Billerica smile, and sinks magnificently, filling the valley with a flood of soft light. High overhead, in silence, two herons pass against the sky, on their way to the North. A good journey, comrades up there; our home is to the Southwest. If you feel as we do, at this heavenly hour of the end of day when two lads, returning from a long expedition, are filled by the beauty of the familiar landscape, you are two very high-hearted herons. The night falls, they row in the light of the few candles a kind providence has set burning above, far higher than the track of the herons. There is no sound on board but the monotonous cadence of the oars, for John and Henry have no desire to talk; silence alone can draw out the thoughts that fill them. They mean to arrive to-night, Friday the thirteenth.

And indeed, late in the evening, the boat of the two argonauts draws up very smoothly alongside the shore whence it had set out fourteen days before, and rubs its wet cheek against the bearded bank. They have completed a stage of fifty miles this day.

John and Henry leap ashore, draw up the boat and fasten it to the wild apple tree. And then! A last look at the dory that has borne them so far out into the wide world, and laden with their traps they turn their steps towards the house. For them now the sweetness of civilised life and soft beds. They are ready to face them with visages bronzed by the wind and the sun of the river. But to-morrow morning, when they awaken, how surprising it will be not to hear the flick-flack of the cotton tent over their heads, to smell no longer the warm odour of the buffalo-skin! What a surprise and what a disenchantment to find the four walls, a motionless ceiling, the glass window. . . . How sad. Meanwhile, a ramble in the woods to-morrow, just to see what preparations are on foot there for the festival of autumn.

The school will soon have lasted for three years. In spite of all, the masters have inspired confidence, and there are now twenty-five pupils. There would be more of them if the building were not inadequate. For others are awaiting the first vacancy, to be taught in their turn. And those pious personages may well ask whether the good morals of the rod are not in peril.

Then, towards Easter, they hear that the Thoreau school is going to close. What has happened? John feels shaky, unable to continue. For some time he has not been well, but he has said nothing about it, in order not to discourage the pupils in their work. But now he is no longer able to keep up the pretence. Whatever the regrets and the consequences may be, everything must be given up abruptly, on the high tide of success, so that John may take care of himself, for it is he who steers the ship. Henry, who had begun the school without his brother, would no longer have the same reasons for keeping it if the latter retired. To keep school with John was perfect. Without him, it was not to be thought of. Better to look for something else.

John is ill, consumed by a slow, tenacious disease. . . . Is the grandfather, lying down there in the graveyard,

demanding him back? Already three of his daughters—
Aunts Sarah, Nancy and Mary, and one of his sons,
Uncle David, whose Christian name Henry bears, have
died young of consumption, like their father. Is his
grandson going to have the same fate? Or is John to
be confronted with a demand more brutal still? To be
condemned without appeal, because sweet souls like
him are out of place on this earth? Yes, for the poor
fellow, as he drags along, is finally carried off, with a
refinement of horror. In shaving himself he makes an
insignificant cut. Lockjaw sets in; and the smile of this
loving soul is extinguished amid atrocious convulsions.
John dies in torture.

In the house of mourning, on this February day of
1842, the younger brother is the most miserable of all.
What is the use of fortitude, of this mask of impassi-
bility, when you are stricken in the tenderest depths?
How survive the best part of yourself? A boy, crushed
under his suffering, does not know. . . . John, my
brother, after these years we have enjoyed together,
and all the secrets we have shared, how can I support
alone the weight of this grief that once was joy? My
comrade, my inspiration, my good genius, my brother.
You whom one read as a beautiful story that everyone
loves to hear retold. You never had to be deciphered
laboriously to yield the meaning of the tale. . . .

Henry remains sitting in the house, with this weight
that overwhelms him. He no longer cares for anything:
everything, in the garden, in the woods, on the banks
of the river, in the neighbourhood of their school, cries
out his destitution. His sisters try to take him out to
distract him. He does not object, he is inert. He is
indifferent to everything. It is as if he had lost the
highest reason for existence, love.

Will he regain his poise, his taste for life? Possibly—

apparently. But there is in his deepest depths an incurable wound that will never endure being touched, however lightly. He cannot make the slightest verbal allusion to his bereavement, so greatly does it pain him. To deceive himself he plays the stoic, writing to a friend that a musical air has brought back to him the sense of the harmony of the universe and that he wishes never again to see his brother in life—that he wishes only for his ideal prototype. But in the confidences of his Journal how much truer he is! "Where is my heart gone? They say men cannot part with it and live." That delightful intimacy they had shared through childhood, boyhood, manhood, he knew very well he would never find again, *never*. John's grave enclosed the youth of two. Twelve years later, trying to describe to a friend those moments when his brother had disappeared in torture, Henry turned pale and almost fainted.

There remained the boat they had built, with which they had unrolled the beautiful watered ribbon of their adventures. To see it rocking against the bank was simply to have before him a sharper image of his grief: John taking sail to face alone a terrible adventure. He would go no more in this boat. That was ended.

In the following spring he gave it to a friend who wanted it.

III

When the Thoreau school unexpectedly closed, Henry was only twenty-four years old. But he had moved forward since he had left Harvard. His convictions, already clear, the presentiments of the college boy, had acquired more force. He had ripened early in solitude and study, and his experience of the world had enlarged. He had had some taste of it, and the face he presented to it held little promise of friendship.

The aversion he had felt in college for an atmosphere dominated by the young gentleman was extended now to the village atmosphere, the realm of the young gentleman's self-satisfied country cousin. The dear little town, preserved in a syrup of sweet conventions, smiled with an air of inviting him to add to its sweetness. The church-tower there pointed toward heaven the sacred meaning of its anxious cares: observance, decency, mediocrity—store-keepers, farmers, townspeople, honourable souls one and all, cast in the same mould, more or less orthodox, good folk, honest folk, so very honest, in almost perfect agreement, as if they were acting together some excellent amateur comedy of manners. Join in the dance, my boy. As he watched them performing their parts he had no inclination to figure in the play. These farces bored him and left him cold. Henry felt within him a disobedient soul.

Where in the world had it come from, this little seed of rebellion that had sprouted in the soul of the child and sprung up in the boy? It was to-day, at any rate, a fine, tough-grained shrub, well-rooted in the soil. The school-less schoolmaster had no inclination to share in the social mill that blissfully revolved about him. Under his hat there was not an atom of the will that animated his forebears, the merchants of the Norman island, or his grandfather, the store-keeper of Long Wharf. A sad fact, but so it was. As naturally as they breathed or said their prayers his family had put on the harness in all docility and taken the road like good domestic animals who never dream that anything else exists in the universe than the shafts, the rack, the halter, the town-square and the street-corners where one turns every day. Doesn't this attract you, this cab-horse's life, with the certainty of a bag of oats at the end of the journey? With a beautiful plume on your head? With your diploma you could easily be the master's horse.

Many thanks. This may very well be, as the doctors say, the good old wisdom of the ages, with an assured recompense in this world and the next, but for me it has a disagreeable taste. If I listen to you and nibble the good oats now, I shall soon find myself grazing in the field and obliged to chew dry stalks. No doubt about that. I don't propose to let your wisdom catch me. It is soft and subtle; it is so powerful because everyone, wherever he turns, not only breathes it in himself and is impregnated at its touch, but passes it on, willy-nilly, to the next fellow. It has its agents at work in the four quarters of the world. To this marvellous wisdom, the crown of centuries of civilisation, Henry gives another name, fraud. It has made itself at home in the village as in the great city. And it has that smile because it knows it is universally accepted.

Henry smiles too, for he is thinking of another universe than that of the hay-merchants. What alienates him from their brotherhood is the ugliness of their existence, pure derision. His own seems to him true, fresh and full of unexpected things, lived in the quick beauty of every moment, demanding no other profit than itself. Munch away your life, then, good citizens of Concord, and permit me to *live* mine. The shadow cast by our elms is not sufficiently enveloping to sweep me along after you into the paths of honourable stupefaction. I know what your society makes of a man by taming him. It will get along very well without my help. If it has held me for a short time, while I was groping my way, trying to get my bearings, you may be assured that this is over and done with. I have no desire to be a bad neighbour to you; you are very worthy members of this parish. But don't count on my aid in making your merry-go-round go. I have my own corn to grind. You say that in refusing to adapt myself to your rhythm I condemn myself to poverty. As you please; why not? He laughs best who laughs last. I am not afraid of my poverty. But I should have a terrible fear of what you call your respectability, your industry, your virtue, if I were ever threatened with having to share them.

But his whole race, all this little world about him, modelled in the image of the great world, had obeyed the commandment: Look after your business, increase your wealth. He listened to the mandate from within— listened in his own fashion. Yes, exactly, look after one's *own* business, increase one's *own* wealth. Interpret this freely, in your own way. This boy does interpret it in his own free way. He counts as much as anyone on "making a position for himself." There are many fine formulas of this kind that pass like counters from hand to hand, from one shop to another, from father to son, while no one suspects their true value. "Make a living" is one of them. Do you mean, make a living and lose what makes it worth while? Then make it, makers of money. We shall see in the end who is rich and who is poor. There is nothing the matter with your formulas. I shall take them and give them a good cleaning before I use them, for your hands have dulled them, soiled them. They will have to be bright and new for my poverty.

Henry is no frivolous boy, make no mistake about that. The great business of existence occupies his thoughts too. He asks himself if life is not too precious an affair to be sold in pencils or lessons, or measured out behind a counter, or at so much the page at a clerk's desk. Yes indeed, the great business of existence. . . . Exactly. But in quite another sense than that of all these poor souls who are much more aware of their dollars, their cattle and their land than of their essential poverty. Henry is quite willing to be poor, but poor like these people, never. By *no* means. Not at any price. He intends to pile up day by day the wealth to which all these well-to-do people, who think they are so comfortable and so shrewd, pay no heed. The great business of existence, in his twenty-five-year old eyes, is to create oneself, to *live*, develop oneself, with respect for this gift that one is—respect and love for this material that has been placed in one's hands in the rough for one to make of it the most beautiful of works of art. Is that clear, you poor souls, with your minds on dollars and cents?

As he watches this world, so diligent in its little wiles, its little thieveries, Henry has no disposition for recriminations and dark thoughts. He is too full of happiness. He feels his own strength. Let them have their gains! A tissue of trivialities, their days, whose comings and goings form the woof and the warp of their life. It amuses him vastly to behold the beautiful acquisitions they pile up around their mediocrity, like so much worthless bric-a-brac. Dull souls, not to see that the first step to wealth is to simplify one's life, disencumber it of endless useless knick-knacks that prevent it from growing. Money, to Henry, represents a pair of stout boots, a straw hat, corduroy trousers. These elements once acquired at little cost, he feels that all the other things—the savoury things the earth freely offers—are given him in addition, as a bounty, as to anyone who trusts. The apples in the orchard and the pike in the river and the joy of the banks are all thrown in. Your money, your absurd money, thanks to which you think you are assured of the enjoyment of the world, simply prevents you from getting it. Your incomes are your jailers; they stand on guard night and day about you. You serious men, you sensible men, perpendicularly set upon your principles, you sly old men of business, dignified heads of families, with an iron belief in the sanctity of your motives, how ludicrous you are in the eyes of a boy who strips away your mask. . . .

A certain mustiness, for the rest, which he finds everywhere in this Puritan atmosphere, offends the taste of the savage and the soul of the pagan that have come to him heaven knows whence. He is not adapted to the moral sanctity which these wooden sidewalks exhale. From his childhood, the meeting-house, the pulpit, the Sunday school and the tedious Sunday itself have made piety unpleasant in his eyes. How does it happen that the church is generally the ugliest building in a village? Is it a symbol? And if, some fine Sunday, in place of the preacher, shouting like a herdsman whose herd is refractory, some honest soul, some simple wood-cutter from the backwoods were to begin to utter, with his accent, before the congregation, a few of the words of Jesus, do you imagine that a single pane would remain in the windows of the edifice, that a single worshipper would stay in his pew and brave the crash? That old story refers across the ages to a fine, frank character who must have been as simple as a wood-cutter, and who could never have suspected, poor soul (otherwise how quickly he would have stopped talking!), that after eighteen hundred years his name would be invoked by all the brawlers of New England and creation to confuse men and women. A splendid fellow, this Jesus, the carpenter's son—too beautiful for us to be able to doubt, in spite of the vagueness of his story or of his legend, that he really existed in the flesh—a boy come from the people to recall the bigots and hucksters to decency, close up the vestries and the temples, put a little manly pride into the heart of the poor, and obliged, after his time and in spite of himself, to be the patron of the most flourishing business of emasculation.

I know you are going to say to me: this is no substantial nourishment, this old gospel of Judea, for a hearty lad who has worked all day and likes to put a jucier morsel into his mouth. I agree. It does not alter the fact that in spite of all the efforts of Christianity to disgust you with him, Jesus, my brother, spreads about him an aroma of godlike humanity. As you read the almost unknown book in which his life is told, you wish, just because you are a pagan yourself, that you could call your friends and say to them: Look here, I want to read to you some pages you probably don't know—they enchant me. . . . What do you think of my discovery? Isn't it fine? Isn't it a splendid heresy, with enough revolutionary force in it to crack the shell of this antiquated world? And how happy you would be to welcome as a comrade the friend of the vagabond if . . . if the fanatic in front did not need him to thrust into his sermon and shoot him at the worshipper at his feet. . . . Poor fellow, soul of love, heart of the poor, what have they made of you? . . .

The famous Pilgrim Fathers, who embarked on the Mayflower to free themselves spiritually and found a new England—did they imagine that in doing this they would be liberated from themselves? It was hardly worth while making this long voyage when, in the hold of the famous boat, the Son of Man was in irons. They had really come to organize, among other solid businesses, that immense conspiracy against life with which every child born under a roof in any of the Atlantic States is supposed to associate itself tacitly, and which he must never betray till death, under pain of eternal damnation and a damned existence here below. What a black responsibility Plymouth Rock bears!

This particular mania is what the posterity of the Pilgrim Fathers call their religion. It taxes with sin the innocence of a boy who sets off for a Sunday walk in the woods, or takes his fishing-line to the waterside at church-time, to feel religious in his own fashion: the Brotherhood of Sunday Bores sneers as the Sunday Walker passes. This religion, with its church-tower, is broadminded enough to tolerate the guile that gets the best of your neighbour during six days of the week. . . . Ugh. . . . Come nearer, good people, and let me tweak your noses and then turn my back and enjoy a good laugh. Your pious, mercantile existence is too dismal; a little gaiety would not ill become you. Your Sabbath bell strikes death into the soul; it sounds as if the continent were groaning in the unending misery of the terrestrial abode adorned by the Smug.

How was it possible for Henry to feel that he belonged to the same parish as these parishioners? As a matter of fact, this refractory soul had early declared his position. Soon after his return from college, at twenty, he had refused to pay the church-tax of the parish and officially separated himself from it with a written declaration in which no deacon caught a hint of humour: "Know all men by these presents that I Henry Thoreau do not wish to be regarded as a member of any incorporated society which I have not joined." This was plain and precise. Take that, clerk of the parish; put this disavowel away among your old papers, so it can bear witness in case there is need for it some day. The parish has carelessly counted one parishioner too many.

This was about the time when Henry, master in a parish school, flatly refused to form the character of his pupils with the help of the rod. Naturally this double rebellion, against the authorities of the village and the church, made him a suspicious character. The following year, when he reached the age for voting, he openly refused to perform the elementary act of a good citizen of a great democratic Republic. Moreover, the very success, for three years, of the Thoreau school had brought him the marked hostility of the mandarins of the village. This stiff little schoolmaster . . . this whipper-snapper of twenty-one who permitted himself not to have recourse to corporal punishment, who taught in an independent, lively fashion, who took the children off boating or gathering huckleberries instead of holding them by fear! Impudent! We shall have to be on our guard against you.

All right, be on your guard, mandarins. If the world speaks through your lips, I shall let the world go. From childhood Henry has been used to walking alone, at his own pace. He will try to find whether there does not exist somewhere another world of which he carries the image in himself. His one ambition, and it is a great one, is to make the finest use of the marvellous gift that he has received—life. He has received it, he is sure of that, and he knows its value. He must find out how to employ his faculties, that is all. Perhaps he is destined for some uncatalogued employment. He will see. But it must be an occupation that dispenses him from conniving with this world of universal hucksering. That's settled. Every line he has meditated in college, every one of his impressions since the time when he drove his parents' cow to pasture, has confirmed him in the resolution to remain himself, cost what it may. The inflexibility which he does not dissemble and which renders him insupportable to the mandarins is merely the outward sign of this will.

In any case, he desires to work only at what is useful, with his hands or his brain or his idleness—fruitfully, that is all that matters—according to his own idea of the useful. Those numberless absurd or degrading interests that absorb the human race he puts aside with deliberate design. He can easily make shift with the little sympathy that is felt for him in some quarters. If he had piled up a lot of rubbish in a shop and sold it at a good profit, like a true Thoreau of tradition, he would certainly have accomplished a work agreeable to the Lord. It's a pity, but he has no desire to please the Lord or his servants. He wants to please himself. This is certainly not the way to get up in the world; but for the moment, so far as that is concerned, to be planted on his two legs and to stand on the top of the Cliffs and watch the sun setting behind the mountains seems to him sufficiently happy till something better turns up.

And then there was another side to the story. Since college Henry had been working with definite aspirations, drawn towards a path that led heaven knew whither but solicited him with an authority as sweetly irresistible as the open spaces, out there, on a morning when he had a hunger for discovery.

This dated even from the days before college. At

Harvard some of his compositions revealed an intellectual curiosity, a boldness, a turn of mind that did not suggest the future lawyer or the embryo minister. Henry was already trying to express himself. As a growing boy he had devoured eagerly the scraps of new thought that came within reach of a villager. They had a fresh, exquisite flavour that left a good taste in his mouth. One day the friends of culture had inaugurated at Concord one of those Lyceums which were being founded almost everywhere in Massachusetts. Henry was only twelve years old at the time; but in future, before going to college, he followed assiduously the lectures and debates. The most beautiful of these lectures was the one he heard there when he was eighteen, delivered by the step-grandson of old Dr. Ripley, the minister of the parish, and a former minister himself, who had come to settle in the village after a difference with the ecclesiastical authorities.

What seized him, exalted him, was not so much the oration itself, composed for the occasion of the second centenary of the founding of Concord, as the sight of the lecturer, his expression, his eyes, the indefinable charm of his words. How right he had been to give up the church and its nonsense, this fellow of thirty-three, to come out as a man among men and talk to them with that voice and that smile that invited you to close your eyes to the wretched spectacles of the world and contemplate the figures which the spheres describe in their sacred dances. This man spoke as one inspired, with a simplicity, a nobility that carried you away. It was said that he had made a journey to Europe and had met a great many people over there, talked with Coleridge, Wordsworth and this Carlyle who was about to publish an astonishing book. He was just going to marry a second time. The year after the lecture, they had recited a poem of his in celebration of the anniversary of the famous battle of Lexington, a historic date from which Concord drew most of its lustre. It looked as if this new inhabitant, who had come to enjoy the natural charm of the little town, had brought it in exchange a superior charm capable of raising it above itself: short as the time was since he had settled there, he already cut a great figure, second only to that of his venerable step-grandfather, the spiritual director of the parish. Henry was nineteen years old. And this very year the poet published a book that was even richer than the most beautiful lecture. What a book! A revelation, a gospel, the music of which made you melt with pure admiration and joy. To think that this man was your neighbour. . . . That simple title *Nature* touched Henry at the most sensitive point. He was captivated, illumined, confirmed in his own aspirations. If he himself, some day, could only write pages that had a little of that subtle and luminous quality! . . .

If he could become a writer, one of those people who have something to say and know how to say it! At certain moments when he found himself really face to face with himself, Henry had the impression that there was something more than a great desire within him, that he had the power as well. Before his twentieth year and aside from his college dissertations, he composed, as an experiment, a few descriptive pages, wrote a rhymed ballad. And since his return from college, his Journal had always been there, scrupulously written up, to receive the secrets of this desire, the more urgent inquiries, the first attempts of a beginner who does not really know if the vein is rich but is heartily resolved to pursue his exploration, even if he is to have at the end nothing but the joy of exploring and contemplating the beautiful veins of the earth cut away by the drill.

Whenever he was not too dissatisfied with a page he had written, he read it to his little sister, for when you have a sister like Sophia, who feels just as you do, a true Thoreau, you can let her into the secret. It was at the beginning of the autumn that followed Henry's return home. A sister-in-law of the new great man of Concord was boarding with his parents. Henry liked her very much: one day in the spring of this year, while passing under her open window, with the gesture of a shy young boy, he had even thrown her a bouquet of fresh violets gathered on his walk, wrapped up in his apprentice rhymes. Yes, Henry liked Lucy Brown very much and he told or wrote her of things that he would never have been willing to confide to anyone else. In talking with this friend, Sophia, who had gone to one of the great man's lectures, could not help remarking: "That is very much like something that Henry has written . . ." It was easy to verify this singular concordance, which Lucy Brown mentioned to her brother-in-law. The great man wanted to see this young neighbour whose thought was so much akin to his own; had he progressed so well, then, the college boy whom he, as an influential and charitable man, had recommended to the benevolence of the President of Harvard? And so Henry found himself face to face with the man whose words, whose expression, whose beautiful book had stirred him.

And now that they had met they were delighted with each other. Each had understood the other at a glance; and before long they felt as if they had always been friends. Waldo was the elder by fourteen years, but Henry's maturity of mind made one forget that he was only twenty. Practically speaking, they were of the same age. The great man, who also kept a Journal, observed in it: "My good Henry Thoreau made this else solitary afternoon sunny with his simplicity and clear perception." Happiest of moments were those when they set out together for a ramble in the woods. At such times it was as if Henry was introducing his lady-love to the author of the beautiful book on Dame Nature. There Henry was at home, his companion was only on a visit. But so happy, this latter, to become acquainted, thanks to his guide, with so many things he had only perceived from a distance, things he had touched in thought but not through the senses. This boy knew everything that a philosopher did not suspect and introduced his friends of the forest to you in such a way that they counted henceforth among your own friends. In an excursion with Henry you were the guest shown about by the master of the estate. The great man became the student once more in the hands of this initiate. Charming student. Charming walks when these two were happy together, the one penetrating into the secret life of the woods with this sylvan creature, the other showing his intimate friend the cherished marvels that had been familiar to him from his childhood. How could a friendship rooted in the mould of the forest fail to shoot up high and thick? When the great man's family planned an expedition to the Cliffs, they sometimes begged Henry to go with them and not to forget to bring his flute.

Who can say what either one or the other of the friends reaped from these walks, these conversations, this exchange? Who gained the more? It would be hard to say. For Henry, in any case, in return for what he brought the great man—an influence that was tonic, real, strong as the taste of some crumpled aromatic plant or even the pungency of a thought impregnated with the raciness of the soil—how comforting it was to find in his elder such a wonderful response to his own

75

youthful meditations. . . to hear, for instance, such
perceptions as these: " Life is an art. When we consider
what life may be to all, and what it is to most, we shall
see how little this art is yet understood. . . The work
of life . . . is self-culture . . . the perfect unfolding
of our individual nature," when, at his own entrance
into life, his instinct had repeated to him in every key
this very admonition. . . . To hear this from the lips of
a sage whose personality was so magnetically impressive
was to yield to the purest appeal of oneself while gathering the sweetest fruit of friendship.

In the warmth of this exchange, which transformed
old Concord and gave it a new relish, Henry's tastes
were developed, along with his peculiar ambition.
From an assiduous listener at the meetings of the Lyceum
he had become a lecturer. At twenty-one he read there
the fragment he was just then writing on *Society*. It
was as bold as the first attempt of a young man is likely
to be, and not very thrilling for the village *élite*, who had
come to listen to a little schoolmaster on his first appearance on the platform; especially as he made no elocu-
tionary efforts to win them. He read his paper to them
as he would have read it at home to his sister, without
any further adornment; it was their business to listen and
profit by it. When people do not understand you there
always remains for them the resource of guessing at
your drift. In spite of this, the following year, because
he was actively interested in the maintainance of this
centre in the grey village existence, they made him the
secretary of the Lyceum, in charge of the lectures—
without remuneration, which gave the post its value and
charm in Henry's eyes. Whether the audience followed
him or not he meant to go on speaking, even if the
things he had to say were a little beyond the horizon
of Concord. Why should Concord not permit itself to

shed a little light, even from afar, upon those who lacked it?

So from now on a luminous centre existed here in spite of the good people who were so busy, here as elsewhere, digesting the dough of their days, without disturbing themselves about an art of living. There were philosophic symposia at the great man's house. A few choice men and even a muse met there, deeply interested in lofty problems and united in the same disinterested worship of the ideal. Towards the third year of the Thoreau school, various wise personages were to be seen there, Harvard graduates, men of learning, a poet, most of them young, attracted from various points in the neighbouring country through their love for a certain new thought. Especially to be noted was one who had the air of presiding over the conversations, with the authority of a man of forty; a pure spirit, lodged by mistake or a singular taste for antithesis in a carnal envelope—thin, lanky, with a pale skin and a head crowned with weeping hair, already white, named after one of the minor prophets, Amos. Amos Bronson Alcott. This noble dreamer had just settled in Concord with his terrestrial family, for he had taken a wife and begotten daughters, after the human law. As for the muse, her thirty summers had brought forth a bony visage and masculine features; her fascination was due to her great learning and her fancy and enthusiasm. Her name was Margaret Fuller. In such company you soon felt disburdened of your clayey mediocrity. You were ready to embark for the various points in the sky which the programme of the meeting indicated. The smile of the master of the house was enough to give you full confidence. Adventurous, intoxicating expeditions on which, after soaring through the clouds, you were never sure of being able to recover your path on the earth. They were veritable skylarkings of the spirit.

Henry listened, sharing in the discussions. Allied as he was to these choice spirits by the noble interests that were common to them, he did not feel entirely in harmony with them. Alcott was very eloquent and said many beautiful things. But while these tours of the heavens have an irresistible attraction for young and generous souls, Henry had never lost his plebeian habit of feeling the grain of the earth under his boots. In this refined game it was the stakes that mattered to him; the game for the game's sake struck him as a little academic. They were neo-platonists. But as these new aspirations required a new name they had adopted that of Realists or Transcendentalists, which the great man had selected with his friend George Ripley, who lived in Boston. Realists, those who pursued the reality behind the appearance—Transcendentalists, seekers of the infinite through the finite: this had the right sound, it told the story, and it was unorthodox enough to disturb all those pious heads that were congealed in the ice of their formulas. The smell of heresy is sweet to the nostrils of one who is fond of sniffing the wind.

Henry rejoiced to feel in himself the soul of a Transcendentalist. A good word this, Transcendentalist. It is long but it goes a long way. He was not quite sure that this "ist" had just the same shade of meaning for the whole gathering. Perhaps it was pale and crowned with white curls like the noble Alcott. Or curved in an exquisite smile like the lips of Waldo. Perhaps Transcendentalism, like its brother isms, had no more value than the individual who happened to pass it round his neck like a collar. Perhaps it was nothing but a tool in the hands of a worker, good or bad. Henry was going to use it as a worker who knows what to do with a tool. As for the word itself, serious as the matter was for him, there were even moments when Henry was tempted not to take it much more seriously than did the outsiders who lost no time in ridiculing the new gospel. Besides, he always had the resource of being a Transcendentalist in his own fashion. Let his friends seek for the real and the infinite as they chose; he was going to seek for it first under the soles of his heavy boots. Of this he was transcendentally sure.

As they were a circle of apostles revealing a new life at the heart of the old withered Puritanism, it was necessary for them to propagate this outside the workroom where they gathered. They founded a magazine; it appeared every three months and the muse of the group assumed the care and the expense of editing it. The great man gave it many pages that ought to have won for it subscribers by the thousand if the public could only have altered its detestable habit of ignoring a magazine supported solely by a belief in the beauty of humanity. If you publish, for instance, noble old bits from the classics, how can you expect to catch readers who ask for things that are amusing and sensational and up-to-the-minute? In the opening number of the magazine Henry had seen himself in print for the first time. A small emotion compared to that which was concealed, to all save one or two persons perhaps, in this poem entitled "Sympathy," under the signature Henry Thoreau. The author was twenty-three years old. He had published. He had emerged from his Journal. He was in a circle of friends who were initiating the renaissance of mystic idealism that was going to renovate the thought of New England and America. This was no reason for giving up his big boots or chinking in his pocket the dollars he had not received, since the magazine paid nothing. But it gave him the desire to write, to collaborate in this rare magazine in which his friends welcomed his manuscripts so cordially—or, when they refused them, refused as friends. They had not refused his "Aulus Persius Flaccus," his first public attempt as a writer of prose. And an unpaid article will sometimes earn one a friendship that is worth more than money. Often one is not to know of this till much later.

But to whom was he to give these little verses, the scribblings of a sentimental and philosophic schoolmaster, since the great man, who did not like them very much, advised him not to publish them? They had the archaic flavour of the old English poets who had helped him to endure his exile in the college library. They were like the work of a boy who amuses himself collecting little wanton butterflies and pinning them on equal lines on a card in some harmonious arrangement of their tinted wings. It was a game at which boys amuse themselves, boys and those older children who re-translate Horace after sixty. Henry was not yet twenty-five, and he was only a child in the sense that his childhood was inseparable from him; but he loved these soothing little old-fashioned verses, just as he loved to play a little air on his flute or whistle the tune of some organ-grinder in the street. Not "smooth and flowing" enough for the taste of the great man of Concord, who made rhymes too now and then. There was nothing to be done then but to keep them to himself, since their rhythm was dear to him in spite of all. There would always be time to throw them into the stove.

But what was he to do with those great chunks of prose interspersed with the little verses in his Journal? And when did he first realize that he was the writer, the poet, in them, and not in these rhymes of an elderly amateur? Aside from the pages that he had used in the composition of his first essay, "Sound and Silence," there were those he had copied and sent to Margaret Fuller, the editor, who did not want them for her magazine. Yet they had rather a strong quality. In a tone of juvenile grandiloquence, but with a firm accent, Henry pronounced his vows, notified society of his refusal to collaborate with it, and dedicated himself to the service of the cause. The editor did not perceive that a writer of prose had been born, prolix and not yet sufficiently sure of himself to break through the weight of words, carried away by his love of paradox, but rich in savoury fantasy, a creator of bold, fresh images. Her copy had been returned to him, with a graceful note of refusal. He would wait, then.

Henry stored his harvest away. Henry worked. Outside his father's little factory, where he made the pencils, there was a labourer at his toil, awaiting his audience without anxiety.

How does it happen that Henry, yesterday a schoolmaster, should be living at his friend Waldo's house? Ralph Waldo Emerson, yes. It has come about quite simply.

His friend, finding him free after the closing of the school, has made him a proposal.

He is greatly in need of someone to look after a hundred and one little matters, in the house and outside, which he cannot attend to himself. When he is away, off on lecture tours, it would be very pleasant to feel that he was leaving at home someone he could trust to see that everything went smoothly, as it should go in the household of a philosopher. He thought that such a man as Henry, who was a famous gardener and understood everything, would be just the person. Was he mistaken? Henry could come and live in their house without sacrificing any of his cherished liberty. How did Henry feel about it?

The latter had accepted. Not as a young man of twenty-four, only too happy to yield to the desire of a great elder, but because this proposal had a sound that pleased him. In that house at least he knew they would accept him, discerningly, at his true value. They were not appealing to a workman whose arms or brain one hires; they were appealing to Henry, raw as he was, with his qualities and his defects. That is why he had said yes. An ugly word becomes clarified when you take a "job" with people who understand you and love you as nature has made you. Heavens, yes, he had agreed without a single reservation.

The arrangement was quite simple. The steward was to work as he chose in the garden or elsewhere, at any hours that pleased him and whenever work seemed good to him; in return, he was to have his meals and his room as if he were one of the family. He was to be one of the family. Wasn't that clear and above-board? . . . If you were a great philosopher, illumined with a serene wisdom, but little fitted for all those small material affairs that have to be reckoned with just the same in the daily life of a philosopher, would you not be very happy to have engaged a trustworthy man to shoulder all these little troublesome tasks and be on the spot, with an alert eye and a sure hand, during your absences? And suppose, at the same time, that you could converse occasionally on the noblest topics with your confidential man, as a brother, an equal, who is prepared to accompany you, to follow or precede you, up the highest peaks of thought: would not this be a famous combination? . . . And if you were a penniless young man, seeking employment for your faculties or your skill with people who would not make use of you simply as a tool that one takes up and throws aside, a tool that one oils or allows to rust, would you not be overjoyed to be the confidential man of a sage who wants to place in your hands all the odd tasks about the house? A sage who knows perfectly who you are and appeals to the man as well as the worker? Would you hesitate? Hardly, for it would strike you that to work for such an employer, such a friend, would be like playing even if the work sometimes were hard; it would be the highest form of collaboration. Your friend is a philosopher divinely adroit in the field of ideas, but far from handy in the practical domain; he needs your workingman's hands and allows them to exist side by side with the soul of a poet. Your friend opens his house to you as an equal.

All right, it's settled, friend Waldo. This environment, this household are sympathetic to Henry; the house itself smiles on him. Coming to Concord, Emerson, after visiting his step-grandfather, in the delightful old manse built by his ancestor where he himself had written *Nature*, had had the luck to find and establish there, as the home of his second marriage, the true dwelling for a sage. At the far end of the village, on the same side as the Poor Farm, it was called, from the name of a previous holder, the Coolidge house. The benediction of the great trees along the road prepared you for the grave smile of a little white dwelling among the pines whose modest porch seemed to say to the new master: I give myself to you for eternity. Be faithful to me. We shall always understand each other. And the nine windows in front approved and the two chimneys took the oath; the Mill Brook in the great meadow was the witness of the engagement. And you felt immediately that what the porch said was true. From there it was only a short quarter of an hour to

Walden Pond, where you found yourself in the wild woods; a spot haunted by Henry since his childhood, where the Sage particularly loved to air his thoughts under the pines. It was a house after Rousseau's heart and after Henry's heart. And when a house pleases you, everything you have to do that depends on the house is tinged with pleasure. It was only a few weeks after the closing of his school that Henry had come to occupy the place offered him in this home, nestling in the joy of the fields at the end of April.

There is nothing like a little white house and its out-buildings in the fields for giving you work to do. This is Henry's business. From the kitchen-dresser hangs a door the hinges of which have come off. Just in his line. The hinges of the door of eternal life are in the best of order, but the genius of a philosopher does not understand kitchen-dressers. The stove draws badly; it must be taken apart. This is in your line too, man of all work. The disfigurement of hands soiled with soot is not indelible. And who is to assume the important labours of the hen-house? A philosopher, of course, possesses like the most ordinary mortal the art of eating a soft-boiled egg; but before and after this beautiful fresh egg is laid for you to go and take it out of the nest, how many little details there are that demand the skill and experience of a man well up in other tasks than the tasks of the study! Fowls have their own life and their own ideas; there is the practical philosophy of the poultry-yard on which neo-platonism has made no profound impression, and there is the hand that knows how to make just the right twist to restore the broken roost. An idealist especially needs good roosts and hens that lay. Not necessarily golden eggs; simple, soft yellow eggs are the thing for your philosophic breakfast. And who but a gardener-poulterer is to prevent the blessed hens from marauding among the flowers in the garden? Then there is a pail that leaks, and here is the tinker. You have everything under your hand with that wonderful boy. He is the universal repairer. The neighbours know him well and have recourse to his knowledge. And he is a great hand at chopping wood. When you see Henry handling the wood you feel that his friend Waldo is going to gain a good deal by this exchange. His trusty man does not measure the pains he takes, he is indefatigable and performs his labourer's toil with the same conscientiousness with which he has elaborated a page of prose, for himself alone, in his Journal.

But Henry's real kingdom is the garden. He understands not merely how to raise melons, but how to prune fruit-trees; he knows how to graft, and how to catch moles and field-mice; he is ready if there is a stake that needs to be strengthened with heavy blows of the mallet, vegetables to be transplanted or trenches to be dug. Sometimes the philosopher and the gardener work together in the garden. Near this invaluable boy, who is like a brother to him, the Sage is happy; it is not merely the garden-work that does him so much good, but Henry's presence acts on him like a tonic. The stroke of this little man's spade seems to stir the roots of his own philosophy; on the clod that he turns up a worm is wriggling. The spade plunges into the secrecy of the combinations of the earth that will make the seed of the idea germinate.

Henry is in a fortunate position. He can really share in such a household. He feels at home there. In their leisure hours the master and his confidential man have long conversations in the study, where the plain board shelves do not look as if they held the books merely for the charm of their bindings. At these moments their everyday intimacy rises to the loftiest comradeship. They prolong these fine excursions in which Waldo remembers that he is the son of a mighty walker before the Eternal. In the open fields and amid this full-hearted intimacy, they make astonishing discoveries. Yes, they are happy, and neither of them would be able to say what it is that so enlivens the landscape when they set out together. The Sage does not walk on Sunday; on that day it is more suitable to stay at home.

So now the master of the Coolidge house can set out with a mind at ease when he is going to give his lectures. He can depend on his young friend, from whom he receives letters that have the fragrance of their garden days together. In his absence the confidential man becomes the protector and the stay of the household. Other ties unite him to the family than those of the hen-house and philosophy. If Lidian, the mistress of the household, loves him like a grown-up son, it is not merely because he looks after the flowers in her garden that she has brought from her parents' house. In the same month in which Henry had lost his brother, she had lost her dear little Waldo, her eldest, five years old. It was to John, the charming John who had brought Emerson one day a bluebird-box for the barn, that she owed that daguerreotype of the child who had now vanished with him. . . . This poignant double loss had touched depths that the Transcendentalist doctrines never reached. From the bereavement they had simultaneously undergone there had sprung up, in the mistress of the house, an affection like that of an older sister for the big boy of the house, which he returned with a deep, tender respect. The good gardener who took such pains with her garden and her flowers gratefully accepted the authority, extending to all sorts of small daily observances, of this woman who confided in him.

They led a very frugal existence in the home of the philosopher, who was familiar with narrow circumstances from his childhood, his mother having been left a widow with five small children to bring up, and he had kept the taste for simplicity. This mother with her wholesome face, always smiling, had come to live with her son and daughter-in-law. As for Aunt Mary, who was also to be seen in the house, still so young at eighty years, Henry had simply won her heart. And it was a holiday when Lidian's elder sister, Lucy Brown, the gardener's very dear friend, happened to be there. Yes, Henry, the philosopher's right-hand man, was very much at home.

Nothing was needed but children to make him feel completely so, for between Henry and the children there was a tacit alliance. There were only two of them, Ellen and Edith, babies or practically so, since the death of little Waldo, but with Henry they formed a new trio. With the children as in the garden he was in his element. Their innocence brought out several Henrys, for he was never at the end of his wits. There was the inexhaustible teller of wonderful tales, a wizard who had no equal for making them little flutes and whistles with the simple reeds they collected in the meadow. And all those tricks he showed them: how to manage the warming-pan in which they heated the pop-corn till it burst and fell in showers like fire-works, the jack-knife that he swallowed and took out again through the nose, with a skill that would have made his Uncle Charles jealous, and the trick of the apple divided so cleverly that it seemed to be intact till he asked you to cut it and it fell into quarters. And how many other inventions! The only person whom Ellen and Edith never saw with their friend was Father Spoil-Sport. When they were bigger he was going to take them out in his boat, and they were going to be Indians and camp out in a hut of branches and live on huckleberries and sour apples and make music. Meanwhile, after supper, they could go on strange journeys on the carpet before the fire; play horse and gallop astride his knee, or perch perilously on Henry's sloping shoulders, standing straight up taller than Grandma and almost touching the ceiling. When Ellen said, "Papa may be coming home this evening," little Edith, who was beginning to talk, would repeat "Papa" and look at her friend Henry. He had a big nose like her real Papa and they were quite willing to accept him as a second Papa. He was not a grave gentleman all in black like those whom they saw coming to the house and who remained shut up in Papa's study. He at least was willing to lend a hand and was not afraid of soiling it. He was a Henry after their own heart with whom they could exchange a knowing smile, for he understood the mysterious meaning of the onomatopoeia of children who create a language of their own before accepting another ready-made; a Henry whom they respected though he did not growl at them and was not one of these respectable people; a Henry who was on secret terms with the world of fairies, strange plants, astonishing animals and corn that burst in the fire, and with the little folk who were in ecstasy before these marvels.

Do not try to play the child with children if you lack the proper physique. Henry's figure contributes greatly to his success with young people. Small, thin as a wolf, with a narrow chest, sloping shoulders, he looks like a wise and cunning gnome. No matter if he is ugly, of an ugliness for which not one of the seven deadly sins would accept the responsibility, for this really makes no difference to them. At the ends of his long arms are veritable workingman's hands; a spindling trunk, rather short legs planted on big feet. His markedly aquiline nose points to a mouth with singularly expressive lips and knows nothing of the receding chin. Sunk beneath the saliant eyebrows are large, clear, wide-open eyes, grey with a tinge of the blue of the sky, that look you through and through. Light-brown hair, abundant and fine. His sunburnt complexion, a certain rusticity of manner, which his association with Harvard and its fine gentlemen has not corrected, would make it very easy to mistake him for some longshore-man on a visit up country. As you see him pass, with his rough clothes, worn alike on weekdays and Sundays, his hob-nailed boots bound with leather laces, with the long, swinging step of a man who is used to walking great distances, hands behind his back and fists clenched, often with his eyes on the ground, the impression of physical resistance this thin little fellow gives is in flat contradiction to the meagre frame. When he lifts his eyes and looks at you it is as if a jet of implacable sincerity and perspicacity had struck you; the whole man is revealed in those eyes. Not a very easy fellow to teach, you say to yourself. But the twinkling of the grey eyes has another meaning which the children and his few friends know; under the bold features of a face that can be serious to the point of desolation, they know what fancy, what a vein of caustic humour and sober gayety is waiting for a chance to be released. And these diverse impressions melt in the aroma of open air that breathes from his whole person.

Not easy to get on with, assuredly no. You can look to him for adhesion or resistance, but never for submission. You can do nothing with him unless you accept him as he is, with his mulish obstinacy, his final "noes," his likes and his dislikes. They know him well at the Emersons': sudden bursts of frankness, resistance

without any reason, fits of combativeness, a bluntness
that does not always conform to the code of politeness
are to be expected from this right-hand man, who shocks
them now and then. But it is always wiser to let him
follow his own fancy, singular as it may be. If they had
engaged a gardener by the year or a day-labourer, he
would have done his money's worth—his money's
worth exactly or a little less, done his job like a duty that
enables you to live. With Henry you always get more
than your money's worth, because money to him means
nothing—or something so different. You have only to
let him choose his own hours and his own way of
working. There is no one who will do a job better
than he, as long as it has none of the grey tinge of a
duty.

For the rest, who could deny the excellence of the
arrangement? A man who can do everything about the
house and yard is very valuable: how much more so if
he can be your literary collaborator as well! Margaret
Fuller, who is finding it very difficult to make a success
of the *Dial*, the Transcendentalist magazine that only
needs subscribers to be the first magazine of the continent, has finally turned over the editorship to Emerson. The latter asks Henry to help him. They will
work in the garden and the magazine together. They
have to assemble the copy, send it to the printer, read
the proofs, put it into pages, canvass for new subscribers. A task not quite so familiar to Henry as graft-
ing and pruning, but he sets to work and does it. Under
his hands the magazine takes a new turn. It associates
the old Oriental sapience with the fresh wisdom of the
Atlantic shores. Henry likes his work as editorial secretary. Here he is at the heart of the movement. And
now it is he, whose manuscripts the amiable editress
had refused, who judges and inserts the manuscripts of

other people. He profits by the change to extract from
his Journal, revise and publish long fragments—accounts
of excursions, impressions of nature, studies of the
fauna and the flora of the country. The editor thinks
very highly of this gardener-subeditor who helps him so
earnestly in preparing the magazine and filling out the
table of contents.

Can you imagine a boy looking back later upon this
time of his twenty-fifth year, passed thus in the confidence of a little white house, and not finding in the
recollection the happiest of tastes? The best part of it
was not so much the privilege of having lived on such
intimate terms with a great man as the liberty they had
given him, the trust they had reposed in him in this
household. Henry, their confidential man—how wise
they had been in giving him their confidence! . . . In
return for his board, they had permitted him to live in
his own way, giving what he was able to give on this
condition. They had not asked him not to be the
Henry that he was by the grace of God, with all his
oddities and his pig-headedness and his nonchalance.

Everything else could be forgotten, but this noble and
affectionate indulgence, this magnanimous faith in him,
a young man who had not yet shown his best, had
warmed his heart at a time when the future seemed dim
to a boy who had nothing to offer the world but what
the world had no use for. Whatever this future might
be, there would remain between his elder and himself
the magnetism of this friendship, the tie of these fraternal years when they had cultivated the garden together.
Even if he said little about it, he carried this always in
the bottom of his shy, remembering heart.

After a visit to New York in February, 1843, Emerson
was at home again by the end of the winter to welcome

another spring in Concord. It would soon be two
years since Henry had come to his house to live: or had
he always been there, and was he to remain always?
It was time to do a little thinking. William, the philosopher's older brother, was looking for a tutor for one
of his children. What would the confidential man, the
Harvard graduate, say to this? He would have to give
up Concord, for William Emerson was living near New
York. A serious resolution, to leave his kingdom and
his own people. On the other hand, the neighbourhood
of New York would be favourable to his literary ambi-
tions, and might help him, who could say, to sell a few
articles. This chance to try was perhaps the most
tempting opportunity that might offer. And then he
would see a new country, another horizon would stand
out against the setting sun. Henry had had no further
glimpse of New York since he had gone there on business, at nineteen, with his father.

So it happened that, in the May of this year, the
confidential man found himself on Staten Island, the
island with its back to the continent like an animal
advancing to sniff that much larger animal, Long Island,
which has come out of the Atlantic, with the bay of
New York crowding between their two muzzles. It
was on the north side of the island that William Emerson
had his residence. A beautiful house, worthy souls
who did their best to be amiable. But one who had just
left a house like that of Waldo and Lidian recognized by
the smell, the moment he entered this house, that these
people were of another species. It was imposing, grave
and stupefying. Henry felt like a stranger among
strangers; even the title of Judge, borne by the master
of the house, weighed upon him. They did not understand one another, they never would understand one
another; but for all that he would do his work as well

as he could since he was a tutor and it was a question
of Waldo's brother. Later on, he would see; meanwhile, the tutor was obliged to stay in his room. For
on arriving he had caught a violent cold that kept him
shut up for a week. A misery to have had such a weak
chest ever since that bad case of bronchitis which had
made him so ill when he was eighteen.

A bad beginning at the Judge's, in an unknown country. In front of the house, deep woods, and a mile
away the sea, which he heard roaring when the wind
blew. The house stood with its back against a hill a
hundred yards high, from which you surveyed the
immense panorama of the Bay, the Narrows, Brooklyn,
New York in the distance, the coast of New Jersey.
The first time he climbed it and took in all this horizon,
he was sure of one thing: this was the place he would
come to for the nourishment he would never find under
this roof, where there was nothing to hold him aside
from his duties as a tutor. His real daily repast awaited
him on the hill. He could live for a few months in a
strange house, situated at the foot of a height that com-
manded such a quarter of space. Alone, up there, he
could collect himself towards evening, watching the
boats and the sea or reading a dear letter received from
far, far over there, beyond the boats and the sea—from
old Concord of which he dreamed and the forest paths
that preserved the imprint of his feet.

Henry felt a void in his soul. A stoical boy has
remedies against homesickness and, wherever he is, his
own company helps him to endure it. Just the same,
the soul suffers from a sudden change of diet; it is slow
in acclimatizing itself. Over there were his own people
and the face of his own country, the voices of the two
rivers and the Mill Brook and the smell of the upturned
earth in Waldo's garden. Here, everything breathed of

exile, and the summer had a different language; in spite of the sun he shivered.

When homesickness prowls about, seeking for some chink by which to worm its way into you, the best thing to do, when you are not shut up between the walls of a college, is to set out for discoveries over the island, to see what it has to offer you. When you are a mighty walker, a born vagabond, you hold homesickness at a respectful distance. From nine to two o'clock Henry makes his pupil work, then he is free. You can see him setting out in his good Concord boots to seek his fortune. The interior of the island is like a great pleasure-park, with its valleys, its woods, its verdure; fruit-trees abound there, cherry-trees are common along the hedges, the tulip-tree flourishes, and the magnolia in July is enthroned like a supernatural bride. A park in which some care has been taken for the views; through the long clefts in the earth you suddenly perceive, over a field, a ship under full sail, passing thirty miles out at sea—as in a magic lantern. In the valleys, shielded by the foliage, are the farms of the Huguenots, the first colonists; the old elm on the shore still marks the spot where they landed, after placing the ocean between themselves and the Dragonnades of Louis XIV—the great-great-grandparents of your own people at Saint-Helier, brought here not by the desire to make fortunes but by their passion for spiritual independence. In the northeastern corner, not very far from Castleton, where the Emersons' house is, there is another Concord. You find them everywhere. The Sundays are free for long excursions. The vast kingdom of an island seems still more vast, for you are surprised that the seashore can surround so much country. The walker annexes it methodically. Everything is new to him. They raise tomatoes and potatoes in the open fields. Henry has not left at home his old vigilance as a rover. Crossing a field he stoops and picks up an arrow-head. It is really almost laughable. At Concord or wherever he may be, when a flint-flake emerges, however imperceptibly, from the earth or a heap of pebbles, you may be sure that Henry, tramping in that neighbourhood, will fall upon it. He smells it. It is as if in his shrewd glance there were a magnet that makes these arrow-heads emerge for his benefit from the earth where they are hidden.

Henry scours the island. A surveyor, no doubt, this lanky fellow whom people see crossing and re-crossing the fields, examining everything with his old habit of inventorying a piece of land, as if he were going to buy it: he cuts across it in a bee-line, whether the ground is good or bad, regardless of the regular road. Or perhaps a man looking for a good site for some speculation. He must be pretty well acquainted with the state of things. A poor devil of a tutor, you say? Come now! . . . More attractive still than the interior of the island are its watery shores, the salt marshes, the approaches of the sea. Henry wanders along the beach, waiting for this enormous presence to define itself. Never before has he had such a chance to be impressed by it. Perhaps it has things to say to him which the pines about Concord have forgotten to convey. He has the whole of space to himself; there is nothing frivolous to distract him, the hidden musicians play for him alone, and he can walk and walk and walk to its ritornello in the dazzling marine daylight. It is grand enough to overwhelm him if he were not made of tough gristle. A pack of half-wild dogs scours the beaches in quest of carrion thrown up by the ocean. The smallest of them stops and barks after him. He has surely rubbed against mankind, this cur, for he was the one you took under your protection yesterday, driving off with stones the big fellows that were chasing him. The only people you see are fishermen who have drawn their boats up on the shore — herring-fishers, with great nets. Far away glide the boats with men on board who think as you do. You feel as if you were one of these boats, and you too long to spread your sails, instead of leaving your footprints on the wet sand or walking on the shingle like the crabs.

Concord, you are in no danger of being forgotten, but confess that you have no such sight as this to offer. The best place from which to take it in is some height where you are the monarch over this immensity. Then, though you are too far away to reach the shore, the ocean seems to you so near that you could touch it. The whole radiant panorama of the sea, islands, bay, shores, marshes, converges towards your own small self that receives it and feasts upon it; your landsman's soul drinks in the sea and the sailors. From an old ruined fort, Henry watches the arrival of the vessels; the health-officer climbing on board, the messenger who has come for his bundle of newspapers. Best of all is the hill-top behind the house which he can ascend every evening, the ideal observatory from which to count the sails in sight as the sun sets, revealing more and more of them the lower it falls—passing, returning, departing, sometimes in a long procession, busy, stately, as if they were coming here, between the muzzles of the two fishes, to conclude their tour of the world.

Before this huge spectacle of the bay of New York, this incessant passing of vessels, this amplitude of ocean that is offered to the eye of the little tutor, sitting and musing there on the ridge, his rustic Concord soul communes with itself and wonders if it could become acclimatized here. This hour is the best of the day, and on this hill-top he recovers his balance. Yes, the sea alone can mitigate the separation. It is like the winds that blow in the woods at home. But if, at the foot of the hill or on his return from a walk, there were only some friend with whom he could talk as a brother! Or if he could merely find himself again in some circle of familiar silence bathed in an atmosphere of trust! For Henry solitude is an old and honoured acquaintance: but never till now has it wearied him as it sometimes wearies him here. There are no human faces about him on the is-land—for all these New York families who come over to spend the summer—save an old fisherman, a neighbour, who invites him to come to the beach and see the beauti-ful shad he has caught. So Staten Island is not a desert island; it is inhabited by old Smith in whose presence he feels happy as a man and a fresh-water fisherman himself.

In a rapid, sloping hand, cut with dashes for punctua-tion, Henry writes affectionate letters to his family and friends in Concord—an extraordinary number of letters for him. This cheers him up when the unsavoury food of his days, served on the Judge's table, leaves on his palate an after-taste of exile. He entreats his mother for details of the life at home, for news of everybody, includ-ing Aunt Louisa, whose benignant face smiles upon him like an apparition from the wall of his room, and Cousin George Minot. The lonely boy ingenuously commits all sorts of enormities: he, with his sovereign contempt for newspapers, asks them to send him the Concord paper. Of course it is perfectly idiotic there, but how good it would be here, alone on the hill in the evening, or in his room, to have a taste of the printed news from home! And business, the pencils? And the vegetable garden? Henry is still so full of Concord that, when he wakes up at night he can hardly believe that the sound of the neighbouring sea is not that of the wind among the woods of his childhood. In his dreams he sits under the poplar behind his father's house, sure that he is going to spend his whole life there. He has bought a new pair of pantaloons which have cost him $2.25 ready-made; the stockings are wearing well, for they are properly made—knitted at home. His mother need have no fears: his outfit will not have to be renewed yet—it withstands the new climate as well as its master's frame. Henry is going through a period of strange mental lethargy, which makes him think of his waggish Uncle Charles, the famous wrestler who was so speedily overthrown by the demon of sleep, in the very middle of a conversation or even while he was shaving. And he also thinks of his brother, in his grave now for more than a year. . . He writes to Waldo. How conceal the fact that he grates upon William and Susan Emerson as much as these excellent people grate upon him? His pupil is clever and is making progress, but nothing about him wins the affection of his tutor. He takes after the Judge. As for your brother, your sister-in-law, your nephews, dear Waldo, you can't guess how much further away one feels from them, thinking of you and yours and the years passed in the little white house! He writes to Lidian. How are the flowers getting on in her garden? Are the weeds coming up too fast? She must have a new gardener. And the chickens? And do they go huckleberrying as they used to do? The poor woman is not well and she has told him about her difficulties; and in his own solitude, in his affection and respect, her old right-hand man feels more grateful than ever to this noble friend. Henry has a heavy heart, but as he breathes these dear odours of Concord his hand does not tremble. His advice to a sick friend is an exhortation to fortitude; his letters to Waldo are as luminous as the conversations they had had when they were off together on some excursion in the fields. The exile dreams, collects his thoughts, struggles against his debility. The penholder and the pocket inkstand which Elizabeth Hoar, Emerson's friend, had given him for his journey, are there like a feminine invitation. He translates the "Seven Against Thebes," and even composes for the *Dial* a piece that is full of visions of dear Concord, *A Winter Walk.* If it comes out well he will send it off for the next number. He can only follow from afar the little review they are making among themselves, imprinting it with a style all its own; but how he loves it as a ray of light, an annunciation—and how he loves its disdain for commercial methods.

As for the nearby metropolis, visible to the North, Henry was not satisfied with observing it from the hilltop when his evening thought interrogated the horizon. Since the first month of his arrival he had profited by his Saturdays to go over and see New York. It was easy: a half-hour's walk on the road that passed in front of the house, then three-quarters of a mile along the shore to the village of Castleton, where you took the boat. In the city he went at once to see two young friends of Emerson, clerks in an office. They had a drink together. Thanks to these pleasant boys he did not feel alone in this pandemonium, where everything shocked and grated on his country nerves. Then he went to see a few sights that would serve as landmarks, the Station, the Reservoir, the National Academy. He was not living so far away; he would come back. Such a big morsel was not to be swallowed at one mouthful. But there was one sight that had struck the Concord boy much more than any of the monuments mentioned in the guide-books: the crowd, the flood of faces in this Babel of a metropolis. The churches, the Stock Exchange, the great pretentious buildings were mean, vulgar, insupportable. But the crowd surging through the canyon-like streets was a phenomenon that surpassed all these monuments, whether they were dedicated to the worship of gold, God or the devil. Nothing like this in Boston; it was a revelation. He would not forget the name of this power. The crowd, yes, the herd that counted for so little beside the individual. But what if the hum that rose from these swarms of nobodies, this surge of faces in the great arteries, did correspond to the waves that he had seen rushing together in the Narrows, or beating the shores of the metropolis? He had the impression that this human flood could, when it wished, submerge these stupid cubes of stone. The crowd had imposed itself on little man.

Henry returned to the city whenever he could. He would have returned oftener were it not for the expense. The boats left every hour, but you had to pay your fare, and he was in rather bad straits. The distances were great in the city, and he would have taken the stage often had it not been for this miserable impecuniosity. If only that wretch of an editor who had published one of his articles with a promise of remuneration and who pretended to be dead would only have paid him! He was obliged to space out his visits to New York. He went to see Henry James, the Swedenborgian, a little plump, rosy, lame man who looked like a broker. Henry spent three hours talking with him: in the questions the latter asked he came into touch with a soul of wisdom and goodness that refreshed him. One of those men who were able to enliven a city whose tawdry buildings disheartened him. By degrees the villager became used to the monster. He went to read in the libraries, where he found the magazines and one or two substantial mouthfuls like Carlyle's last article; especially the Mercantile Library, the keeper of which, an old Harvard tutor, had given him a card of admission for a month. Moreover, in spite of this mental lethargy from which he suffered, he did not forget one of the reasons that had led him to try New York. He had come with the idea of seeing how the land lay in the literary world. Horace Greeley, the editor-in-chief of the *Tribune*, upon whom he called, made a good impression on him. They talked over the experimental phalansteries, in which Horace had more faith than Henry. Horace was a strong and important connection. He recommended the beginner to the *Democratic Review* which accepted his paper "The Landlord," for its October number. This was no great source of wealth, for the magazine was poor and only paid famine prices. So he thought it would be a good thing to find something else, for there was always this irritating question of money. Henry held his lethargy in check and boldly called upon publishers and editors; there might be one who needed a young writer like himself, just fresh from his village, a fruit of the orchards of Concord with their bloom still on him. One of them proposed some work that an honest man could not do. Another jingled the $50,000 in profits which he made year in, year out, just by letting well enough alone. No doubt, no doubt. This chinking of dollars made Henry feel that he was rich enough to despise them. There was nothing much to tempt him indeed among fellows like that. It was just as it was in Concord; no one needed him, and those who would have liked to give him a welcome were unable to pay him. He had gone the rounds of the magazines; those that he had thought of as possible had obliging contributors by the dozen. There was, to be sure, the *Ladies' Companion*, which paid; but he was not likely to stray into that company. Ask somebody else, dear lady. And yet he was absolutely obliged to earn a little money. So Henry spent a whole day hawking *The Agriculturist* about New York. This was less humiliating than scribbling for a trashy publisher. If there was nothing for a writer to do in New York, he would wait for luckier days. The Republic of Letters would not die, nor would Henry either. He would retire in good order, as light in money and the hope of money as when he arrived. His flat purse, on his return as on his departure, would serve to identify him. . . .

But have you reckoned up exactly what you are bringing back, my friend? It is more than your purse would hold. Or even your portmanteau, between your socks and your books. Your wealth, young man of Concord, is solid and durable in a different way from the ready-made trousers you have bought in New York. The experience of the literary market—how much do you think that is worth? You have watched these shopkeepers, big and little, at their counters; while they were talking, you have caught the odours from the back-shop. These few glimpses were enough for you to divine the flavour of their cooking, their motives, the quality of their trade. The most generous of them could not pay for your collaboration a more royal price than that of this experience. At twenty-six, when you are beginning, to know once and for all that the literary market is a market like other markets, to which you bring your merchandise, which will remain on your hands if it does not suit the taste of the customer; to know that the career of letters as you understand it is not a trade that enables a man to subsist and that there is no profit of money for you to hope for in this way . . . tie up this truth tight in your handkerchief and keep it as the rarest of your arrow-heads.

And this ocean of faces in the streets, on the wharves,

the human flood of New York—how much is it worth, from your point of view, to have coasted along that and felt it beat against you? The passionate individualist is in rebellion against the power of the mass. But it has fascinated you, disturbed you; its magnetism has impressed you at the first contact. A mob, undoubtedly. But with a movement as grand and sweeping as that of the clouds and the winds and the waves. And the watery surroundings of the city, that luxuriance of ocean and horizon and ships, absorbed from the hill-top, and those long walks on the shore—do you imagine they have not affected you also? Recall those crowds of immigrants you have seen passing, stopping for a day or two, pent up on a wharf, men, women, children, tattered but so very human, so real, washing their linen unconcernedly, cooking their dinner in the open air, whole families come from the four corners of the Old World to seek their fortunes in the hospitable West. Always the mob, observed with a distrustful sympathy by a savage who will never admit that man can keep his quality as a man by mingling in the mob. Yes, but in this swarm of poor wretches, encamped on a wharf, among these playing, whining children, these mothers sitting on their bundles of clothing, has it not occurred to you as you observed them with the eye of an artist fascinated by this picturesque parade, that there might be some Henry going West with his tools and his fortune and a soul as rich as your own or even greater? In any case, your glances have scrutinized this horde on the march and recognized human faces in transit. And what remains to you from this must not be forgotten when you balance your accounts.

Have you lost your homesickness? Has even your health been strengthened by the air of the bay? When you go home, you will remember, with a leaping of the heart that will warm the November air, how much you have been repaid for your months of exile by all that those crowds, that ocean, those wharves, those steamers have left in you—yes, and those hours of solitude when, from the top of the hill, your sick soul was fed by the play of the storm and the sunlight and the moonlight at midnight over the bay. And that sound of the sea which you have heard in your bed in the silence of the Judge's house, and the spectacle of the sun rising from the Atlantic—do you think they will not add something to the magnificence of the sunset when you have contemplated it anew from your riverside heights of Musketaquid?

IV

The dear presences are ranged about you there, in the centre of that universe for which you have longed; it is good there, and what does the reſt matter? For a lover who has been nourished exclusively on his dreams for six months, the joy of return surpasses everything. It is winter; but what warms Henry is not merely the ſticks in the ſtove. All Concord offers its warmth for his return.

He finds his father ſtill busy with the pencils. What if he were to turn in and help? All right, the pencils. The lead seems less grey in the delight of his return. Since he has nothing to look for in a literary way, and no opportunity offers for the moment, he will ſtay at home and attend to the pencil business with his father. Doesn't it occur to you that a miserable little piece of lead imprisoned between two ſticks of cedar-wood may be unworthy of your attention? It is not quite what you have dreamed of, perhaps. But Henry knows the secret. For there is a secret. So much so that it would be a miſtake for anyone who has no business there to approach the workshop where the Thoreaus, father and son, manufacture their produ&.

The business had made progress since the time when the unlucky ſtorekeeper had bethought himself of competing with Monroe, the Concord pencilmaker. It was quite a ſtory. The native pencils were not good for much, even Monroe's, in spite of the process he had invented; they had the disagreeable grain of poor, scratchy, brittle, inefficient pencils. No chance of holding out in the market beside the imported English pencils, and especially the incomparable Fabers from Germany. So something better had to be tried if they were to satisfy people who liked good pencils. To obtain a good pencil, everything depended on the treatment and the preparation of the graphite, which came from Sturbridge, then from Canada, and which the elder Thoreau had especially ground for him at Acton. The first thing was to reduce the graphite to a very fine powder, which was obtained by means of an ingenious, primitive machine that enabled them to collect exclusively the finest dust from the material ground in the mill. This was a great point gained. After this the softness of the pencil depended on the product mixed with the pulverized graphite, upon so composing the paste that, once hardened, it would produce that delicate, firm substance that glides on the paper between your fingers, leaving a fine, vigorous mark, of a beautiful grey-black, and not that dim, vague mark that bad pencils have. Hitherto the elder Thoreau had produced this effect, like his predecessor Monroe, by the use of spermaceti or bayberry wax mixed with glue, while there entered into the composition of the Faber pencils a certain clay that was found in Bavaria. They succeeded in procuring this. The result was remarkable. After much groping and difficulty they at length arrived at the goal of their efforts, the perfect pencil. It was awarded a first medal at the exposition of mechanical arts in Salem. Henceforth they could hold their own in competition with the English pencils of pure graphite or even the Fabers with their skilful proportioning of graphite and Bavarian clay. But they could not think of turning out a pencil as cheap as these. The Thoreau pencils cost twenty-five cents, in spite of which many teachers of drawing who saw how excellent they were recommended them to their pupils. A friend, Horace

Hosmer, was the traveller for the house. So the business was not bad. But they also had to watch carefully lest someone else should steal the process. This explained the mystery that surrounded the great work—the mystery of the mill at Acton where they ground the graphite, the mystery of the very primitive workshop, adjoining the house, where, with a workman who could be trusted not to give them away, they manufactured, finished, packed and shipped the choice article. Six dollars a gross, and the daily bread of the family depended on it.

In these researches, these experiments, this final success, Henry played an ample part. It was he who had found out in some reference-book about this clay which the masters of the pencil industry used in Germany, and who had contrived two or three pieces of apparatus of capital importance, notably for the cutting out of the slabs of hardened paste and the drilling of the blocks of wood that were destined to receive the lead. So long as it was a question of producing a fine pencil that would be satisfying to exacting draughtsmen, you could count on his skill and his zeal; to conquer a difficulty was the business of the admirable Henry, master of ingenious arts. But when the end was attained the pencil-factory left him rather lukewarm; it was a simple affair of exploiting an invention and reaping profits. All very well for his family who lived by it. But if the equilibrium of the family rested on the lead-pencils, his equilibrium had a less friable foundation. He would help his father, yes, as much as was necessary. But sell his entire life in pencils, no, thank you; he had other fish to fry. With his life he wrote poems—even without a pencil.

Working in the paternal factory was then, after all, only a makeshift. Always the same story: the pencils

were his father's business. Even though it was enough
to keep them all afloat, Henry was unwilling to be a
charge on his family. He must earn a little outside and
butter with a little independence the bread that he ate
at home. But how? School-teaching, tutoring, already
had a rather ſtale taſte. A page turned—look further.

This thing that is rolling in his head, turning over and
over, this trifle of one's daily bread, is a great problem
when you don't follow the beaten track that leads to
ease and self-disguſt. He is not ſtupider or clumsier than
other people; he is qualified in all sorts of lines and has
plenty of good will. Who is going to profit by employ-
ing him in some way in which he knows he can do a
good job? Myſtery. Unless you are looking for a
flogging schoolmaſter for your children, or a scribbler
of copy, or a clerk, or a servant by the year, or an animal
that will place himself in the shafts, here I am with
hands at the ends of my long arms, five ſtrong fingers
on each hand, a trade at the end of each of my ten
fingers, and a head full of resources. I am twenty-seven
years old and have not travelled very much, but I know
enough about the world and myself not to sell you my
beautiful liberty, except in bits. Ask me for a day, two
days, three days of work; from childhood I have been
used to manual labour, I have always been a good gardener, in a house I have taken the place of several workmen, I can build a boat, and in the woods I am as much
at home as a wood-cutter. Give me the tools and you
will see. My hands and my brain and my good will
are for anyone who wants to take them for a dollar a
day.

And you will get something for your dollar, I promise
you. *Noblesse oblige.* When one has the honour to be
called Henry Thoreau, one doesn't do one's work by
halves. One respects one's work, whether it is for

someone else or for oneself, because one respects oneself.
At your service.

After various experiments, Henry, graduate of Harvard, son and grandson and great-grandson of merchants, has already made his choice. The lot he desires most, as the happiest and the freest, and the worthiest as well, is that of a day-labourer, who cuts off a slice of his time to sell, when he must, but takes good pains not to sell the whole loaf. He knows that fifty days of work a year will be enough to pay for his keep, such as it is. And all the other days, six each week, will be for God and himself, for his own private affairs.

Manual labour is not only the most congenial to his tastes: it is that which agrees the best with an intellectual worker. Above your toiling hands, the spirit cheerfully pursues its free play, thanking the hands for placing it in so cordial a relation with this beautiful material world, so richly veined, the sight of which refreshes and attracts it. The day-labourer who treasures his time escapes from the damnable routine of the salaried work that devours your soul. When you engage me, I shall do for you everything that a clever, skilful man who puts his heart into his work can do. But when your work is finished I shall go back to my own which requires no assistance. I append to my offers of service a programme of the things you can ask me to do: fence in your land, plant your young trees, dig, build a wall, set up the frame of a house, cut your wood, whitewash your walls, hang wall-paper, etc., etc., etc. . . . And if you have a leaking pail or a door that is off its hinges, I shall attend to them into the bargain. I am not particular. Work has no terrors for me. There is not an Irish labourer of them all—you see those strapping fellows who are laying out the ground about the village for the new railroad?—who has waded in the swamps as much as I have done, for my own pleasure. It knows me well, that mud. Tilling the ground for Tom, Dick and Harry for a few days for the sake of earning five dollars is what you call servile, back-breaking work. (You tell me this, you who spend the day adding up figures for an employer, you who bow and scrape to customers from behind your counter, morning and afternoon, sunshine or snow. . . .) Come! Do you expect me to shudder at this rough work? Feel the callous on my palms. You don't know how cheerily the handle of a pickaxe or a hoe slips between fingers that have smoothed and stroked it as fellow-diggers and delvers. Servile labour? Fine masks with white hands, look at Henry toiling out there in the field if you want to see a fellow whose work does not enslave him at all. While you are adding up your ciphers or calculating your phrases, I am adding up my strokes of the pickaxe or the billhook, and smelling the earth and the turf and the bark around me. Yes, hire me to do work in my own line and I shall do it less for the money than for the love of the labour of my hands. Don't worry, I shall not give you time enough to disgust me. So take me for what I am worth, and you will have a workman who will treat you as he would like to have the other fellow treat him.

Henry looks about him. Who wants a fellow like this? Don't all speak at once. If he could secure a day here and a day there it would encourage him to believe that it is really possible in this world for an honest man who can do everything to earn his bread. But the lovers of good work do not seem to be very numerous. Only the friends at whose houses he drops in for a meal or who stop as they pass him seem to appreciate the varied talents of a clever young man. And if you only knew what a pleasure it is, for a fellow who flatters himself that he is no bungler, to feel that he is appreciated, without any compliments, at his real worth. As a general thing, you have to work for some dull soul who naturally takes you for a creature of his own kind; all he wants for his dollar is the strength of your hoofs and your back, without the slightest regard for the real extent of your competence. The employer, in short, in all his worldly splendour.

Suppose he were to try some of those little trades that do not catch a man up in the greedy machinery of their routine, only to leave him at the end empty of his pulp, flat as an apple in a cider-press? Henry has often thought of this. In summer when he sees the boys bringing back baskets of huckleberries to sell to the important villagers whose dignity or lofty occupations prevent them from running about the fields, he says to himself: I am as much of a vagabond as they are. . . . I should like to do that too. Or he could make baskets, trays and all sorts of fine, durable, useful things out of birch-bark. Why not? The manufacture of sand-paper would be lucrative if he could get a few customers. He invents various contrivances that might be exploited, such as a rule for measuring cords of wood. But the superintendent of the city hay-scales in Boston tells him that the wood-dealers would never hear of this because it would put an end to their swindling. No, the best thing is to try surveying. Henry has devised his own compass and chain and is ready to measure other people's property to the very confines of the earth. He can be relied upon as a surveyor.

But whether or not the world offers him employment for his faculties, it will never get him into the mill of "wholesome work," extolled by the preachers and held up as an example to the sons of the family. Let the parish make the best of its bereavement: he has not the makings of a respectable citizen. "You must get your living by loving"—isn't that so, Henry? And not earn your bread by being turned into dough? That's the main thing. He will make shift as he can on the ragged edge of society, if society has no place for an individual like him. Meanwhile, far from groaning over his lot, he loves it to the very marrow and would not exchange it for an empire. Concord is richer than all the empires in the heart of old Asia, and Henry Thoreau, a day-labourer without a job, feels that he is in the heart of rich Concord, the king of a limitless country of which every day he brings back a little of the earth sticking to his boots. Though he may end his days in a poor-house, nothing can take away this triumphant happiness which he experiences in living responsive to the instinct that rings in him like gold.

If you are industrious in your own way and not in the accepted fashion, you must not be surprised if you pass for a loafer. That is the way of things. In the eyes of the sober folk around you an inaptitude for business is the very mark of inferiority. Think of it, an American who cares nothing about getting on. . . . What's more, a Yankee, without the slightest relish for trading, who seems to be positively bent on remaining poor. . . . It's preposterous, it's even rather presumptuous. Among the mandarins of the village there is scant sympathy for this little whipper-snapper of a schoolmaster who has audaciously pronounced against the rod and holds aloof from church, charitable circles, politics. And that surly eye, the gruff tone of his replies and his cutting words . . . When they see him passing down the village street, under the dome of the great elms, or crossing their fields, a Henry who lives heaven knows how and seems to have his pockets full of leisure, the good people sneer, smile knowingly or shrug their

shoulders as much as to say: "You bleed yourself to
send a boy to college. . . . He's been spoiled. . . . Behaving like a millionaire . . . running about the woods
all day like a schoolboy, lounging in his boat on the
river. . . . If he had no brains it wouldn't matter, but
he's clever enough when he wants to take the trouble,
the lazy good-for-nothing. . . ."

If they were able to read the mind of this "lazy good-
for-nothing" who marches along, with head bent,
sloping shoulders, clenched fists, in his old workingman's togs, they might hear a much finer sermon for
their own sins present and to come. But the good
people are a little hard of hearing, and they would not
understand, anyhow! On the other hand, he has taken
their measure as exactly as if he had used his surveyor's
outfit, when surveying their precious land for them.
If they are "society," Henry, the simpleton, the ne'er-
do-well, the good-for-nothing, the village fool, is of the
unsociable kind. He sets out for adventure in disgust
at money and the evil-smelling varnish with which
money covers existence. There is no spite in this retirement, none of the peevishness of the misunderstood
soul who has been deceived in his hopes. He goes
simply to seek elsewhere the feeling of another humanity that must exist somewhere, perhaps under the bark
of the trees. Even in the main street of the village, how
much more moving is the presence of the great elms
than the fronts of the neighbouring houses!

Come, good people, would you like to see a savage,
a real one, not one of those of whom your grandfathers
told you, whom they perhaps never saw? Watch this
little man passing at the bottom of your pasture, avoid-
ing the habitations that are set about like snares through
the countryside, on the way to his daily rendezvous.
Do not waste your precious time attempting to follow

him, natives of Concord. His savagery would soon leave you behind.

When you are neither the lawyer nor the doctor, nor even the principal shopkeeper of the town, you naturally have to go without the legitimate prestige that attaches to these functions. To be a day-labourer, even though you are the son of a pencil-manufacturer, is to be condemned to live outside the luminous circle in which these incontestable powers move. It is to dedicate yourself to an obscure destiny.

No doubt, but this has its compensations. They are insufficient, you will tell me; but are you sure of this? The great advantage of being a day-labourer, free to hire yourself out as you please and cheerfully pocket your dollar or two, is that you keep the brightest of your time for your own affairs. These little personal affairs are nobody's concern; but, great or small, they are your own. Admit that they have the same claims as a vocation and everything yields to what is most important.

Henry's vocation is to start out every afternoon, rain or shine, for half the day, three, four hours or more, according to the occasion and the season, half for adventure, half with an object, in search of . . . In search of what, indeed? Does one ever know? Simply in search.

He does not set out for amusement like a sedentary man who is taking his constitutional; he sets out like an artist towards the studio where his work is awaiting him. This excursion is the very core of the day, the condition of the creative hours that will give him his knowledge and his reward. Ask Henry for anything you wish, money, a good pencil, a helping hand, but do not suggest that he might sacrifice his precious afternoon; he will send you packing. The afternoon is reserved for work, his work. Amid the little tasks of the day, this is the big affair. Henry punctually responds to the call of the hour, which has no sound of duty for him: it has a commanding charm. If some obstacle interferes with his outing, some urgent task or illness, he is as miserable as a lover who has missed his rendez-vous. The day is spoilt. It is the empty day of one who has failed in his work. And if he is forced to keep to his room for several days running, he is as despondent as a girl over a sad story. Henry in a cage feels himself becoming soft. It is as if he were deprived of his food.

As a rule, he goes off alone, for labours of love demand this strict intimacy. No annoying person, no idler, no lover of the "joys of the country" to pester you with his questions, his chatter, when you are out on business. Not at any price. But when your friend, who is a congenial soul, accompanies you, there are three of you, for William's dog is of the party. The dog hunts for his profit, as the two companions seek for theirs.

On occasion Henry devotes himself to fishing, but this is rare. He never hunts any more; he has sold his gun. The game that he starts to-day is no longer that which he pursued in his boyhood, with his brother. Instead of the fowling-piece on the strap, he is likely to carry under his arm, if it is the season for flowers, an old music-book in which he can press specimens of plants that he wants to keep. And in his pockets, which are as roomy as wallets, you will be sure to find his field-glass for observ-ing distant objects, his magnifying-glass for examining the ground, his big knife, a ball of twine, and perhaps a bite to eat, if he has set out for the whole day. But you don't know him if you think that without the old music-book he would have any difficulty in bringing back some occasional vegetable discovery. He drops in at your house for a moment on his way back from some expedition, and you notice the care with which he sets down his old straw hat in the hall; its interior is skilfully arranged for receiving frail plants or flowers without bruising or crushing them. Henry carries his herbarium on his head and braves under this friendly protection the rain and the sun. He is indeed equipped from top to toe for the most perilous expeditions, for the leather of his brogues is proof against mud and brush. His trouser-ends are thrust into his boots, a sign that he is not going out for an afternoon call or even going to follow the main road.

Concord is connected with the world by the roads. A villager only sets out from the village when his business takes him to some neighbouring village. What lies between the roads is indifferent to him, unless he happens to have something to do there. For this reason there are vast, empty stretches between the roads and around the farms where you never meet a soul, for no serious man could possibly find anything worth his while there; haunts of animals, weeds, thickets, mud-holes and trees that are allowed to grow as they please. The surroundings of Concord abound in solitudes, and these are Henry's studio. He has his favourite nooks and corners where the soil is bad or barren, untilled, abandoned, chaotic, marshy, with clumps of trees, large ponds, cliffs. The luxuriant, aromatic vegetation of swampy ground is a feast for him, for he is a regular glutton, this lean little fellow. Around Fairhaven, to the South, there are stretches of country that will return to haunt him in his last hour—Conantum, Baker Farm; and over there, towards the west, as far as Second Division Brook, one can walk in a veritable cloud of revelations. It is just the same to the north, the Easter-brook country, and Mason's Pasture—abandoned orchards that have surrendered again to the moss, the rocks and the underbrush, fields of huckleberries and barberries, and wild apple trees among the birches and pines. And the Great Meadows and Walden Woods. . . And those old grass-grown roads, wandering at their own will, without a living soul, without a house or a landmark, their forgotten tracks leading heaven knows whither, but where you feel so much at home; brotherly roads that take you by the arm as you leave the village behind and lead you along till they are lost themselves in the wilderness. The wild grasses that people call weeds seem sweeter to you than the tractable plants of good family. They belong to your own family. They like to straggle along the old roads, just as you do, far from the little gardens where the sober box-wood grows.

Concord is also united with the world by two rivers, the lively one and the sluggish one, which are not navigable for trade. The domain of the waters which, in the spring and autumn floods, lops off an inordinate amount of the surrounding country, belongs to no one and is free to all. The two rivers are yours if you want them. Accept their gladness and their freshness; no one will dispute them with you. That fisherman over there wants nothing but their fish.

It is towards one or another province of this domain that Henry, freed from the little tasks of the morning, turns each day with the soul of an explorer. The house where he has slept and spent the morning between four walls has a musty smell. He must leave it behind to get the poison out of his system, set out at midday to receive the shock of the wind and the sunlight. He is off for discovery. Soon the village and its rancid taste are far in the walker's rear.

The point now is to keep clear of the tilled lots that bore him, like those people who are so cultivated that he wants to turn his back on them. It is to foil the eye of the house-fronts that are watching among the trees, to avoid the roads and those people who, flourishing some phrase of village wisdom, are capable of spoiling his whole day. By foot-paths and short-cuts known from of old Henry steals between the farms, like a marauder who is anxious to escape the owner's observation. At last he has emerged from the danger-zone; he is on the threshold of a region where his studious sauntering will be troubled by no further undesirables. The beautiful hours of the day begin, the fruitful hours. The inspector visits a corner of the bad ground, pauses, examines, calculates the harvest. How much this poor soil yields! And how vast the domain is! Within a radius of ten miles about the village, the surprises that await him are so marvellous and so numberless that his whole life will not suffice to exhaust them.

So Henry is the busiest man in Concord. The rest of you on your little farms cannot imagine the concerns of a great farmer whose lands cover more than the whole township. Nor can you imagine them, you men of business. Henry does not close his store on Sundays and holidays. Henry has no master who employs him. He is an incomprehensible donkey who works for himself and never stops. In other words, a skulker. Such is the opinion of those great toilers who, after the day's work is over, twist about in their chairs with their newspapers in their hands, enjoying their poor hours of liberty and fulfilling the rites of the Sunday boredom. This fellow seems to pay no attention to the rites. Active in his silence, without appearing to be so, he is off at his work. He alone knows the demands of this work and the wages. A true loafer, this lad after whom a certain farm-hand, emboldened by drink, shouts: "Hello, Mister, what do you think of the walking?"

HENRY THOREAU

Henry's work? Yes, walking, juſt that. But how explain to this country simpleton and his kind what walking means for a born walker who praċtises the art of walking, with all its emotions, its discoveries, the great expeċtations that it arouses and the work at which it aims? Two, three miles away from the village square you are in the midſt of the unknown, familiar as the place may be to you. In you there awakens a world of relations that Main Street in Concord has never been able to set vibrating. It has a reality so ſtrange that sometimes you ask yourself if the country of the Arabian Nights begins on the outskirts of Concord or if it is the village ant-heap itself that is unreal. These ſtreams of living things flowing beyond human control for the mere joy of being are fragments of a great poem that will find their completion perhaps only in you—ſtrange man who comes day after day to surprise them, observe them, weigh their words and penetrate to their rhythm. All the confidences of which you have been the depository since childhood have woven between this wild life and your own (less wild?) a web of intimacy so ſtrong that to break it would be to tear yourself to pieces. In what language, through what images, can you make the tame people underſtand the force of this old passion that drives the heart of an untamed man into the heart of this wild nature?

The objeċt of your expedition? What does it matter? At the end there is always some conquest, big or little. Follow the direċtion that is indicated by the magnetic needle of your inſtinċt. Perhaps the thought of some particular chum that you have promised to go and see has decided you. For you have well-tried friendships out there amid the waſte of trees, weeds and ponds. To-day Henry has passed and heard the news from this old boy that lives far away over there, like a squire on

119

his lands.   He walks with an alert step, stops, his eye
watching,   listens,   bends   over,   picks   some   flower,
examines it, full of spirits, transformed, his heart high.
All these familiar faces salute him as he passes.   He has
acquaintances on every side.   No one who has known
him at such a moment as this could ever see him as the
stiff, purse-lipped fellow, bored and hardly concealing
it, who has to keep such a tight hold on himself and his
sarcastic impulses in polite company.   It is a new man
that these friendly presences stir into life.   Among his
own kindred he has recovered his humanity.   He keeps
his wry face for society.   Here he expands, he is himself,
he is real.   Sometimes it is as if these open spaces were
all one fast friendship that intoxicates him like a drink
between old cronies.

   Does all this astonish you?   Perhaps the only things
you know are the four walls of your room, the door-
mat that lies before your threshold and receives without
a tremor the petty dust of your routine, and the grey
ribbon that leads to your daily bread.   This may be
enough for your imagination.   But confess that you
have never set out for an adventure beyond your dooryard.   You have never risen well before dawn to go and
watch the awakening of the water-lilies and bring back
a dozen or so to put in a dish of water; you have never
got up at the first peep of the birds to climb the Cliffs
and watch from up there the white sea of fog strewn
with the crests of the mountains like islands of which
you wonder if the inhabitants are not at this very moment watching your own.   At the end of the day, when
the summer moon is in its first quarter, you have never
turned towards Conantum to listen to the sounds of
the   twilight,   while   you   study   through   your   spy-
glass the neighbouring slopes that look as immense as the
Andes: a scrap of the song of a boy on his way home,

the trumpeting of the bull-frogs or a horse in the distance neighing in a meadow. You have never walked miles and miles at a stretch to go and watch, from one season to another, the growth of a plant, as many as ten times in a fortnight, making detours and digressions to pass other great friends of yours. You have not scrambled up to the summit of a pine-tree to balance there, facing an astonishing horizon, and climb down again to the ground besmeared with resin but proud of having picked the unknown flower that opens up there every summer for the sole joy of adventurous man. You have never even bent your spine—not once—to study the land-scape through your legs and observe the surprising things in a sky that is hung with pictures of the earth. No, you have never dreamed of the resources that pro-cure for a born walker a thousand means of feeling himself live.

Surprised by a heavy rain, he remains for hours under a tree, in the shelter of a roof of bark that he has made in an instant with his knife, delightfully occupied in studying the texture of the liber or the minute vegetation at the foot of the tree, while the shower tumbles and splashes the earth about this man who feels a strange well-being (he never feels less alone than in this laughing cascade of merry drops).

He finds himself before a clump of shrub-oaks, as compact as a thicket, and instead of going round it he plunges into it like a savage, going through it in a straight line, bending down, pushing aside these branches that are as hard as iron, regardless of rips and scratches on his hands, regardless even of blinding himself, lost in the embrace of the foliage but happy in bending its tough arms.

He becomes so infatuated with a swamp that he thinks of remaining for a whole afternoon weltering in the mud,

121

not to doctor his aching limbs but for the sheer delight of breathing the rich aromas and listening to the hum of the insects, not as a stranger, an intruder, but as an equal, as if he were himself a sweet-flag meditating on the strange happiness of its fate.

He listens and listens again to the ineffable evening song of the woodthrush . . . *hi willy willy—ha willy willy—o willy oh* . . . which sounds continually, like a tender prayer to the heart of man that he may remember, or the *de-de-de* of the chickadees, trooping about him as if they were in a playground.

He watches the departure of the balloonists when the ripe down of the milkweed embarks, free at last, on its great voyage, after having awaited this moment all summer, one seed crowded against another. He returns from his expedition in the brush, covered with clinging burs that absolutely insist upon travelling with him.

He remains for three-quarters of an hour motionless in the most uncomfortable position to watch a turtle laying its eggs, or to observe a female nighthawk, rigid on its nest and peering at him through its all but closed eyelids.

In mid-July, he takes his bath walking, as if on a road, down some shallow river, his straw hat on his head, the water up to his knees, then suddenly up to his neck, observing the incidents of the road, the wayfarers whom he passes, the irregularities of the ground, the water-plants as shapely as sea-weeds, the molluscs, moving along like himself, a turtle shambling by, the entrance to the apartments of a musk-rat and that mother pout advancing toward his naked self with her procession of infants behind her . . . a thousand of them at least and all so credulous, so confiding . . . the mother, frightened at first by the monster barring her way, returning to them, then becoming accustomed to the monster . . . the little ones approaching and examining his legs, tickling his toes. . . . They form such a cloud that he can no longer see his feet in the clear water.

He takes his boat and listens to the grinding of the oars in the locks, which evokes for him all the odours and sounds of a harbour, the swinging of the vessels in the docks, or spends hours on the water fishing up driftwood that he will carry home and use for making a trestle to pull his boat up on the shore.

He feels, as he witnesses the felling of a great pine-tree a hundred feet high and four feet in diameter at the base, as much anguish of heart as if he were present at an execution, and he curses the executioner.

He leans with his companion over a rippling brook and sees their double image, two black heads, as big as thumbs, William and Henry, looking as if they were bending towards one another in this mirror of convex bubbles, with the reflexion of the branch of a young elm crowning them.

He feasts like a blackbird on those huckleberries which they call low blueberries and carries them home by the pocketful, thinking that if he were a Canadian he would also call them "bluets" and that if he were a native of the country about Oulme in Normandy, not far from the home of his great-grandparents, he would say to the little girls: "Let's pick some *maurettes;* we can eat as many as we like and keep the rest for preserves.". . . As a connoisseur he runs the whole gamut of the whortleberry family, the wild grapes and the cranberries, not forgetting the barberries.

Best of all, in the old abandoned orchards, he gathers those wild apples that are sour and crabbed enough to set your teeth on edge but that later, when you eat them after they have been softened by the frost, refresh your palate with a delectable cider.

He inhales the fragrance of the plants in the moon-light when the earth is breathing and the sounds have a supernatural delicacy in the silence, or listens to the hooting of the screech-owls whose wisdom is older and greater than that of all the sages. He would like to trifle away the whole night.

He feels that everything has a message for him and is awaiting his response—the layers on the sides of the railroad cut, the fireflies in the meadows, thistles, puff-balls, migrating birds, and the immutable mountains that he sees over there by the setting sun with their grassy slopes where he pastures so often the flock of his thoughts . . . as if the vanished Indians still spoke to him, those Indians who sprinkled the soil with arrow-heads (look here, one more for his collection) and left the very embers of their fires intact under a crust of earth.

He is like a trapper who sets his traps after sunset and visits them before dawn, a skilful trapper who knows the likeliest places and varies his bait, and keeps from his catch only the thing he is looking for, a thing that is better than fur or meat.

You think there is nothing here to sustain a man, saturate his life, fill him with the desire to spend in such company not just a few hours of afternoon but the whole day? The beings whom Henry comes to visit may not communicate with the aid of articulate lan-guage, but they have a soul just the same: how happy he would be to find a soul so expressive among his own kind! Did you suppose that such company was to be found only in drawing-rooms or the halls of the hotels in the city? Pretentious human race that regards itself as the salt of the earth! A little modesty, my neighbours. Out beyond that stretch of space where the murmur of your words is no longer heard, a man sees and hears many things, but never one that is absurd.

Think of calling oneself inpecunious with the great, beautiful day before one and this swarming life around Concord! This poor fellow goes off every day on his visit to the waste lands to watch the growing things their two mingled poverties yield. . . . Henry enjoys that elemental happiness which is the breath of the soul, freed from the load that burdens it—knowledge, morality, prudence, laws. If he did not have so much respect for the skin of a tree, he would like to cut with his knife in the bark of that oak three simple letters:

H H H

Henry Happy Heathen. It would be a curious design on the bark and would recall those mysterious signs which the Indians engraved to mark their passing. Or Three Hatchets, to puzzle passers-by still more. And then dance a wild jig around the tree at the thought of the beautiful epitaph there, to be cut off some day and set on a flat stone among the crosses and urns in a grave-yard.

He is happy without reason, because things are as they are . . . happy just as the river is happy as it hastens to join its great sister and run with her down to the sea . . . or as the leaves of the poplar, fluttering as they prattle the news which this gay little wind has whispered to them as it passed. In the delight that he shares with all these things he strews the landscape with imaginary beings after his own heart. There are whole families of them of whom he has never caught so much as a glimpse, but who, as he knows, live there in the spots where his dreams place them. From afar he greets them as he passes, sure friends who must not be disturbed at their work or in their serenity; it is enough to know that they are there. Their presence helps him to endure cheerfully the misery of the town.

With his own happiness chinking down in his pockets like an arrow-head against the steel of his knife, Henry marvels that he never encounters anyone on his expeditions. So he is the only one to profit by all this? Not one of his own kind dreams of disputing his pleasure with him. I am greatly obliged to you all. How kind of you to abandon the earth to me, while you, sober souls, measure cotton behind your counters or spend the whole afternoon sitting with your legs crossed on your bench like a penitent! Take care or some green sprig may thrust itself between the pages of your existence; this would spoil the pious images that slip into your book. Work on, and let me carry off in peace what you despise. You will not prevent a lad who is up earlier than you and passes your yard in the moonlight without waking you from drawing from your land the profits he is pleased to put into his own pocket. Let each have his own share: you bear the costs and the risks and take the money, and he in his poverty will collect the tithe. The hail that ravages your harvest will be music in his ears. You will never believe it; but unaware of it as you may be, it is for him that all your work is done, good people. You think you are the possessors, but it is he who possesses you.

Henry exercises with impudent freedom the privileges that are common to all men. He has not surrendered for the ownership of a miserable field or two his claims to the whole earth. Henry knows his rights. He will build a fence for you now and then at so much a yard, but you cannot talk to him about Holy Property.

Henry is the largest farmer in Concord. He collects the revenues of a whole township. There are other men in this world who, through carelessness or lack of skill, utterly fail to perceive what belongs to them by right. They are the indifferent souls who forget to

take their share of the spectacle of the setting sun, the
beauty of men and women, the sea, the day, the night,
the trees, the lands of their neighbours. Well, it is for
them that the little god with the big boots, the great
nose, the thin chest, the long arms and the sloping
shoulders collects the inalienable share of the common
property.

Suppose, some day, the village authorities, perceiving
the value for everyone of these journeys of a little god
who so carefully keeps up the forest paths and maintains
the right of way wherever men might like to go, were
to coax him into accepting an appointment, as, let us
say, Conservator of Waste Lands or Inspector of Swamps
or Curator of Indian Relics? Something like a liaison
officer between the wilderness and civilization. Of course
they would have to be tactful and appoint him without
any formal appointment. For in what form could they
make him accept the frightful idea of being any kind of
town official! With a little imagination they might be
able to find the formula that would permit him to remain
his own free self and yet receive a small allowance just
the same. Perhaps a little fund, or a commission, as in
the case of an explorer . . . Yes, assuming that you
could find in the bosom of the town-council the slightest
sense of these fine shades. Hm . . . let's not be too
sanguine about it. But what a fine thing it would be
for the town to be assured for some trifling sum of the
services of a young man who has an eye for these treas-
ure-chests to which everyone can go and take what he
likes when he feels his soul in a cage behind the bars of
his dull days. . . . Have you no sense of your own
interest, you poor silly people? He demands nothing,
he complains of nothing. He has had his choice and
finds that he is amply indemnified for having squandered
all his capital in tilling the wastes; but it would be rather

nice now if they were to assure him a pittance. . . . So Henry dreams and scatters his fancies to the wind along his path. Yes, of all possible employments it strikes him that this is the one he would have accepted most gladly, for he is prepared for it by a long apprenticeship, and he could put into it so much of himself, so much love.

If it is for the sake of one young man of Concord that the seasons arrange and vary their pageants, you may imagine what obligations this favour imposes on him. Henry sets out in all weathers, from one year's end to another, favoured by a porous soil that is sandy enough to absorb the water. The festival of summer offers the most plentiful programme, of course, for there is room then for the longest of processions from dawn till dusk, and the manager of the show is a spendthrift. It dazzles us and leaves us with the impression of an unequalled pomp when, after its mad extravagance, it has vanished in a golden stream, sounding a glorious fanfare amid the blazing bonfires of October. The illumined brow of the tiniest hill is a murmur that mounts, swells, ends in a clamour of farewell to the great artist who is disappearing. Every tree unites in this in the words of its own language and the accent of its spot of soil. Listen. . . . The hickories express their thanks with orange words, the oaks cry out in scarlet that makes the blacksmith's forge seem pale, the maples shout with a mad note of crimson and yellow that spreads panic among the soberminded. A red flag unfurled would disappear in the fires of this conflagration.

It is as if a whole wild race of beings at the point of death were confessing at last without reserve the delirious thoughts of the year that have ripened in the August sunlight. Every weed, to the very rim of the forest, every leaf tries, before it vanishes, to be as sumptuous and beautiful and tempting as a flower. Even in the streets of Concord, under the golden ruin of the great elms, one asks oneself how the passers-by can still cherish such beggarly thoughts. Then Henry's eyes, gorged with the purple, the red, the lemon-yellow, the flame-colour, do not lose a crumb of the feast. They devour the oriflammes of the great flag-day, offered once a year to children and barbarians to satisfy their joy in lively colours. And at this season, when the villagers no longer go into the woods and he is alone under this great rose-like oak, the deep scarlet of which forms so intense a contrast to the green of the pines, he feels stirring in himself a veritable troop of bohemians, good-for-nothings, ne'er-do-wells, burning to join hands and dance, shouting as if possessed. . . . The long festival of summer at its mad end! It returns later, appears for a moment to offer a last farewell, with a calm, purified serene magnificence, in the golden days of Indian summer with their flavour of ripe fruit, ruddy, sweet and sunny. . . . Yes, the summer bears on its brow the assurance of its triumph; it has the easy pride of wealth. But the other seasons . . . Are you so blind as to ignore them?

Admit for yourself that you have never discovered what a different face the seasons wear at home from that which they wear in the calendar. You may know what it is to walk with great strides over a bed of dead leaves, hearing them whisper like a crowd in a church at the entrance of some expected personage. But it is a safe wager that you know nothing of the real quality of those naked, desolate, paralysed days at the end of November when a man feels that the best thing he can do is to stay in his own hole, that there can be absolutely nothing for him to glean amid this death of all things. But Henry has set out just the same, without much hope in his heart; and lo and behold, in the course of the journey through this windy desert a beautiful surprise is waiting to feed and enchant his imagination. He returns with the sunlight in his heart, "as if from an adventure." What he has seen it has required the nakedness of this dying November to permit him to discover, and it is the very thing perhaps that he has been vainly seeking so long in the abundance of the year. There is not a living thing abroad but himself, not an insect, not a flower, not a reflexion of real light, and here is this wandering lunatic, marching along with his hands in his pockets, waiting for the dismal day to confide to him for safe-keeping the particles of illumination and warmth that are hidden under its desolate exterior. At this season, when the wild geese pass in echelon, a thousand sometimes in a single day, the fancy seizes him, when he is out of doors, to imitate their cry. The means are at hand. You flap your elbows against your sides, then utter through your nose, with your neck stretched out: *snowack*. It is so good that a flock on their journey up there are positively deceived by it and do you the honour to take you for a goose—a wild goose, let us hope.

Winter has come. His visit is due, and since the first snow-flakes a new joy has come to take the place of the little old pleasures that still linger on. For this jolly newcomer, who has the blood and strength of youth, needs all the room there is. Henry's fingers are so numb that he cannot open his knife, and he buries them in his pockets to feel the pulse of this youthful joy. He puts on his cloak and mittens: it is time for him to start. Walking is hard work; he has to plough his way, and he turns round now and then to look at the furrow he has dug in the melting snow that covers the earth. In this cheerful little soul who walks along with padded steps, the warmth of this pleasure is like a log-fire in a hut in the woods in January; it is as if the evening crickets had left their snatches of song in some nook in the timbers to keep it cheerful till their return. Weary of all this whiteness, his eyes fasten upon a twig of brier glimmering with such an intense green that it seems to be the bearer of all the memories of the shrouded earth. Two men, seen from afar in this frame fishing for pickerel through a hole cut in the ice of the pond, look as if they had come out of some legend.

Henry has walked into the land of metamorphoses. The pine-tree, in its contentment, has deepened to a brown green; with its arms trimmed to support the weight of the snow, it rises like a mass of fantastic architecture. The miracle has spread even as far as the store in Main Street, where the arborescence on the shop-window makes you forget the beautiful Christmas presents that are on show there . . . spread to the very panes of your own window, which are being covered with a fern-like growth. Winter is blossoming like the orchards in May with these miraculous trees, each one wrought like a shrine.

He has put his boat up for the winter. But the river is still there for those who enjoy the wind, for them more than ever. It has prepared for them a solid floor on which they can whirl as if they were on a race-track. The skater has a double joy; he is the horse and the rider at once. He moves swiftly wherever his fancy takes him; the best runner is the merest lout beside him— the man on skates makes him look like a fool. The heavy boat was not of much use, anyway; its clumsy body was never able to follow all the windings of the river, and it was too timid to lead you to all the things you discover as you dart over the immense ice-sheet of the flooded fields where the little wooden bridges emerge

like islets. Henry, an accomplished skater from childhood, can make fifteen miles an hour against the wind
without straining himself. While the good William is
covered with perspiration from the strenuous efforts
he makes to keep up, Henry merely has a little watering
of the eyes from the wind of the race. No, without
winter and the kindness of the river offering its hard
back, the master would never know many of the aspects
of his domain.

Winter, the severe winter that is not a mere picture
in the almanac . . . When the snow-storms block trains
and roads and shut people up in their houses . . . When
there is not a single sleigh to be seen in the village
square, nothing but a saddle-horse that has just brought
a farmer into town, Henry has gone out just the same,
as far as the post-office . . . The bitter cold creeps
into the house, freezes the bread, the milk and the food
in the pantry till you dread the moment when you have
to go upstairs to bed, thinking of those sheets as stiff
as boards against your cheek . . . Indeed, you no longer
know just how cold it is because the mercury of the
thermometer has taken refuge in the bulb, as a snail
in its shell. The earth cracks and splits; in the house
the wood-work creaks. This is no reason for ignoring
what goes on out of doors; after all, your skin is somehow related to the skin of the earth. If it cracks too,
well, you will look through the cranny.

No need to go far to find a polar landscape. Here is
Baffin's Bay, there is Nova Zembla. The snow is waist-
high. No longer any trace of the embankment of the
railroad. The farmers have become cave-dwellers; the
houses are buried half-way up the windows, but the
smoke rises from the chimneys. The houses breathe.
The silence is prodigious, it hums in your ears. The
colours sing on the white sheet, red, blue, straw-yellow,

purple, green, orange, russet, tawny. The light is pink, and your shadow a deep indigo.

What has the finest log-fire to say to those slippered folk who have never left the chimney-corner when the moonlight on the snow leads you by the hand through an enchanted palace, or on those days when the south wind melts the snow and the uncovered earth exhales an odour that invigorates you like the scent of strong meat, or on those evenings when you come back armoured in ice because it has rained while you are out and you are coated with rime like a gingerbread man?

Is there any romance comparable to the events of a walk on a winter's day? The song that rises to your lips . . . the echo that comes back to you deadened because the snow has kept a good share of the sound of your voice . . . those vermilion berries sparkling with ice . . . that hardened ground offering you a footway in all directions where you were never able to take a step in mild weather . . . the living warmth that smoulders under the red catkins of the alders and in the blue of the silhouette of that Persian, with his hatchet in his hand, so tall, so imposing, so admirable that you would like to present your respects to him, just as if he were not your own shadow on the ice of the pond. . . Winter, hard winter, great banks of snow without which you would never have known that downy intimacy in the padded hollows of the old earth, season of the warm, quick heart under the frost! Now, remembering the summer, you ask if winter is not also a person of substance, concealing under his white furs the rarest jewels of the year.

And that matchless moment when the spring breaks, just begins to break—what do you make of that? If you remain in the back of your shop while outside the wings of the swallows brush a man who is seeking for

an answer to the disquietude he has borne within him
in the bleak February or March landscape, you are a
poor wretch who has deliberately deprived himself of
the cream of earthly emotions. You are to be pitied if
you have never prowled about then to receive the surprise of the first signs. The winter for you has been
merely a torpor, and the end of winter will only be a
renewal of the same old play, Rubbing Along—with
the same old scenery.

The first bee has come out with numbed wings in
search of the first calyx. This man has come forth too,
for he has been on the alert ever since that day at the
end of February when he found on the willows and the
osiers an unusual lustre of red and green. He is expecting
great news. Amid the dead leaves and the melted snow
of a ditch he has seen two yellow-spotted turtles moving.
He is greatly stirred because of a certain quality in the
air which makes him think he is going to hear a blue-
bird sing. He looks for signs that will bear out his
presentiment. On the watch from the ridges, he scrutinizes the deep blue of the inundated fields where cakes
of ice are drifting about, and upon this mass of water
which covers a good quarter of the land of the township
there is a little shining white spot that catches his
attention: he discovers through his glass that this is a
little sheldrake which, with its companion, has taken
possession of the waters. So one couple is already there,
awaiting the coming of the procession. No more does
he himself intend to miss the first measures of the music
announcing its approach.

March thrills with the anxiety of a man who is following the steps of the resurrection. A robin has called,
svit, svit. The black waves of the river have almost a
grassy smell. There are sea-gulls in the air. The look-
out-man scrutinizes the earth: bare and tawny, it

reappears in spots, its bosom exposed to the rains that are going to fertilise it. The buds of the red maples are swelling. On a beautiful clear day, after a night of frost the sap flows if he makes an incision. Henry collects the sap to make maple sugar. He draws from his tubes four and a half pints, boils them down and obtains an ounce and a half of sugar. Fine. But his father cannot understand why anyone should bother to make bad sugar when it is so easy to get good sugar at the grocer's. His father is right, as fathers always are. It is because he does not feel the maple-sap flowing in himself. There is no sap in his pencils.

Walking along his favourite path, the railroad-track, towards the middle of March, when he hears the blue-birds and sees them flying, Henry has a feeling of deliverance, as if some band that confined his chest had burst. He would like to fall on his knees and embrace the earth. The sound of a wood-cutter's axe in the forest lightens his heart. What doubts can he have henceforth? From a pool deep in the woods comes the faintly perceptible *wurrk, wurrk, wur r r k wurk* of a frog, a treasure to this keen ear that catches it. The air grows softer, an overcoat becomes troublesome. When the brooks break up, the saunterer sets out along the banks to hear the song of their awakening and watch the floating procession of the little rafts of ice. The fish hasten up-stream, for they too have heard the great news and wish to have the details. New arrivals are to be observed on all sides, a procession of travellers returning after a long absence. How many things they have to tell one another!

One day a boat appears, freshly painted, setting out to reconnoitre in the cold clearness. In the distance the village looks like a low island lying in the water. The wind brings you an odour of musk. The note of a bird that has come back sounds joyously in the woods as if he were giving a house-warming there. Since the birds have returned, there is one man in the village who rises before daybreak and goes out to hear them in the dawn of things, a man who can sleep no longer when he has heard that call flung from the tops of the elms along the street. A man who must needs inhale the scent of the earth in the early morning, a gardener who, when he plants his spade in the soil of his garden, once released from the frost, has a feeling of victory, not so much perhaps at the thought of the seeds he is going to entrust to it again as because of this new life which, stronger than the shoots of April, he feels germinating in himself.

No use for you to say, to excuse your own inertia, that this man owes to the unique quality of his senses the enjoyment he derives from a spectacle in the midst of which the village is monumentally indifferent. For nature has made him all nerves—visual, olfactory, auditory, gustatory, tactile. Henry, the virginal New Englander, is repaid for his chastity by the most voluptuous delights of the senses. It is a great pity if you have not been repaid for your own; but is that an excuse? The voice of sex has remained silent in him, or he has silenced it by a strict discipline for reasons of his own— because his race, his temperament, the gods of Concord demand it, and then because . . . because that is the way things go, it makes no difference: nature will have her due. Henry drinks water, but the essences of the waste lands intoxicate him. There is no symphony orchestra in the village, but a common accordeon or a hand-organ in the street is enough to wring his heart, and a simple music-box enchants him. He eats little or no meat but no epicure could scent with a more delicate nostril the savour of a solitude that is peopled with secret lives. If carnal emotion at the sight of the human body has not been annihilated in him, it cowers in the darkness of so deep a cave that you will never catch a glimpse of it. But he has at his command five scouts who always have marvellous things to relate when they return to their master. They are able to put such delicate perception, such freshness into their reports that he could listen to them forever. Seeing, tasting, touching, hearing, smelling are a matchless intoxication when you are served by such stewards and have a soul in which their least declaration echoes and re-echoes.

Henry's virility lurks in his eye. He has a look that envelops and penetrates pitilessly a piece of the landscape and probes you to the bottom if you form a part of it. Among the plants, the dead leaves and the debris he distinguishes some tiny creature which, to the ordinary passer-by, would be lost among the colours of the soil. But this man with the senses of a savage relies especially upon his ear and his sense of smell: a thing betrays or confesses its presence by the sound it makes or the odour it gives off. The thrush's song in the woods touches the depths of his soul, but all space is strewn with fragments of music that ravish him, as a child is enchanted by the tinkling of crystal or the tick-tack of a watch. When he wishes to hear the news of the world Henry puts his ear close to the telegraph-poles along the railroad. You could never explain how astonished you are by this murmur of the ocean that reaches you from the heart of a vibrating mast. It is the same continuous story that a shell tells you when you put it to your ear, but far greater, infinitely richer and more sonorous. The listener, alone at the foot of the pole, far away from the post-office, receives a flood of communications; he cannot make out the words but their music is enough for him. It is as if they had been round the world before coming to ring through the pores of the wood; they have travelled so far that to receive them you wish you had a larger frame. The dispatches vary according to the humour of the day, the direction of the wind, the quality of the air. Henry never fails to stop as he passes and listen to see if there is a message for him. Very strange, the playing of this harp. You might pass twenty times and hear nothing but a vague trill; and then, all at once, some fine day, as if tremendous things were happening in the world, the wires begin to vibrate with an unheard-of intensity and volume. What you hear is yours alone; you may be sure that no one is eavesdropping at any other receiving-pole unless some youngster is amusing himself as you are, listening to the music, so much more beautiful than that of the locomotive passing along the track.

Henry's big nose is no useless ornament: when he breathes the smoke of burning leaves or the first water-lily of the season that has just opened at dawn, all his quick sensibility flows into the sense of smell. Of the five messengers, this is the most faithful; its report carries conviction. When he picks a plant, Henry first smells it to see if he knows it; and even in re-reading some page he has written he *smells* what is good and what ought to be rejected. The surrounding country is full of floating aromas that have come heaven knows whence, varying with the hours and the seasons but always there, and sometimes so fragrant as to make you think that your adventure has led you to the shores of the Moluccas, the Spice Islands.

And you speak of renunciation in connection with a penniless man who has for his daily bread such delights as these! When you see the wanderer returning from his rounds, perhaps chewing a stalk, you would not

138

fling him a glance of contemptuous pity if you knew what he has brought back with him. First of all, good folk of Concord, the satisfaction of a man who has not wasted his day. A good walker, he has zigzagged about for miles. On the way back he has spent a quarter of an hour perhaps on the cliff, watching the sun sinking behind the Peterboro hills and blazing in the windows of the first houses in the village. Wachusett, all by itself over there, looked like a whale this evening at sunset. And with this sumptuous vision he returns, as the bats are flitting about, just as you are on your way to the post-office to get your own news.

In his pockets he carries the spoils of the day: notes that he has scribbled on his walk as a painter jots down a hasty outline in his sketch-book, and perhaps a few lucky finds, plant or fruit, egg or bit of moss, flint or bark. But among these finds there is one you would never count, if you were allowed to plunge your hand to the very bottom of his big pockets or even into that surprise-hat. It takes up much less room than a handful of huckleberries or chestnuts. The best of the spoils— can you guess what it is? It is the invigorated mind, the soul that has been stretched by the adventure of the day. . . This imponderable that he has brought home from the wastes to fertilise his life and enrich his humanity is a rather big affair, you see, brothers. . . This lesson he has received from the plants and the trees in the art of self-expression. . . These spoils that a rambler has taken from your orchards and fields, you farmers of Concord. . . This barely visible green which the plants and the mosses have left on his elbows and his knees. . . This earth that he brings back on his boots, full of things to be born which have made the journey with him and for which he cares so much. . .

In the evening, in his room, when the shop-keepers

are making up their books and the farmers are counting the loads of hay that have been brought in, Henry does not forget to note down these discoveries. They are not expressed in figures, hardly in words. They are not even palpable. But they fecundate the page that he is adding to his Journal.

For is it not a Henry-still-to-be-found that he has followed as a hunter follows the trail through all the zigzags of his walk? Is it not, after all, a reflexion of himself, in these faces in the verdure and the water, in these cries, this silence, this wildness, these odours, this swarming growth, these blue shadows on the snow— is it not himself that he has glimpsed at the end of the path?

Extraordinarily enough, one April evening in 1844 the man of the wilds returned from his walk not alone nor with one companion but accompanied by a whole troop of villagers. What was the meaning of this unusual spectacle?

It was Town-Meeting Day, a serious ceremony in a democratic community and one at which every loyal citizen, proud of being a necessary unit, was expected to be on hand. Henry, who had no love for voting and debating, nor any pride in the exercise of his civic rights, did not feel that his presence was indispensable. If he failed in his duty as a citizen and a unit, well, he could survive it. This little celebration was not for him. Let every man mind his own business. This day was plainly intended for a spring-time exploration; young Edward, still in college and Henry's comrade because he was the brother of his friend Elizabeth Hoar, was going with him. They were to set off by boat on the river, and they were not coming back till they had found the sources of the Sudbury River. They were going to camp on the bank unless they found a farmhouse where they could spend the night. They were taking their fishing-tackle with them, having decided to live like savages on their catch. A magnificent prospect, while the citizens, conscious of their duties and their rights, were worthily spending the day palavering.

So they had set off, light-hearted, as in the old days when the big brother had gone off with the younger on a long adventure. They had forgotten the matches for the camp-fire, an omission that could be repaired happily at the cobbler's, near the point of embarkation. It would be no sort of day without matches for two fellows gaily setting out over the world.

As the spring had not been rainy, the river was low and they caught some fish. When the time came for lunch they landed on the shore of Fairhaven Pond, the big bay with its little island adjoining the richest provinces of the domain. The two explorers had started a fire in a sunny hollow, a long way from the woods; they were about to eat their fish and they had the appetite of cannibals. But, lo and behold, if the tall, dry last year's grass didn't catch fire like tinder about the camp! They tried to put it out with their hands, then by beating it with a board, but all in vain. The flames were already eating their way up the slope and the underbrush was crackling. . . They were stunned for a moment. "Where will this end?" asked young Edward, whose father, the old Senator, was one of the bigwigs of the village. The flames in their headlong joy were rushing towards the top of the slope and the woods in a transport of victory and Henry was sure they were going to devour everything. The woods once reached, it would certainly be the village next; the fire would descend upon the assembled citizens who were debating and voting. So there was nothing to do now but to run and charitably warn them of what was threatening. Edward, very much excited, leapt into the boat to go back by water. Henry, speeding through the woods by his usual shortcuts, would reach the village before him and give the alarm.

It was a bad business, but how could they have foreseen it? Many and many a time they had lighted a fire out of doors and burned a little of the surrounding grass without doing any harm. These furious flames had the most definite and perverse intentions: they were like a tidal wave of red rebels, even surer of their rights than the citizens over there. Henry raced through the woods, and, looking back, saw the great cloud of smoke behind him. The first man he met was a farmer driving a team who, when he was told what the smoke meant, cheerfully jogged on again: it was not his woods that were burning. But that other man over there in his field happened to be the owner of the woodlot where the flames were crackling at that very moment. He followed the messenger on the run towards the fire: but what could they do, two men, even if one of them was the owner, before that crepitating wave of assault? . . . A hundred cords of wood, ready for delivery, were threatened with disaster. They must go for help.

Henry was out of breath. He was going to stay there and wait for events, while the owner went for reinforcements. The battle-front now extended over half a mile. Henry watched it rushing on. It was a fine spectacle. He had forgotten all about Wheeler, the man to whom the largest of the threatened woodlots belonged. He was a deacon, yes, just so, as chance would have it. You go off fishing and light a fire to cook your catch and innocently set fire to a deacon's woodlot. Just Henry's luck. It was too bad about that fellow—but the devil take him anyway! Perhaps these woods that

praised God in their own fashion were tired of belonging
to a deacon. So crackle, beautiful flames, be as red as
you like, beautiful logs! It will take away from you
the taste of the deacon. Henry climbed to the top of
the cliff to enjoy the spectacle better; and sitting on a
rock he watched the flames leaping for joy, escaping
with a hiss from their old prison under the bark, spreading so rapidly that they threatened to surround him,
high up as he was—watching with the satisfied eye of
an artist. The fire licked the roots of the pines, then
sprang with one leap to their tops. The squirrels beat a
retreat, the wood-pigeons flew away through the
smoke. He heard the alarm-bell in the village. This
was a moment worth living. Just before, when he was
running to warn the people, Henry had felt rather
sheepish; but now a pure joy blazed up in him at this
conflagration that seemed to have been decreed by the
solitary Nero calmly seated on the top of the rock,
enjoying the spectacle while the rescuers were approaching.

For several hours he fought the fire with the others
who were dashing about. Result: a hundred acres
burned over, including many young trees. He had no
reason to feel so proud—or to be astonished at being
called a "damned rascal" by those whose woods had
suffered. As for the crowd that had rushed up from the
village, they seemed to be tacitly grateful to the good-
for-nothing who had provided them with this free
conflagration to crown their Town-Meeting Day.

After all, if anyone had reason to be grieved, was it
not Henry himself, thinking of the beautiful young trees
that had been destroyed? He who owned the woods
by a different right than the persons who had paid their
market-value in mere greenbacks? He who loved them
for themselves and not for the number of cords of wood

that could be got from them? Walking through the burned woodland alone that night to see if the insurrection had been entirely quelled, the incendiary thought of the fresh shoots that would spring up with new life through the charred surface.

On the spot where they had had their interrupted lunch lay those blessed fish, shamefaced and shrivelled, as if they were the real culprits.

V

In spite of all, dear Concord, a man would have to be very perverse and strangely made not to accept you with all your faults, your absurdities, the petty prosaicness of your townspeople. . . Not to embrace you as heartily as the river-bank embraces your Main Street, without debating your good and your evil. . . Not to respond with a smile to the smiling unison of this little world where farmers and citizens, tradesmen, workmen, store-keepers, educated people, after the purest tradition of democratic equality and simplicity, are scarcely distinguishable from one another. . . In the shade of those great elms that spread harmony over all, how can one fail to feel tenderly sympathetic with this family of honest souls?

See the two white churches there, the tavern and the jail, where they will receive you without the least compunction. Few of the things are absent from the village that make the solid happiness of the world. Not even a bowling green and a centre of high culture. There is the Mill-dam, where the people gossip and munch the news of the day, the blacksmith's, the post-office, the shops. And the little wooden houses with their Doric pediments, painted white, with the gardens stretching down to the willows to reach the water. Everything is in its place, everything in concord. The village sings in its grey-white, in the green of the meadows and the pine-crowned hills, with the approbation of those beautiful big maples on the common, as serene as philosophers. And on Sunday, when no townsman would have the bad taste to abuse the peace of the Sabbath by playing the piano or taking his skates to the river, and an awful silence reigns over the wooden sidewalks, how good it would be to allow oneself to be carried along by the godly simplicity of the town, dozing blissfully to the sound of the clock that spreads the enchantment of submission.

Yes, indeed. . . And there are moments when Henry could envelop in his affection all the households of dear Concord. For example, when he sees the roofs smoking far away over the crests of the young elms; when humanity melts into the landscape or is only heard in the sound of an anvil, the shout of a ploughman with his team. At such moments as these he was in concord too. From a distance it was so easy to believe that people lived there whose daily life flowed like the river that bears you along as it gives you its freshness. Why, when you have taken part since your infancy in the activities of the village, are you not the dupe of appearances? The smile of Concord hides so many ugly thoughts, mean habits, dull conventions; there is so much tacit deceit in its simplicity. Why has not nature made you complete by granting you the adaptability that accommodates itself to the little frauds of ordinary life, to the devious path that discreetly spins the thread of its days?

It is not Henry's fault if he is at odds with it all. Instead of the treasures of indulgence that nature might have given him, she has provided him with a sense of smell too subtle not to be offended by its odours of routine and rapacity. He thinks of that old farmer, living alone on his big farm with a man to do his housekeeping for him, who gets up every morning in midwinter, when everything is frozen hard, between three and four o'clock, puts on his boots and his coat, lights his lantern and goes out to the barn to milk his seventeen cows. Of course it is warm in the stable near the cows, but just the same. . . Rich, without heirs, he yokes himself to this task of milking, his one satisfaction in life being to fulfil punctiliously the function of a miser. You see him returning to the house, his morning task ended, and eating the breakfast his man has prepared while the master was at work at the seventeen udders. All very fine, you say. But how surprised he would be one of these nights, when the animals begin to talk, if he heard a sisterly cow say to him: "Go back to bed, old man, and when you wake up glance over your accounts again. See how much cream your life has given you for all that your pails of milk have furnished." . . . Obstinate soul, perverse rebel, not to be able to forgive these virtuous farmers because, while their first concern is to fill their barns with good hay, they think they absolve themselves from the sin of avarice by posing as protectors of letters and the arts.

In the good society of Concord he finds himself among notables of Philistia who like to feel that they are the choice spirits of New England. These are the upper spheres of the village. Henry avoids them, for his lungs are not adapted to the air they breathe there. The language and attitudes of society people have the unfailing effect of precipitating the mercury of his thermometer to the bulb. On the rare occasions when he has been exposed to the hostile and malign influences that float in the humblest parlour, the experience has left him with a bad memory. It is there that you encounter those people who say to you, with their faces shining with amiability: "Oh, my dear fellow, how well I understand your love of nature. . . It is so poetic. . ."

The victim has his ferocious words or silences for cases of this kind. If the lover of "nature" and "the poetic" were shrewd enough, he could collect a good pint of the most acid disgust this mouth and these pursed lips are able to distil.

He cannot always avoid the peril under its most artful forms. When he has charge of the lectures at the village Lyceum, he cannot refuse to carry the manuscript of the distinguished lecturess who is going to discourse this evening on Woman: she has rolled it up in a handkerchief and he has thrust it into his pocket before returning it to her. He would be very glad to fulfil with stoical politeness for half an hour the obligations of ladies' man, but he would be happier if his pocket, the next morning, did not retain such a fragrant reminder of the lady, of her manuscript and her dressing-table. Feminism and perfumery have craftily conspired to get the best of his lining. Similarly, when he has allowed himself to be taken across the threshold of some stifling room where, under the pretext of a " soiree," thirty-odd idle women, young or not so young, are chattering, simpering, warbling, in company with various gentlemen who are dumb with admiration, the sad thing is not merely the two mortal hours that he has passed there, wretched and humiliated: the worst is the shame afterwards of his own weakness which has prevented him from fleeing on the spot or committing some enormity that would spread panic in this dove-cote. The pretty girl to whom they have presented him would have been charming perhaps if she had been willing to keep still among all these ladybirds. In masculine society, after a social dinner well seasoned with anecdotes, he feels just as unhappy till he is past the door and free. In vain Henry holds himself on the defensive: on another occasion there is that benign soul who intrudes upon him with an oily affection for his person, an odious, vulgar familiarity.

In the presence of these samples of cultivated humanity, Henry's natural stiffness is intensified and he becomes so icy that it is difficult to imagine him ever laughing—as a good lady had the hardihood to remark to him one day: she had never heard him in his gay moods, for she had encountered him only during a call in a region where, owing to the atmosphere, the laughter of this laugher was extinguished. The polite people of the village, the church-goers, those upright and self-sufficient folk, provoke his curt witticisms, the sharp rejoinders that suddenly rivet a fellow, with outstretched wings, like an owl over a barn door. Henry inevitably reaps antipathies and lasting enmities. The clever ones think that he wants to astonish and scandalize people by his paradoxes. They think he is pretentious. His reputation for merciless satire and a cynical misanthropy, odd to the point of perversity, is of his own making. If you roundly abuse philanthropy and philanthropists, of course it shows that you are not very anxious to win the esteem of the world. The plain-dealer sometimes amuses himself with this game of massacre, delights in sharpening his sarcasms, but without wasting any considerable time on the characters who play in the village comedy: the keenest of his sarcasms is to ignore them. When they come to his attention he packs them off as intruders: let these fine-mannered gentry air their graces somewhere else and leave common mortals alone. A substantial citizen, whoever he may be, is always a slightly ludicrous animal in the eyes of a workingman like Henry. A man's virtue is all nonsense if it is disconnected from his sins.

Happily Concord has something more than the silence of its elms and maples to unite it with the true humanity. It also possesses those congenial souls who gather about the Sage in the household where Henry has been living, a spiritual family whose friendship has a far better flavour than all the sarcasms. The pipe and frock of Edmund Hosmer, that shrewd farmer who knows what the earth is made of, make up for all these mean peasants. Amos Bronson Alcott, who has returned from an adventure in which he has vainly tried to consummate the marriage of dreams and reality in a paradisical existence, may be a cause of wit in others, but his presence is really like an anticipation or a recollection of the golden age. Henry has no particular taste for the sky-blue tint of his idealism, so delightful to old maids who are devoured by spiritual love, but he feels a brother in this poor dreamer who is so helplessly unfitted to follow the ways of the world. He lends him a good hand and digs beside him, when Alcott is settling at Hillside. In every stroke that he takes with the pickaxe, as they sweat side by side on the slope, the beautiful Platonic dreams incarnate themselves in the shape of friendship. Henry is not unhappy as a comrade and handyman in the service of philosophy. Who knows but the good Alcott's immense generosity of soul does' not exist to counterbalance all the miserliness of the neighbourhood?

With Hawthorne one doesn't turn up the earth. In the company of this imposing personage, a simple heart sheathed in solemn gravity, Henry is inclined to present rather an iron visage: like black cloth and corduroy, they are somehow unable to be friends. In handing over his boat to him—the boat of the great voyage, which he manages like a virtuoso—Henry, the dry joker, remarks: "It's a boat that manages itself, you see." The grave Hawthorne tries it, with the awkwardness of a beginner, and the boat, deprived of its soul, obeys no more.

Of this spiritual family, however, the one who is most closely akin to him is William. They have been comrades since the days before Henry's departure for Staten Island. William Ellery Channing, one year younger than himself, is the nephew of a Unitarian minister, a professor at Harvard. He has married a sister of Margaret Fuller, the animating spirit of the *Dial*. An odd soul, whimsical, fanciful, not very sociable, childlike, hard to please, charming, full of imagination and in other respects the best companion in the world. William also writes verses, but in other respects, in spite of his independence, he is not wholly exempt from a touch of Philistinism. He has a knack of sharpening Henry's love of paradox and leads him rather to force the expression of his cynicism in regard to the civilised; but he is an invaluable friend for toning you up again when you are feeling a little slack. And when they set out together for an afternoon's ramble they are the happiest of comrades, welcoming the surprises of the road in the intoxication of an open-air chat. Of all possible cronies he is almost the only one whom Henry accepts, the only one who does not throw a blot upon his afternoon landscape; with William he can have a silent understanding. To whom but William then, and those fields that are free from fine manners, do you show yourself as you are, with your boyish zest, your fits of gaiety, the bursts of buffoonery that make you dance and leap over the ice when you are skating? William is the witness of those spontaneous moments when the spleen of a young man who has been frozen by the sight of stupidity breaks and falls into pieces like a mask of clay. What is under the mask reveals itself only to this friendly nature, this friend after one's own heart.

A lover of the wilds can enjoy friendships like this that establish in the greyness of the village a few luminous points proclaiming the presence of his own kind.

Why are they not always complete enough to satisfy him fully? Too often Henry feels a kind of embarrassment in his relations with brotherly minds. The impediment is not of his own willing. He asks to be filled to the brim, and these half-unbosomings leave him dissatisfied with himself and others. When he is away from them, alone in the woods, it seems to him that the silence of his surroundings speaks of a truer friendship than that which he feels in their company: it is a silence whose "yes" melts all discords. A tree knows the art of winning you without discussion, while in the presence of a human face you resist, you are a stubborn mule, a bellicose intransigent who will not appear to approve of what he condemns and then demolishes his adversary—his friend—with blows of crabbed speechlessness or bitter irony. A human face is a provocation; at the least pretext you discharge a "no" that shoots like an arrow.

Even among such friends as these, if an opinion, a gesture, an attitude happens not to suit him, Henry rolls up into a ball and erects his quills. Touch him then if you dare. Look at him, bristling with resistance, ready to defend his position against all comers, fiercely resolved not to yield an inch of ground. No doubt the ground is too precious for him to sacrifice an inch of it. Pride? Conceit? Touchy susceptibility? It is rather an excessive, irreducible, militant devotion to various axioms that he identifies with himself. The gods have made a Henry who is all of a piece, and they have placed him on the earth among objects and souls that are different and queer. He reacts. He has no particular desire to please you. But you happen to be his friend. Well, one owes a friend the purest truth one has. If friendship ceases to be a perfect harmony, it is a struggle, not an exchange of concessions. So Henry abruptly says his "no": forces rush from all the provinces composing the individual Henry Thoreau, throwing into disorder everything in their way. He must attest, amplify, exalt the difference, to establish the fact that he is this and not that. The Sage, a friend of long standing, knows something about all this: the ferocity of this instinct of contradiction shocks the man with the exquisite and conciliatory smile, though it does not cool his affection for this headstrong soul who sometimes puts his patience to a severe test. The other friends are also very familiar with their "terrible Thoreau" in whose eyes esteem seems to be the strongest of reasons never to capitulate. And they allow themselves to be cut by his plain speaking or bitten by his caustic spirit, on occasion, since he will not give himself on any other terms. A naked simplicity is necessary to this fearfully difficult man. Manners fill him with horror, like an indecency. If you allow him to see that after all you belong to a world in which the desire to be correct and respectable taints your gestures or speech, well, for the moment that is the end of your understanding. You have shown the tip of the black cloth from which the frock-coats are cut. To be a man, a plain man, would be so fine and so sincere. Why this smooth, mealy-mouthed parlour-talk? Henry retires into his shell of silence. This is not the sort of thing he was expecting from you.

As for those people who are as sober as a church-pew, they cannot understand why a savage wants to whet his fancy and his paradoxes and gravely make a butt of their respectable heads. Innocent souls who are skilled in cleaving the interstellar spaces but whose terrestrial envelope is of a prudently bourgeois cut have difficulty in adapting themselves to the diapason of an artistic sensibility. That is why Henry, who is both savage and artist, never feels so fully as at the times when he is away from his friends the value of a friendship that would have the serenity of a landscape in which every blade of grass has a true word to say.

However it may be with men and their manners, Concord is in the centre of a territory that is rich in living springs where all deceit is drowned, and Henry has his home with his own family in the heart of Concord. In the great kingdom of the afternoons—wind, sun or snow—the little kingdom of morning, evening, night—shelter, stability, ties: the house, the garden.

The little kingdom is peopled, not like the great, with secret lives and furtive encounters as he passes, but with beings to whom he is united more closely than by blood: by the memories of childhood and their sweetness, strong as the memory of a brother, the sharing of every day, and the tenderness that cannot refuse itself. There is his mother, lively, talkative, full of geniality, the animating spirit of the little house, skilful in the art of making a little go a long way when times are hard, a housekeeper as heedful of the comfort of the boarders who are entertained at the family table as in mending the pockets of her son's trousers. There is his father whom nature has endowed with a middling stature and an air of prudence, a rather retiring man because not destined to command but to find his way in a tacit submission to the justifiable authority of his wife. As nature has not developed in him to excess the imaginative and poetical sense, he is the better able to play the part of a cautious, circumspect little father who looks after his pencils, attends to his work, silently, sedulously, with a mind set on details, good man that he is. And then Sophia and Helen, Henry's two sisters—Helen, the elder, with the big eyes, the strong nose and a mouth as expressive as her brother's. Finally, Aunt Sophia and the devoted Aunt Louisa, when one or the other happens to be living with the family.

This is the harmonious household the thought of which filled with such ardent melancholy the heart of the exile in the Judge's house, as if he had heard from afar the shrill sound of the delicious music-box, the gift of Richard, Margaret Fuller's brother, with which the family regaled itself in the evening. At home, the ne'er-do-well, the jack-of-all-trades cheerfully does his share of the work, taking charge of all the small tasks that need to be done.

The valuable little services that he renders his family extend even to his boat, which not only bears occasionally the two noble dames, Sophia and his mother, who enjoy a trip on the river in the evening, but serves him for gathering driftwood to stock the wood-pile. The wood that he hoists on board with a pole and then carries on his back to the house, saws and splits with his hands, has a tawny life that warms you a great deal better than the rotten wood these silly rich people buy at so much a cord; for you have already sweated in transporting it and cutting it up, and when you see its flames dancing the trouble it has given you makes them dance all the more merrily. It is wood which, far from costing you anything, gives you returns. It is of every kind and has plenty of stories to tell you—old pickets, old planks, old stumps, dead trees, condemned, adventurous timbers which, instead of rotting in their abandonment, are going to give the Thoreaus before they vanish the last rays of their glowing hearts, leaving beautiful ashes that will be valuable for washing.

In the garden, it goes without saying, Henry's function is as important as that of his mother in the house. He raises enough potatoes for the needs of the table and occasionally has some to sell. You can order them by the bushel from the market, if you prefer. You can settle yourself in your slippers in a corner by the fire, without knowing what it is to have logs from your own wood-pile. You can taste the joy of living like a potato or a stump. But he is a gardener to whom the potatoes, even before they have been gathered, have given something more nourishing than their starch. Henry's work in his garden brings with it another recompense than the beauty of the melons, the pumpkins, the fruit-trees, the rose-bushes that he cultivates. Besides, the garden is that one place in all the world where the home is contiguous to the earth.

When the family is obliged to leave the big house where they have lived for seven years, the Parkman house in the centre of the village where the school was begun, a scheme is adopted which they could not have conceived, still less executed, without the boy's aid. For the question is one of building a house. They are going to live at the end of the world, in a lane on the other side of the railroad. A big undertaking, a man's work, to excavate the earth and lay the foundations, pave the cellar, take the measurements, collect the materials. He would be happy to do it for other people; he is still happier to do it for his own family. Henry does the digging, the masonry, the carpentry, the slating with his father. He plants the fruit-trees. There is a fine view from the house; and besides, it is somewhat sheltered from the routine and the tittle-tattle of the village. He will be able to sleep well under this modest roof that he has put up himself.

Aside from the aid of his skilful and inventive hands, the man of the wilds does not refuse his family that best of himself of which he is far from lavish outside. What the chestnut is to the bur the big child who amuses himself by the half-hour with the kitten or dances a jig

with his intimates is to the "terrible Thoreau" of those
sharp replies. Is he tamed then? Well, perhaps so, if
you mean by this that his resistance, in the family circle,
adopts a tolerant and courteous manner—which his
friends would greatly appreciate. If, at table, the
maternal voice occasionally interrupts your dialogue
with a friend, why vent your ill-humour instead of listening till this gifted woman has had her say? Her son
patiently lets the downpour pass, as if he were under a
pine-tree in the woods, and at the last drops acquiesces
with a little bow: "Shall I take the liberty . . . my
turn?"—then resumes the interrupted discussion. Because he himself despises the newspapers, is he going
to cast a scoffing or disdainful glance towards his father,
deep in the paper he is reading from the first line to the
last, with the touching faith of an honest shopkeeper?
Nothing more natural than that the good man should
like to roll the lollipop of the "latest news" in his mouth
to get rid of the taste of the lead. Let him roll it as
much as he likes and go up to bed: his son will not
plague him with demands for advice, for he relies for
everything on his own personal experience and looks
for little or nothing from the knowledge of his elders.
Henry's indulgence is not blind. He knows the prejudices, the limitations of this beloved little house, and he
notes them on occasion in his Journal. But his home is
an indisputable reality to which he comes back every
evening, on his return from an adventure, finding there
certain special ways that may not have very much in
common with his inner life but that belong to him just
the same, exactly how he could hardly say—his father's
love of good work, for instance, a perfect pencil or a
phrase that hits the bull's-eye, and his mother's vivacity
of imagination and lively spirits that are always ready
for a little mischief. And if the sisters, the excellent

aunts alone had been there to warm the wanderer, all his roads would still have converged towards this fixed light.

Is the little flame of the family fire fed at the same sources as those wandering lights that attract his eye on his walks and make him stop as he stops before his friends the trees? But that is another story. These lights are not will-o'-the-wisps but miraculous beings that win the favour of an unsociable soul, as if they had no connection with a humanity that he has tried and condemned. Go and ask the cleverest person in the village to explain this strange fact to you: you have heard of a young fellow who is intolerably conceited, who affects a gruff, stiff, top-lofty air when he is in company—such is the report of the polite people—and this workingman here, if you happen to ask him whether he knows this boy, tells you that he is the most amiable of companions. . . Then there are two Henry Thoreaus in Concord? The workingman tells you about a delightful boy, sincere, simple, always ready to do you a good turn and always to be depended upon; in describing him he uses the sort of words that come to you when you are speaking of a brother, without the least allusion to his conceit, his stiffness, his sarcasms. He does not know of any other Henry Thoreau; there is no other in Concord. . . It is simply incomprehensible. And you will never understand it if you are not of the understanding kind.

There exist, in fact, among the human fauna of this village, of all villages, magicians who have the power of calling this other Henry instantly into life, the Henry whose friendship is gained for all time by his own kind. There are certain characters who have no part in Concord society—obscure little nameless people, men who do odd jobs, farm-hands, small farmers, and there are

people of dubious reputation, bad boys, who are akin
to the waste lands, fishermen, Irishmen, wood-cutters,
small fry, loafers, weeds in the eyes of the village bigwigs. Henry finds them very much to his taste. These
latter are real people, not play-actors. The artist is
touched, the heart of the man is captured. The grain
of sympathy that is buried in the depths of this unsociable soul can rise to the surface just the same. And
he shows them his true face, which is unknown to the
prosperous townspeople, the well-to-do farmers and
the deacons.

When he sees one-eyed Goodwin, the tough old
fisherman, making for the river-bank at any hour of the
day, small and thick-set under his old oil-cloth coat,
carrying his basket and pole or fetching home in a hand-
cart the wood he has collected in his boat, or dressed in
his short blue frock, chopping stumps for his winter
after having laid wall all day, Henry feels less isolated
among men. Goodwin, the vicious character, as the
good people call him, puts a little poetry into their
sanctimonious dullness. He lives his life cheerily in the
freshness of the river and the fields, far from all these
souls who are so poor in imagination and sincerity.
It is the same way with those hunters, drunkards,
rascals who are periodically sent to serve a term in the
House of Correction, like that big, lanky young black-
guard of a Melvin, with his baskets and his game-bag,
accompanied by his lean, bluish-white, black-spotted
hound, who are so much more your own kind than the
village lawyer. Their gunshots sound so free in the
woods, and you remember the time when you wandered
about the country like these blessed pagans for hours
with John. Melvin is an antidote to the morality of
the deacons. Melvin is a part of the beauty of Concord.

And there is Rice sawing the planks in his workshop.

He is a master of the art of living. Whether he is digging in the earth or going off hunting or fishing with his boy, everything seems to amuse him. The sacrosanct law of stupefying labour was not invented for him, for he always consults his own time and pleasure when he works. At the mere sight of him you forget the ugliness of humanity, you graze the reality of a life that is strong and leafy as a poem; you are no longer alone in the world with your dreams and your sadness. Rays of joy that warm you as you pass, the gift that the poor make to the solitary walker. . . How could you fail to be enlivened after days of misery by the childlike gaiety of old Brooks who, at eighty, bent double with age, sets out every day with his basket under his arm to gather a little wood and whatever else happy chance may offer to cheer his old days? To-day, dressed in an ancient frock-coat, he has come back from an expedition, barefoot, an axe in one hand, in the other carrying the boots that he has filled with apples because his pockets would hold no more. He has also brought back a thrush with a broken wing that he has found, and old Brooks is very happy in his find—as happy as yourself as you stop to hear him tell about it on an autumn evening made still lovelier by the old man's delight. Bit by bit he has gathered in two cords of wood for his winter; but they will certainly warm him less than this school-boy's joy in roaming the countryside which has remained intact in the heart of a poor old grandfather who blesses the life that puts thrushes in his path.

Why are there certain beings of whom it is enough to have a glimpse to be happy? When you meet old Minot and cross a woodlot with him, everything seems to sing at his mere presence while he tells you stories of the days when he used to go hunting. One glimpse of his little cottage on the hillside is enough to make you forget that there was ever an ugly house in this world; it is the first to show signs of the coming of spring and the last to bid farewell to the beautiful season. How easy it is to understand why old Minot has never wanted to budge from Concord, when even his rheumatism cannot keep him indoors! It is up there you must hear him, surrounded by the old furniture that he has inherited from his ancestors, to the tick-tack of a clock that was sounding before Massachusetts existed, reciting to you the stories that he knows almost by heart, stories that are engarlanded with minute details and good old solid and obsolete words that gratify the ear of an artist. He has a tiny bit of land that he has always cultivated himself, without help, mingling his work and his pleasure, drawing from every inch of ground the great happiness it gives him with his bread and asking for nothing more. He lives with his sister, and his only regret is that because of his rheumatism he is no longer able to go out and cut his own wood. But what a clear flame his life yields! He has the finest ear in the village for the thread of a bird's note, however thin it may be. How you would love to toil away for an employer like that, to be the man-of-all-work for the master of the little house on the hillside where the spring first breaks!

You perceive, solitary walker, how the ugliness of humanity dies away at the foot of this hill? And how it vanishes at the foot of other hills than old Minot's? You may not have realized this, you who walk with your eyes on the ground, meditating, but look: the sunlit smile of this old woman ironing at her window, which is full of blossoming daisies, cleanses the whole earth as you pass, as if you had never seen it before. Take a good look around you, as you go through the world. You may find that it is strewn with men and women whose beauty you have never suspected and who belong to you as much as Goodwin or old Minot.

Henry is certainly not at war with humanity when it presents itself in the form of this wood-cutter who knows the woods so much better than the finest naturalist: his clothes have a wholesome smell, he is happy enough for two, and you could work beside him all day. And you would like to follow old Hayden too as you see him pass and repass with his team, with the serenity of a good workman. The world of labourers is a friendly world where you cease to feel that you are among strangers. There is nothing in them that irritates you; your love of sarcasm vanishes in their atmosphere; there is nothing awry, nothing that you could find fault with in them, nothing that is not assured of your affectionate indulgence. No parlour, no store, no model farm in the village shelters a face as human as the faces of these Irish labourers, camping under their plank shanties along the new railroad. Simple digging-machines, ridiculous louts, in the eyes of noble, pure-blooded Yankees, are these brawny souls condemned to their killing tasks for a tiny wage. The scantiness of his own respectability is confirmed in Henry's eyes in the friendship he feels for these slow-witted fellows, navvies, ditch-diggers, scavengers, ice-cutters, indefatigable executors of the heavy tasks of the earth. To his mind their accent, their awkwardness, the dirtiness of their big, boyish, sunburnt faces are far less to be sneered at than the unctuousness of some doctor of divinity whose hands have never rubbed against anything but a cake of soap or the Holy Scriptures.

How could one fail to like that big-hearted Michael Flannery who toils away all day with such bubbling good spirits! It is as if the more energy he spent the more inexhaustible were the good humour he has drawn from heaven knows what miraculous fountain in his native Kerry. Naturally the respectable exploiters of other people's work take advantage of this and abuse his simplicity. Michael has won a prize at the Cattle-show, and the farmer who hires him has taken the prize-money away from him, maintaining that his wages pay for his time and that his good luck belongs to his em-ployer: to swindle a lout of an Irishman is a good Yankee joke that will never shut you out of the kingdom of heaven promised to prosperous farmers. But this is an act that completely upsets Henry's serenity: he im-mediately takes up a collection and returns to Michael the money which the miser has cribbed. And when he sees that little Irish monkey of a Johnny going to school all alone through the snow from the shanty where his parents live in the woods, as sober as a judge under the rags that so oddly cover his four or five years, Henry thinks of the satisfied air of the alms-givers and osten-sible philanthropists who brave the winter courageously muffled up in their rich fur-coats. What does a mere little weed of a wood-cutter's child matter, toddling along without stumbling through the intense cold with scarcely a shoe on his foot or a rag on his back, looking as if he found this world royally well made for little Irish boys who go to school where there is a bench to sit on and a fire in the stove? And in his mind he strips these worthy rich folk and puts the rags of the poor Irish on their backs to drape their philanthropy—takes their purple and fine linen and tenderly envelops this little scrap of half-naked humanity. Henry himself has no purple and fine linen to give Johnny, but what he has he takes to his parents: an old pair of pantaloons and a coat from which Mrs. Riordan can work up some trousers and a schoolboy's cloak so that he will not have to miss school for the futile reason that the snow is too deep this winter.

For the rest, whether it is Irish Johnny or some New England youngster, the world of childhood is an irreducible power that tolerates no assumed formality nor any veil of reserve. To make an end of the "terrible Thoreau," nothing is necessary but the two black eyes of some little boy under a big cap or the manoeuvres of four small kiddies bringing back a big horse from the pasture. You will find then that he is just a big boy himself, touched, captivated, won, a boy whose shyness feeds upon solitude and wild nature and who, in order to love you, asks only to be able to find in you that simplicity and candour, that true and savoury quality for which his childlike heart is greedy.

Henry feels affectionately sheltered under his own family roof: nothing in the world could induce him to leave home as his grandfather did for good and all to seek his fortune far away. But when he meets on his path these poor, ignorant, simple people, small folk, little souls, a strange feeling of kinship awakens in him, stronger than the affections of home, as if at bottom they were his real family.

It was an old desire that had haunted him very often, a desire that he had cherished no doubt from his childhood, when he had been a great chief who had withdrawn into his cave to inspect the spoils of conquest and dream of future expeditions, to go and live alone in some solitary spot—as Wheeler had done, a fellow at Harvard who had established himself in a shanty on the edge of Flint Pond to devote himself in all tranquillity to the study of Greek. A well-tempered character, this Wheeler, who slept there on the straw like a stableman or a soldier and later went off to study in Germany, where the poor fellow died. Henry liked and admired him greatly.

Yes, it was the dream of having some sort of shelter bathed in silence where he could listen to the things, both within and outside himself, that were lost in the Babel of the village. He had once been on the point of realizing it when he had just missed buying the Hallowell place, the beautifully ruined and solitary old farm he had seen on the river as he passed in his boat; but he had not come to terms with the owner and it had remained nothing but a charming fancy sheltered behind its screen of maple-trees. After all, it was better to have missed this opportunity, to have been spared the humiliation of seeing his name printed in the records as a property-owner.

But the old desire had not died. It spoke to-day with more authority than ever. At twenty-eight, with some experience of the solutions the world offered for the problem of a livelihood and no inclination whatever to adopt any of them, there still remained the old question of supporting himself. His little jobs as an occasional day-labourer gave him at best a precarious and insufficient means of living. It had become clearer and clearer that Concord was not very anxious to employ the particular talents of an "amateur" who undertook to do his work with the respect of an artist for his art. Well, suppose he were to free himself from all these needs that were not worth the trouble he took to satisfy them? Suppose he were to simplify his life?

Existence in his own home, to be sure, was frugality itself. But when you looked closely, how encumbered it was with superfluities! Cut down, cut down! This luxury perverts the life of a man. It usurps the place of true values that only ask for a chance to blossom. The truth of life is a fragile plant that a gardener should protect against evil intruders. A house brings with it innumerable duties. A village is a buzzing, trampled thoroughfare, poisoned with gossip and neighbours. You could get away by yourself for a few hours, but there were times when domestic thoughts, village thoughts clung so tight to your skin that you could not shake them off in the open air and they reduced your adventure to the vulgar proportions of some cockney's holiday in the country. You would give anything to rid yourself of these leechlike thoughts, not just for a few hours in the afternoon but for good and all, for days and nights together. You would give anything, for example, if the first sound you heard when you woke up in the morning were not to come from some neighbour who is clearing his throat. You would give anything not to squander so many precious hours, sacrificed for the privilege of being a citizen who is taught his P's and Q's on the lap of a parish. And what wouldn't you give not to dream any longer of the beauty of living, but to experience it completely for a while, without alloy, unrestrictedly, in all its freshness, free as the open air, naked and real, from dawn to the day's end, and the same to-morrow—to feel that you were *existing* on this good green earth?

There happened to be other needs that quickened this desire for a little retirement. Henry had already written a few pages with which he had reason not to be too dissatisfied. His articles, his studies were only a prelude, an incentive to exercise himself more rigorously at his trade as a writer. There too he had to strip himself of vain ornaments and find out exactly what he was capable of and whether he was really worthy of doing something. He would work well in this peaceful seclusion. The outlines of a book were vaguely taking form in the pages of the Journal. He would see.

Henry needed a retreat, to audit his books with all care and discover just where his personal affairs stood, to examine various true, essential matters, including himself, face to face.

It was a more serious business at bottom even than the desire to clarify his existence and live more or less alone, after his own fashion. It had the charm of a great difficulty to be overcome; instead of running away from it or trifling with it, he wanted to come to grips with it and find out, without any beating about the bush, which was the stronger. It was a tempting opportunity to prove to himself that he could provide for his subsistence with his own hands, without aid, giving himself the beautiful margin of leisure that is indispensable to a man if his life is to have a meaning and yield its flower. We shall have a good try, my shopkeeping friends. You set yourself up in business. Henry is going to follow your example and launch out in an enterprise of his own, at his own risk and peril, with his ten fingers and the wits of a ne'er-do-well for his capital. When you are the son and grandson and great-grandson of merchants, you may turn your back on your patrimony, but you do not discard from your destiny the taste for certain kinds of operations. On the other hand, you are not going to puzzle your brains trying to calculate your profits if you succeed. And if your speculation is unfortunate, you will still have the pleasure of telling about your failure.

A boy had been turning these thoughts over in his mind while tramping over the fourteen acres of woodland which his friend Waldo had bought for a little more than $200 last September, a spot that had taken Henry's fancy above all the paradises of the domain of vagabonds. It was on the banks of Walden Pond, where the Sage carried his philosophy into the woods,

drawn there by the sound of the name: Waldo . . .
Eden . . .

The circle of sombre branches reflected in the calm
blue waters was an impression that he had preserved
from his earliest infancy, and later it had been the goal
of many an expedition. As a child, as a boy he had run
off to go fishing, hunting, skating there, or to stretch
out in a boat in summer, letting himself glide over the
water to the waves of wild foliage that enclosed the
pond. The spot had an incomparable charm and wildness, and although it was only half an hour from the
village it was so retired that all the villages of the earth
were lost and forgotten there in a distance beyond the
sea for the explorer who prowled about its banks. An
evil fame, a legendary mirage floated about these
regions—an additional attraction. On the borders of
the woods of Walden, on the neighbouring hill, in former
times, all sorts of lawless characters, pariahs, escaped
slaves, negresses who told fortunes and other riff-raff
used to live whose presence in the shadow of the church
would have been an offence to the purity of the village.
The blackened remains of their cabins were still to be
seen there. Henry liked to think of black Zilpha, who
spun linen and had such a beautiful voice, and Wyman,
the poor potter, unfortunate souls indeed. But the
pond itself! Sunk in the shelving semicircle, a dark
green mass drank in the deep blue of this miraculous
glade under a great stretch of sky. The whole world
was still, and he himself was a flood of silent wonder
amid this population of pines and oaks.

How good it would be to come here and taste the
quality of the silence! Who knew but this pond, meditating in its immemorial solitude, folded in upon itself
in the quiet of the woods, might not have some important secret to whisper to him, if he became its confi-

dant? . . . Many a time on its banks he had dreamed
of a Waldenic existence and had taken the road home
again to the village and his old ways. But now the
little voice murmured among the reeds: My secret is
not for a boy who has merely come on a visit. It is for
the faithful soul who will come and live beside me,
spending his nights and his days and mingling with his
existence every hour of my own. . . The little voice
possessed an all-powerful sweetness for the senses of a
lover, a solitary. Yes, to come and savour there the
interminable summer evenings, drink in the first draught
of air before the dawn, allow the winter to blockade
him with snow as he listened to the beating of his heart
in the frosty silence. To plunge into the pond every
morning! To feel at home there, like a wild duck or a
skater-insect! . . . Suppose, instead of the summer-
house which the Sage planned to set up there, some day,
on his land, he were to build himself at once a house
under the pines, on the side of the knoll that dropped
off by a gentle slope into the pond?

When a beautiful castle in Spain that has been tenderly
cherished for years finds a foundation like this upon
which to rest, one hesitates no longer. The business is
settled. Spring appears like a notification. Towards
the end of March, in the year 1845 of the Christian era,
Henry goes to his friend Alcott and borrows his axe; it
does not cut very well, this philosophical axe—perhaps
it has been blunted at Fruitlands, in that unhappy phal-
ansterian enterprise—but he undertakes to sharpen it .

The builder has chosen his site, felled the trees to
clear the space where he is to erect the house. The plan
is already settled. Those pines will do for the frame-
work. The other materials can be found at little cost.
Why new planks when second-hand planks will serve
perfectly well? A labourer's shanty will give him plenty

of timber, and he will only have to unnail it and transport it with all the accessories, not forgetting the old
nails, which will serve a second time. For four dollars
and twenty-five cents, an Irishman who is working on
the railroad is quite willing to sell him the one he lives
in; it will only be necessary to let the planks dry a little
so that the air can absorb their Hibernian moisture.
The materials are all ready for the work. The cellar
is dug in the sand, where the provisions are to be kept.
There is nothing impossible about setting up the frame
for a man who helped his father to build their new house
the year before; no need of a gang of skilled hands to
plant a post upright at the corner where the roof is to
rest. But if his friends offer to come and give him a
hand with this heavy job of the timber-work, is he
going to renounce the rare pleasure of working in the
woods there with a few cronies who are not such good
carpenters as himself perhaps but who are full of hearty
good will? Alcott and Edmund Hosmer join in the
party. Everything they say sparkles in the resinous air;
all the preparations have taken time and it is May
already. A philosopher, a farmer and a ne'er-do-well
in collaboration nail together with affection the frame
of a cabin that is going to support the weight of solitude.

It may be weeks since spring came to surprise old
Minot. But it has been just as long, if not longer, since
it took possession of the heart of a boy who, since the
end of March, has turned his steps every morning, with
his lunch in his pocket, towards his workshop in the
woods. The little glade is covered with shavings; the
work of building goes on amid the cheerful clatter of
axe and hammer, and the surrounding pines gaze with
a curious eye upon this neighbour who is coming to live
there as if they had never seen old nails driven by so
young an arm. It is only a house that is going up, a

motionless house overlooking a motionless pond, but
for the workman, blissfully alone in the woods. . . .
April, May, June . . . the light sings as in former days
when he was building his little boat for those faraway
expeditions—sings a chaplet of songs as long as the
work that he pursues unhastingly on this piney knoll.
The cabin is fixed to the earth by its roots, and it is to
shelter the sleep of an explorer who is promising himself
not a week or two but whole seasons of discoveries and
adventures . . . seasons that will be reflected in the
eye of this big high window, seasons upon which this
door that hangs here will open with a gesture of welcome
and familiarity at the entrance of the cabin where Henry
is going to sleep on this holiday evening—for it is the
Fourth of July.

Up before dawn on the first morning, the builder
stops on his threshold, goes out, takes a turn around his
castle, comes in again, goes out again, looks up at his
roof with perfect confidence in its power to resist snow,
sun and rain, and only asking himself if it is not going
to burst with the happiness contained between these
four plank walls. In the woods some neighbours are
singing and chirping. The fresh air pours through him
as if he had come out of a tent. But the cabin is not a
tent, it is spacious: ten feet by fifteen. You can stretch
your legs in it. It contains everything: bed, table, a
chair and, at one end, facing the door, a place for the
hearth which is not yet built. The household utensils
are in a cupboard. Under the floor, the cellar, and an
attic above, each with its trap-door. The room is
lighted by two windows, one in front and one in the
rear. It has all the comfort and brightness of a living-
room with the compact intimacy of a ship's cabin.

Thirty to forty square yards of ground, which do not
belong to him, offer their immovable base to this new

man who has built the home of his dreams and come
here to sleep and means to sleep here to-morrow and
another tomorrow—who has touched with his feet, as
he leaps out of bed, the realization of his vision, touched
it with his hand as he opens his door, as he slowly makes
the rounds to reassure himself that it is all true, as,
from the threshold of the cabin, in the innocence of the
earth, emerging from the summer night, he sees down
there forty yards away the rocky little bay, his haven,
the great blue lake and the woods beyond, nothing but
water, sky, waves of foliage, without the least sign of a
human habitation, a whole corner of the world that
has kept itself intact to enchant the eye of a newcomer.
Like everyone else he had had his black and his grey
moments in life, but he cannot imagine at this instant a
discontent the vexation of which would not vanish
under the benediction of such a morning, in the air of a
hillside where he has planted his cabin to live an eternity
there. He is not cut off from the world: on the left is
the road to Lincoln and on the right the railroad to
Fitchburg. But the squatter cannot see a roof. He can
fancy as he awakens that the human race has gone
away for a time to nurse its sorrows under other skies,
leaving the place for the fresh happiness of a solitary.

Yes, it seems as if one could live here. Everything is
clean, there is none of the litter that encumbers existence.
The true wealth is in the open; you can weigh it, drink
it, breathe it; it is solid, fluid, has a good resinous smell,
refreshing as ice-water, fills your arms like the stones
you pile up to build the fireplace. There is so much to
do, in the first place, living is such an absorbing, delightful
occupation, that the most beautiful page you could read
would seem like an impertinence: it would interrupt
your collaboration in the poem of the whole day. You
are no longer an afternoon stroller. The slow task of

taking possession of the surroundings demands all your hours, a continuous employment, going and coming on the path that leads to the water, observations, saunterings, surprises. But the hours about the cabin are free from everything you have left out there beyond the woods, the habits of a household, the family table, the routine with its taſte of pencil-lead, the house-fronts in Main Street, the regimented faces. They wear new robes, these hours, cut in the workshop of Walden; they marvel at themselves and their labour is like play.

What is there to do, all the blessed day long, living alone on the edge of a pond? That is what puzzles those charitable souls beyond the woods. Ah, good people, if one were alone! . . . But Henry has never felt less alone than he has felt since the day when he put that little space between the village and himself, not for a few hours but for good. He can feel alone in a Judge's house but not in a cabin in the woods which he has built after his own heart. When is there a moment for loneliness to worm itself into the course of the day? When he is preparing his meals? Hardly. His main dish every day is a gruel of corn, rye or rice; the preparation is simple and pleasant. No need of a lot of saucepans and ingredients, no need to devote himself to those rather repulsive manipulations that are demanded in expert cookery. And this is very nourishing too. If he feels like it, the cook may also broil a little rasher of bacon. When he wants to vary his ordinary diet, it is quite simple for him to boil some acorns for breakfaſt as an homage to the gods of Walden; boiled acorns are a little more bitter than raw acorns, but you soon get used to them. And what other bitterness can you imagine a man feeling who does his housekeeping in the open air, in front of his cabin, where he eats sitting on his door-ſtep, with his bowl on his knees and the lake at his feet and the whole day entirely at his disposal? He has the best of table companions around him, all drinking to the health of a happy man. Music plays for him, and it is a different music from that of the human voice. Henry oversees the baking of his bread, placed in an oven the mouth of which is covered with stones as unceremoniously as in the days of the ancient Romans. But the bread that is baked in this way has no flavour of antiquity; a savoury odour comes from this rustic bakery improvised on a piney New England slope. How could a baker like this, watching his ovenful in the open air, feel lonely? Nor is he any likelier to feel so as he does his housekeeping, chops his wood or sets to work to give his room a good cleaning. All his furniture is taken outside—there is a whole wheel-barrowful of it—the table faces the broad daylight without flinching, the bed stretches itself in the open air, while Henry carries up buckets of water and scours and rinses his floor with the water of Walden. Imagine a boy who does his housekeeping under the eye of the pines, carries his furniture in again when the floor is dry, happy as a king who is going to sleep to-night in a room that has a good, well-washed smell—imagine a boy so happily busy feeling himself forsaken! Solitude may prowl almost anywhere, on the very pavements of a populous city, but what could it ever find to pick up in the tracks of a boy like this?

To deserve this life he has chosen he must first make sure of his subsistence. The cabin is not a philosopher's country cottage; it is a farmhouse, and the farmer has his mind on his farm and his harvest. This bread that smells so good when he takes it out of the oven is not to be earned by listening to the hooting of the owls. On Emerson's lot at Walden there is a stretch of waste land which, with a good deal of work and a little imagination, he ought to be able to turn into a field. It is a piece of poor, sandy ground which the woods have covered for the laſt fifteen years: virgin soil, ſtill full of ſtumps but with plenty of vigour and good will, in which he can have some confidence—even if it did belong, at the end of the laſt century, to a great uncle by marriage who was a deacon. It certainly needs manure, but he has not come to Walden to apply the methods of model farms. The labour of his own solid muscles will have to take the place of the manure, after the clearing, ploughing and harrowing of the ground, for which the work of a man with his horse and cultivator is indispensable. Certain expenses are unavoidable in every enterprise.

Henry has sown some potatoes, a little corn, a few peas, a handful of turnips and a lot of beans, and they all come up—all but the seeds which the worms have eaten—come up, sprout and form an immense field. But the weeds, encouraged by the ploughing, also spring up merrily, and he has to grub them out to proteċt the life of the beans and his own honour as a rash adventurer. And what work! The sower has sown his beans generously, as a farmer who sees things in a large way. He has rows and rows of them, innumerable rows—seven good miles if he placed them end to end—four times longer than the diſtance from the cabin to the village. On this immense battle-front the general defends the land ſtep by ſtep. It is very painful for a man of the wilds to see himself condemned to assuming the defence of culture againſt these hordes of barbarians that have grown so beautifully. But what is to be done when the deſtiny of a legion of beans, threatened with being surrounded, hangs in the balance? Since five o'clock in the morning, hoe in hand, the squatter has been out in his field, firſt in the dew, then, as the sun mounts, in the glare of the summer day, weeding, putting fresh

175

soil about the stems, without giving up till noon, his bare feet in the burning sand, as steady as a negro in a cotton-field.

The man with the hoe is not slaving away under the eye of an overseer. He works with a will, first because that is his way, and then because he is not a hired man but an obstinate soul who means to carry out with honour a difficult undertaking; he must justify Walden with the sweat of his brow. Walden is not a phalanstery; there is only one person responsible for it, and that is much more serious. The villagers who pass in their carts on the road see a little skinny fellow bending over his bean-stalks in his half-wild, half-cultivated field and wonder why this strange workman is breaking his back over such a piece of ground at such a season. It is Henry the simpleton, toiling away cheerfully and letting the world go by. He is thinking, under the heat of the sun, of the sweet bath he is going to give himself in the pond, after this glorious sweat, and how good it will be to stretch out on his grassy bank near the spring, in the shade of a vast white pine, with a book for a companion. . . But it is not enough to work himself to death defending, weapon in hand, these wretched beans that are surrounded with enemies; the woodchucks, which are very partial to them, eat up a quarter of your acre. For these blessed beasts the attraction of the tender shoots is stronger than any fear of the trap; Henry kills one of them and eats it in revenge. But in spite of all, as the reward of his labours, the farmer harvests twelve bushels of beans and sells them for $16.94, plus $4.75 for potatoes. Something of a result!

In all, $8.71½, deducting the original outlay, a total that might not satisfy one of those knowing souls who go by sneering on the road, but enough to yield the farmer of Walden a good profit—if he adds it to the others which, shrewder than these shrewd folk, he gathered in long before the harvest. The sneerers know all about the sort of soil that produces a big crop, but what do they know of these magnificent days of combat for the beans? They have no Ganges in which to cleanse themselves every morning, to begin the day as if with a prayer; they have no poor field on a hillside on the edge of the woods, where you sweat for hours scratching the earth to persuade it to yield well-podded stalks; they do not know the reward for all the toil of the toilers of the world, or the delight of feeling one's skin exhale its gratitude after the bath and the rubbing. They do not have the rest of the day for dreaming, observing, wandering, turning their laziness into thanksgiving, listening to one's own life amid the throng of things. They are clodhoppers.

The summer has its great sunny spaciousness in which friendship hangs like a scarf from every branch. Just wait for autumn and winter, when some evil animal cowering in the solitude of the cellar comes up from below or descends slyly from a corner of the attic, in the long evenings, to clamber up the legs of a solitary in his cabin, or glide under his shirt and bite him—some insect, some black beetle, some blue devil of doubt to plague a boy who thinks he can get along without the village. But there is nothing under this floor but the field-mice, and they only want the potatoes. And there is nothing in the attic but an old tent-cloth that dreams of distant adventures and the wide air of the river-banks. The spiders may have hung up their webs, but they are the friends of man, weaving decorations for the roof-timbers of a castle in the woods.

No, there are no foul creatures prowling about this cabin, not even an importunate cockroach. Henry has made everything ship-shape. A log is smouldering in the fireplace and the thoughts it has kept shut up till its laſt hour surround him, dancing gaily. For the cabin, finished at laſt, breathes. A house without a chimney through which you can see the smoke coming out is not a living house. It is a mere vulgar barn, a ſtore-house, a dead thing. Before the bad season William comes and lends his friend a hand in setting up the fireplace; he ſtays fifteen days, fifteen beautiful days of comradeship. From now on there will be wood in the woodshed to keep Henry warm in winter and in the evening when he sits up late. He is living here like some old bachelor of a foreſter who has juſt finished his supper, his day's work ended, and tells himself ſtories before going to bed. The latter would probably have his pipe for company, or some yellow-haired mongrel with grave, tender, vigilant eyes. Henry's only companions are his thoughts, the ladies of the house who brush him lightly as they pass as if they were siſters who had come out with him to the woods. Henry reads or writes at his table in the deep silence, where the singing of the fire gives him the feeling of a presence. He revises his manuscripts, works, writes an essay on Carlyle. He takes a good measure of his inner powers in the silence of the cabin and toils over a sheet of paper with the heart of a workman who has swung his hoe through the furrows under the glaring sun. There are the weeds to be dug out, the beans to be defended. Sometimes Henry works at his table in the morning, when he is in the right mood, in the freshness of his ſtrength. At the approach of spring the red squirrels come and make love under the floor of the cabin where a solitary meditates in his twenty-ninth year; when he raps with his foot to silence them, their squeals redouble, as if the lovers were affirming their rights in the face of this scribbler whom their gambols do not greatly diſturb.

And in winter, when the snow covers the paths and the approaches of the dwelling, weighs down the pines, weighs upon the roof of the cabin, when the village is further away than ever, in the overwhelming silence of the snow and its dazzling splendour, what joy to feel himself in this hollow in the woods, like a nest stamped with the warmth of his body, and how the stumps he has toilsomely split repay him for the difficult time he has spent in loosening the embrace of their fibres! What joy walking on the stiffened pond, making a hole in the ice with his axe and bending over the opening, lying flat on his stomach to peep into the aquarium where the hermit fishes look as if they did not find it so bad living in Walden, even under this opaque glass that hides the day from them. . . .

And now, if by chance a friend comes to call on you in the woods, you can do him the honours of your castle. When there are two between the bed, the table and the fireplace, the reception-hall is almost filled, but it is large enough to make room for this chance accession. One Sunday it is dear Edmund Hosmer—no miserly peasant, that fellow—who comes to look in on his colleague, the farmer of Walden; or his son Joseph perhaps, whom the latter has invited to come for a feast at his table. On this occasion there is a choice of dishes and the cook has surpassed himself. You cannot do too much when you are entertaining one of your own kind. He has prepared a banquet: fish from the pond, beans, corn, bread from the Walden bakery, all seasoned with that fine salt of which there is always a full box at Henry's. It is Sunday twice over in the cabin. Nor does Alcott refuse to make it the object of a walk to go and see one of the two or three friends with whom alone he can embark on one of those endless conversations in which time and space are abolished. There is not much philosophical talk at Walden; you don't press wisdom there between the leaves of an old book; you live it, freshly every day, as naturally as you turn to the water in the pond. But with the master of the axe that Henry borrowed to fell the pines for his house, what a feast he has! The bean-field is soon left behind; they are in full flight, and in a few hours they have surveyed numberless continents and unknown archipelagos. If the visitor is only William, who lives a good three miles from the pond but whom neither snow nor storm can stop when the fancy seizes him to go and say good morning to his friend, there are no culinary preparations or voyages into the empyrean: there are simply orgies of laughter in the hermitage. They must say and do all sorts of foolish things to express their joy in finding themselves there in the woods as brothers, free from bores. How the laughter resounds in the cabin on the hillside! Listening to the response that comes from the heart of the woods, you might think it had been built just for this day. . . They chatter like magpies, they chirrup louder than those amorous squirrels, they roar, their boisterous mirth shakes the plank walls. They have no good old wine to drink as they eat their dishes of gruel, nothing but a nut to put under their teeth. But they are able to intoxicate themselves just the same, with the pure gaiety of old cronies.

Now and again some prying busybody also comes to the woods. A boy who has had a little experience of the world knows various tricks for getting rid of these gentry—though they are not always successful. But what a charm spreads about the cabin when other visitors pass, those strolling railroad men, for instance, who are not afraid to violate the Sabbath occasionally by turning in towards the little house in the woods. They are quite a gang, half a dozen of them, walking together and stopping in as neighbours, for Henry often meets them on his comings and goings along his boulevard, the railroad. They have put on their white shirts and saunter along, airing their leisure and waving their Sunday idleness like a little twig one cuts on one's way, the older ones with seamy faces, the younger giving you a friendly greeting and wishing you good luck, without showing the least surprise that a man prefers the company of the pines to that of the villagers. The language and bearing of some of these fine fellows reveal that exquisite, simple, unaffected courtesy that bears the stamp of the workingman and leaves you with the impression that you have received a visit from great personages.

One of those good apostles of the village who knows Henry only as a harsh, dismal mask should pass at a moment when his tempestuous laugh is sounding over the knoll; he would understand better then what this mock hermit has come to seek in the woods. Henry has not broken with the world. He is simply holding it at a distance for a while in order to find space for something he wishes to create. Almost every afternoon the anchorite-in-his-own-fashion crosses the woods and descends again among men. There is an unimaginable charm in taking a trip of this kind as a simple visitor into the regions of the civilized, where he sees human faces. When you have behind you a cabin that is waiting for you in the heart of a kingdom of your choice, the Main Street of the village is as pleasant as possible. You see the strangest things there and you judge everything indulgently, for you see it from another point of view. You have all the enjoyment of a traveller in a foreign town, observing the manners of the natives, the sights, the shops, the fashions, the things for sale. Henry, in spite of his change of domicile, remains on the same old intimate terms with his family and ſtops in regularly to see if everything is going well at home, lend a hand in the workshop, if it is necessary, or busy himself a little in the garden. When he goes home again he sometimes has to carry some tidbit cooked for him by his mother, who is rather afraid that the gruel at the cabin may be too slender a diet for a boy accuſtomed to the family table. Sometimes too, at the end of the day, if the fancy takes him, Henry knocks at a friend's door and invites himself to supper, as the bearer of the lateſt news from the woods; then if night has fallen on the road, as he gropes his way through the darkness after the evening he has passed with his friends, it only deepens the serenity of his return. And this is not to mention the times when, even for a man who has no complaint to make of his business, a dollar comes in very nicely and he undertakes to go down and work for a day or two in the village as a painter, gardener or mason. It is juſt so much to add to the revenue of the farm.

The farmer of Walden does not deposit his wealth in the bank like big landowners and prudent citizens. These good people lock their tills and bolt their doors for fear of robbers. They are so afraid of being relieved of a crumb of their bothersome money! When Henry leaves home for a whole day, and even when he sets out for several days on some diſtant excursion, it never occurs to him to lock his door. One bother the less. The door of the cabin has neither lock nor bolt; nothing but a latch. It is open to all comers. The scorner of men has confidence in humanity, in the unknown. Come in, gentlemen, if you happen to be passing, and you too, Mrs. Paul Pry. Inspeċt the bed, the fireplace and the cupboard. A little something to eat? Eat to your heart's content. You will find a dipper to fetch the water if you are thirſty. Make yourself at home.

And if you have a mind to, after the feast, read a page in one of those books lying there on the table. It will not do you any harm. And if you like the book so much that you don't want to leave it, take it away with you. It has gilt edges; the man of the woods makes you a present of it. The principal of his worldly wealth is there between those planks. But what are the sneak-thieves thinking of? They never come to Walden.

One evening, when he sets out for the cobbler's to take a boot to be repaired, the village resorts to a singularly rough way of testifying its regret at no longer seeing him except as a passing stranger. The town constable places his hand on Henry's shoulder and takes him off to jail. He has refused to pay his poll-tax. His intention in doing so was to protest against a power which protects the purchase, the sale, the practice of dealing in men, women and children, those colonial wares from Africa—and which, on the other hand, makes war on one of its neighbours in order to seize its territory. To say "no" flatly to the tax-collector is a much more serious matter than to refuse to pay the tax of a parish of which one is not a parishioner. It is revolt, dis-loyalty, the crime of treason, the perverse act of a bad citizen who disowns the institutions and the enter-prises of his country. Off with his head!

So here is a boy who only wants to return to his home in the woods and who is invited to spend the night in the middle of the village in a beautiful stone house. Modest as he may be, this pressing and irresistible way of showing him that he is indispensable to the equilib-rium of the village does not fail to touch his pride a little. They lodge him in a princely fashion, for this is not the old wooden jail where, in the days of the Revolu-tion, two of Henry's great-uncles were imprisoned as Loyalists—and from which their sister, his grandmother

Jones, coming from Weston to bring them something to eat in prison, helped one of them to escape. No, the world has made great progress since then, and the jail is in harmony with the world.

On the threshold of the fine modern building, Henry is accosted by his friend Sam Staples, whose cheery bluster is not insensible to the honour of receiving under his roof the son of the pencil-manufacturer. A former innkeeper, Sam adds to this quality the importance of the part he plays in the village; he is at once the jailer and the tax-collector. He is almost everything but a deacon. Sam is also the son-in-law of the innkeeper celebrated by Henry in one of his best pieces, published three years before in the *Democratic Review*. Sam owes it to himself and his father-in-law to be polite in return to Henry. His first remark is: " I'll pay your tax, Henry, if you're hard up." The pity is that Henry is by no means hard up and does not want money. The only thing he wants is to go to jail to meditate at leisure on the beauty of the institutions of his country. Walden is not propitious for this meditation; the hours there are too precious to be wasted in such unclean thoughts. But in this beautiful stone edifice, behind the stout, bolted door, he is in a better position to think of his country, and its laws and law-makers, while he is held there between four firm walls, under the guard of a jailer-tax-collector-ex-innkeeper who is going to sell him at auction perhaps like a mere negro for refusing to bow down to an enslaving and conquering State.

The noise of Henry's arrest spreads through the village. Waldo hastens over to see his friend. The Sage is a little shocked; it spoils the harmony of his universe to find Henry in such a place. "Henry, why are you here?" "Why are you not here?" the prisoner replies with the cool impudence that great criminals have. You can be

a sage and yet never be able to understand certain things.
The best thing Henry can do is to remain in the company
of his own thoughts, which, in spite of this magnificent
masonry that seems destined to annihilate them, have
not lost a jot of their serenity and their liberty. Yes, and
to talk with his cell-companion, an honest soul, accused
of having set fire to a barn, who had been imprudent
enough to go to sleep there in the straw when he was
drunk with a lighted pipe in his mouth; or to listen to
this other prisoner, whose voice comes from a neighbouring cell and who never stops repeating in his misery:
"What is life? . . . So this is life!" . . . Through the
safe bars of the skylight there comes to you the clear
sound of the village bell, a strange sound to hear in this
way from behind these prison walls and this bolted
door. You have never felt so close to the soul of the
village, so close to its citizens, to the beautiful souls of
the builders of the prison, the makers of laws, the buyers
and sellers of human flesh, the plunderers of other
people's territory. This voice of the bell, falling in the
naked intimacy of a jail, is just the one thing necessary to
strip you of the last shred of respect you have kept, without being aware of it, for these blessed institutions. The
prisoner actually has a feeling of deliverance: when he
first came in he did not perceive that the parish was
really imprisoned on the other side of those bars and
that he had been summoned there as a judge to judge it.

A man can find his happiness anywhere if he has room
for happiness in himself. Many a time Henry has said
that he would be able to live very well in an almshouse,
among the humble souls whom one saw about the
grounds of the Poor Farm. He is quite ready to remain
Sam's boarder till Authority recognizes that it has made
a bad blunder. But he has reckoned without the indis-
creet solicitude of his family, who are all in a flutter

over the incarceration of their Henry. While he is
meditating in his dungeon, his good Aunt Maria haſtens
out after nightfall, concealing herself in a neckerchief to
avoid scandal, and deposits the sum which the tax-
collector demands, plus the coſts. All the serenity which
his evening in prison has confirmed in this enemy of the
laws vanishes at dawn when the jailer comes in and
tells him of this transaction. The beautiful ſtone building is to lodge him only for one night; he muſt leave it.
Sam is very happy to set this sympathetic boarder free,
but the latter is furious at finding himself betrayed by
his own people. Confound them! So he leaves. The
village has become odious to him. When he goes to the
cobbler's for his boot, he exhibits on the visage that he
reveals to the gaze of his sly fellow-townsmen the
defiance of an army marching, with flags unfurled,
through a conquered country. That evening the dis-
charged prisoner looks like a man who has come back
from a long journey. As a matter of fact, in order to
efface the memory of that night and that awakening and
the humiliation of that enforced release, he has gone off
and spent the day gathering huckleberries.

Ineſtimable hours of Walden! Do you really imagine,
you poor simple souls, that he has nothing to do here,
nothing more important than to contemplate the image
of his own blessed purity in the mirror of the pond, or
to liſten to himself playing his flute on the water amid
this encircling verdure? It is perfectly true that the
pond is a liquid gem, where the myſterious little rayed
breem lives, as perfect as a jewel. It is not bottomless,
as the good people say. Your sounding-lead touches
the bottom in more than a hundred places—a bottom
of pure sand, without mud—and you can draw up an
outline of its basin. But how far the discoveries you

make here surpass the miracle of its limpidity! Why does this prowler about the woods find more soul in these desert places than among his own brothers, the bipeds of the villages and cities? Is it possible that a narrow-chested fellow with sloping shoulders carries the whole load of it on his own back, scattering it about the roads as he passes? And so saturates the earth with his own feeling as to make it murmur, sing, pray, utter words, force it to say what its religion is? Or does the human quality reside in a diffused state under the bark of the trees and in the sap of plants for the soul of this vagabond to collect it and feed upon it? . . . In any case, every hour at Walden is like the measure of sand passed through the sieve of a gold-seeker; it leaves enough of a residue to make a boy comfortable for the rest of his days.

These fresh things that flow about the cabin surprise him in the midst of his labours with a beauty so pure and so exultant that he is obliged to drop his spade, his book or his housekeeping, sit down on the doorstep and simply surrender himself to the unknown things that are passing. You would say then that the earth had chosen this poor, shy boy whom you see absorbed there, on the threshold of his cabin, as an instrument for thinking in peace of its own unity and eternity. How can he say where he is? The planet is silent, time and space are strangely annihilated, the notion of any journey is lost, he may be at the antipodes. Under the pines of Walden, this man who is lost in his dream is Mir Mohammed Ali, perhaps, the painter of Ispahan; his American profile is drawn in miniature in the colours of a precious stone on the blue of the pond. Or is he some Chinese poet-philosopher in whom mingle the souls of animals and plants and hermits sitting under an arbour near a little lake? There comes to this man, as he listens to sound

187

beyond sound, a music that is deeper and more ample than the music of his everyday life; he feels on his palate as it were a taste of immortality—it grows clearer than the clear morning about him. This beetle that buzzes by, this sweetflag swaying on the pond are like messengers charged with transmitting to him the friendship of men who have dreamed the same dreams in the depths of the old Orient. He knows those men, he has invited them now and again in the evening to come and bear him company under his roof; they have never felt out of their element or constrained in a cabin as big as one's hand in the open woods. And the beautiful stories they have told him are not discordant with the cry of the whip-poor-will.

At such moments as these, you would take him for a fellow who has laid his hoe aside like a workman about to take his rest. In reality, he is a man in ecstasy, ravished by this miracle, and his life grows more and more exalted and ascends in a perfume of thanksgiving till his contempt for the little men whose stupidity has made him flee is unravelled like smoke in the wind. Some fine morning he will find them almost rehabilitated in his eyes: in the first rays of the sun, at the first notes of the thrush after the winter, it will be the end of all that; there will be nothing left under the pines of Walden but a man who is all feeling and who is ready to pardon his kind for being such sorry automatons, repeating their mechanical gestures in the dullness of their days. This light of early dawn will be enough to set shining at the bottom of their poverty a precious spangle which they themselves do not know they possess, and which redeems all their shabbiness.

Two such years as these, two full years quite to himself, far from every discordant sound, impregnate the very tissue of an existence. The anchorite can leave his cabin. Very foolish would be the person who supposed that the experience of his life in the woods had played him false. It had crowned him. To have proved to himself that a man, when he wishes, can be entirely self-sufficient without hiring out either his arms or his head, was one result: but he had derived something else from it as well. He had not only provided for his needs; he had learned how to economize. He could choose, according to his mood, like a man of leisure: return and stay with his fellowmen or remain by the pond.

At the end of the third summer he abandoned the cabin to the squirrels. Why, exactly? Will those who know be good enough to tell him? He scarcely knows himself. Changing one's dwelling-place is a vestige perhaps of the old migratory instinct. Was he right or wrong in leaving? Did he have any reason to regret it? Vain questions . . . He simply went away in 1847 as he had come in 1845. But aside from this? Perhaps because it was better that an all too beautiful experience should be interrupted before habit destroyed its freshness. Or merely because he could not resist the invitation of a great friend who begged his old right-hand man to come and live in his house again during his second voyage to Europe.

For Henry Waldo's house was like another home. He had spent two happy years there; he would be glad to spend another eight or ten months. During his stay in the woods he had read to Waldo, under an oak on the bank of the river, some pages from the book he was preparing. He would be able to work in the Sage's house. He intended to include in this book a piece on friendship that he would be able to write most fitly under the roof of a perfect friend. On October 5th, Henry went to Boston to see the traveller off and say good-bye to him in his stateroom. (How small and dark it was after the cabin!) The boat was called the "Washington Irving"—a favourable augury. The great man was going to deliver some lectures before the choicest spirits in England. He was going to see Carlyle. He planned to make a tour of the Continent, stopping at Paris. Bon voyage, and may the gods of Concord protect you, dear Waldo. Have no anxiety about the garden or your family.

Once more in the little white house the children find their Henry. Ellen has become a personage of eight; Eddy, a new personage, is three and a half. And the parties begin again. The right-hand man has not forgotten in the woods how to win the confidence of childhood. When they turn over together the pages of a picture-book, the savage takes as much interest in them as the little figures perched on his knees. He is on very good terms with Ellen. He must never ignore these important details in giving the traveller the news of the little house. It is the middle of November, a good time for long letters. In a hand not always easy to decipher but one which the recipient will read without any hesitation, Henry writes to his friend Waldo:

I am but a poor neighbour to you here,—a very poor companion am I. I understand that very well, but that need not prevent my *writing* to you now. . . .
I have banked up the young trees against the winter and the mice, and I will look out, in my careless way, to see when a pale is loose or a nail drops out of its place. The broad gaps, at least, I will occupy. I heartily wish I could be of good service to this household. But I, who have only used these ten digits so long to solve the problem of a living, how can I? The world is a cow that is hard to milk—life does not come so easy,—and oh, how thinly it is watered ere we get it! But the young bunting calf, he will get at it. There is no way so

direct. This is to earn one's living by the sweat of his brow. It is a little like joining a community, this life, to such a hermit as I am; and as I don't keep the accounts, I don't know whether the experiment will succeed or fail finally. At any rate, it is good for society, so I do not regret my transient nor my permanent share in it.

Lidian and I make very good housekeepers. She is a very dear sister to me. Ellen and Edith and Eddy and Aunty Brown keep up the tragedy and comedy and tragic-comedy of life as usual. The two former have not forgotten their old acquaintance; even Edith carries a young memory in her head, I find. Eddy can teach us all how to pronounce. If you should discover any rare hoard of wooden or pewter horses, I have no doubt he will know how to appreciate it. He occasionally surveys mankind from my shoulders as wisely as ever Johnson did. I respect him not a little, though it is I that lift him up so unceremoniously. And sometimes I have to set him down again in a hurry, according to his "mere will and good pleasure." He very seriously asked me, the other day, "Mr. Thoreau, will you be my father?" I am occasionally Mr. Rough-and-tumble with him that I may not miss *him*, and lest he should miss *you* too much. So you must come back soon, or you will be superseded.

Alcott has heard that I laughed, and so set the people laughing, at his arbour, though I never laughed louder than when I was on the ridge-pole. But now I have not laughed for a long time, it is so serious. He is very grave to look at. But, not knowing all this, I strove innocently enough, the other day, to engage his attention to my mathematics. "Did you ever study geometry, the relation of straight lines to curves, the transition from the finite to the infinite? Fine things about it in Newton and Leibnitz." But he would hear none of it,—men of taste preferred the natural curve. Ah, he is a crooked stick himself. He is getting on now so many *knots* an hour. There is one knot at present occupying the point of higheſt elevation,—the present higheſt point; and as many knots as are not handsome, I presume, are thrown down and caſt into the pines. Pray show him this if you meet him anywhere in London, for I cannot make him hear much plainer words here. He forgets that I am neither old nor young, nor anything in particular, and behaves as if I had ſtill some of the animal heat in me. As for the building, I feel a little oppressed when I come near it. It has no great disposition to be beautiful; it is certainly a wonderful ſtructure, on the whole, and the fame of the architeᵈt will endure as long as it shall ſtand. . . .

I have had a tragic correspondence, for the moſt part all on one side, with Miss—. She did really wish to—I hesitate to write—marry me. That is the way they spell it. Of course I did not write a deliberate answer. How could I deliberate upon it? I sent back as diſtinᵈt a *no* as I have learned to pronounce after considerable praᵈtice, and I truſt that this *no* has succeeded. Indeed, I wished that it might burſt, like hollow shot, after it had ſtruck and buried itself and made itself felt there. *There was no other way.* I really had anticipated no such foe as this in my career.

I suppose you will like to hear of my book, though I have nothing worth writing about it. Indeed for the laſt month or two I have forgotten it, but shall certainly remember it again. Wiley & Putnam, Munroe, the Harpers, and Crosby & Nichols have all declined printing it with the leaſt risk to themselves; but Wiley & Putnam will print it in their series, and any of them anywhere, at *my* risk. If I liked the book well enough, I should not delay; but for the present I am indifferent. I believe this is, after all, the course you advised,—to let it lie.

I do not know what to say of myself. I sit before my green desk, in the chamber at the head of the ſtairs, and attend to my thinking, sometimes more, sometimes less diſtinᵈtly.

I trust a common man will be the most uncommon to you before you return to these parts. I have thought there was some advantage even in death, by which we "mingle with the herd of common men". . .

Oh, yes, he must also send him the news about Hugh, the gardener, who has been intending to buy Henry's cabin and the old bean-field. The fruit-trees he promised to plant there are not set out yet. Hugh is busy elsewhere: on the day after the Cattle-show he was among the missing. The same old story, too much beer. . . The field at Walden is in good hands.

They have had a peace meeting here . . . Some men, Deacon Brown at the head, have signed a long pledge, swearing that they will "treat all mankind as brothers henceforth." I think I shall wait and see how they treat me first. I think that Nature meant kindly when she made our brothers few. However, my voice is still for peace. So good-bye, and a truce to all joking, my dear friend.

VI

Henry weighs in his hand a book that has just come from the press. A duodecimo, bearing on its back: H. D. THOREAU—A WEEK ON THE CONCORD AND MERRIMAC RIVERS.

From it rises a faintly insipid odour of glue and ink. But it is no cardboard tomb that he has wished to raise to the memory of the dear companion to whom these pages are dedicated. He is wondering how the delight of a week like that, two adventurous weeks passed with his brother, could possibly be contained between two layers of brown cardboard, and he has half a mind to fling the volume into the corner. It is less true than that arrow-head there on the table.

He is examining his first book, which has at last appeared. It is a mere trifle of pulp or dirty rags, boiled down, flattened into sheets, dried and finally blackened with ink. And beyond that? How about all the things he had meant to put into it? The best part has been lost between the manuscript and the composing-stick. A book that is nothing more than a book may be a very attractive accessory among the drawing-room furnishings of people of taste if the shade of the binding harmonizes with the hangings and the rugs. To a man of the woods whose eye prefers to linger on bare boards and plain whitewashed walls, a book is a useless knick-knack, a rather sorry one, mere dust in a cardboard box.

In this scrap-book of verse and prose (the verse—old verse, for he has ceased to write it—like dried flowers pressed between the leaves) in which the glorious voyage . . . yes, ten summers ago now . . . serves only

194

as a pretext for personal digressions, he would have
liked to put the whole world, with its blowing winds,
its floods of light, the fragrance of the river-banks at
dawn and all the surprises under heaven that had been
gathered in by a twenty-year-old heart. A book of
which the first outlines had been sketched under a tent
and the chapters had been assembled in a cabin in the
woods was not intended merely for the mahogany
shelves of Mr. Pettifogger the bibliophile. It should
dance and plash like the boat that had borne the two
conquerors; it should preserve a little of the flavour of
the melons they had carried on board. What was the
use of it otherwise? There were enough cemeteries of
books already, full of the other kind, with mortuary
emblems watching over them.

Did they amount to as much as one dip of an oar in a
river spangled with reflexions, these few hundred pages,
black on white? (See if you can find any black in
nature.) Well, anyway, the book had come out. Not
without difficulty. The publishers would have nothing
to do with it. In the end he had had to resign himself to
a "published by the author." Another fling of the adventurer, launching his bark for the conquest of the world,
with the good Jersey blood of the mariner in his veins.
It was for the public now to do its duty by demanding
Weeks and *Weeks* from the booksellers, enough weeks
to make up the life of a centenarian, or at least the age of
the author. Here's a book for you, just out, a thousand
copies, by Henry Thoreau, out of his own head, every
word of it, from the title to the last period. Quite a
different affair from an article published in a magazine,
between a cream-puff and a sermon.

When you have cherished from college days an ambition to be a writer there is naturally a little warmth in
the hand that holds the back of the first book. You have

made your bow in the world, you have started, you have
set out for the antipodes; you are off on a voyage that
will never end. You have openly confessed your secret
passion, accepted the ordeal of the daylight that shines
on a larger world than Concord. The Sage has encouraged you to try your luck. You are going to see. The
author is not greatly troubled in advance about the
judgment of the world on the first fruits of a writer of
thirty-two. In his silent communion with his note-
books, during the dozen years that he has been preparing
himself to write, Henry has fortified himself with assur-
ances that have nothing to do with success or failure.

Curious Journal, curious confidant, a work that is to
be continued through many volumes—eight or ten
already exist—and that will never be finished till the day
when the universe ceases to surprise him, the day when
his two eager eyes are closed at last. As the farmer has
been in no hurry to sell his crop while he was reaping it,
his barn contains the harvest of several years. It has
been necessary to add one floor after another in order to
get it all stored away. Heaven knows whether all this
will keep; but he has taken good care that all the gar-
nered sheaves shall be quite dry.

On his rambles the explorer scribbles on the spot a
note or a few cabalistic signs, while he is under the
direct impression of the phenomenon or the landscape
he is observing. On his return the note is copied out,
more deliberately. Later, in its final form, it will be
incorporated in the Journal. What Henry, the writer,
adds in the evening to the visions and thoughts of the
day's walk in no way destroys their freshness, for they
are thoughts of a true Pilgrim, flowers that have unfolded in the rhythm of the walk and that he turns over
in his hands at home, in the evening, with his spirit
bathed in the open air, so as to study their tints. It

might be called, this Journal, the account of a journey that never comes to an end, for the world about Concord is immense and has a genius for metamorphosis; or perhaps the review of a spectacle that is performed for himself alone, with a programme that is constantly renewed, action and setting, with the strange encounters one has after a performance, the people one likes, the people one laughs at. Or the "love story" of a boy who is looking for his own affinities and finds them oftener in the world of plants than in human form. It is illustrated now and then by rude sketches carefully recording some observation or discovery. But whether it is to be called a report, a review, a story or the music of the day, the notebook contains nothing that is not veracious testimony. A descendant of merchants and like them a hoarder of treasures, Henry reckons up in the Journal the gains of the day. He too is in business, and he keeps his accounts with the meticulous exactness of a book-keeper. You can examine his books. Observe the debits and the credits. If the profits do not strike you as very clear, it is because you have singular ideas about wealth, my dear fellow.

The harvest might well have remained in the barn. No purchasers appear, but at times the desire seizes him to sell a few armfuls if only to see whether or not it is keeping well—perhaps, too, for the fun of having a little cash. Now and then Henry wants to buy some fine old book, if only to escape the bother of having to go to the library to read it, or he needs a good pair of boots. Then he draws from his Journal the substance of an article and sends it off to a magazine. Horace Greeley, whose acquaintance he has made in New York, has been of great service in finding a place for his work and has even agreed to advance him a small sum. But Concordians propose and editors dispose. The manuscript is too long, or they will not countenance some of his audacities of thought. Or, what is more likely to happen, the article is printed and the author is swindled. What, dear sir, you are not satisfied with the honour of appearing in print in my celebrated sheet? You expect to be paid for it? You can dig in your own pockets. This misadventure befell him long since with the editor of a certain *Boston Miscellany* and more recently with that of *Graham's Magazine*, who published his essay on Carlyle, written at Walden. There you are! You are a Concord hayseed, and these fine gentlemen are giving you a lesson in humility. One doesn't write for money. Pocket the lesson and clench your fist. And get back to work at your Journal.

And now it has appeared, after all, this volume he has just brought back, freshly bound, from his printer Monroe's, at whose shop he has been to see it through the press on this twenty-sixth of May. Henry examines his first book, and he does not feel so very proud. He is the author of *A Week on the Concord*. It has been introduced to the public. What next? One must sometimes have confidence in one's fellow-men and place a figure before a line of zeros.

(Yes, a book is born, and almost at once someone close to you dies, someone whose loss hurts you deeply and blots out all thought of books. Henry loses his sister Helen, the eldest—called back, she too, to the grandfather—Helen who had his features, his eyes, and was so sympathetic with his ideas. Helen has gone, not yet thirty-seven, to keep John company in the cemetery.)

The writer also appears in public when he gives a lecture. It is in the Concord Lyceum that Waldo distributes the honey from his hives. Since he made his first appearance at twenty-one, Henry has spoken there every year. He has been chosen secretary. The honour of addressing one's fellow-citizens from a chair that has been occupied by a sage of European fame is worth the effort of trying to do it graciously. From the fund on which he can draw to organize his series of winter lectures, Henry can offer in exceptional cases ten dollars to an orator of note; he himself pockets only the thanks of the committee. But the neighbouring Lyceums ask him to come and speak in other towns. Last year his friend Hawthorne, who has left Concord and now lives in Salem, arranged for him to be invited there and asked him to stay at his house. Henry received twenty dollars for his trouble. A fine haul. This year he is taking his eloquence to Worcester, where Harrison Blake lives.

What do you think of the lecturer? Hm, hm. . . In the first place, he doesn't speak, he "reads" a paper elaborately written; he doesn't drop his manuscript for an instant, and he utters it all in a desperately earnest, monotonous voice. A bad method. He pronounces his r's harshly. And he is not exactly engaging, this young man. He doesn't give himself. The people listen attentively to this sober soul who talks to them about things that interest them very little; they are not repelled, they are not indignant, they are simply bored. And the worst of it is that Henry not only believes in what he says but is quite aware of the freezing effect his little discourse has upon people; he plods along with imperturbable gravity. It is as if he had started with some such little preamble as this in his mind: You blockheads down there listening to me, what do I care whether I interest you or not? You seem to think I've come here to give you lollypops. Here are a few sour apples and some acorns I've collected for you. Do what you like with them. What can a man expect from such frozen wits? It's quite useless to waste any finesse on these dolts.

They wouldn't see anything in it. They make no personal effort; they don't come half-way to meet you. . . If you go on speaking just the same, it is because you are sustained by the hope of finding one or two living beings among these mummies, a few simple and impressionable souls thanks to whom your pains will not be lost. As a rule, no one comes up after the lecture to tell you how extraordinarily good it is. Well, never mind; you can go home, ladies and gentlemen. There is something to be said for you for having listened without a murmur to such a trying pedant.

No, Henry doesn't hit it off with the audience at all. You don't get very far with these good people with paradoxes and ferocious affirmations; you must have the art of flattering and tickling them, putting them into a good humour and touching their hearts. This fellow here doesn't know the first thing about his business. There is nothing these people like better than to be amused in a sociable kind of way, and he doesn't even know how to make himself agreeable. He is the worst bore in New England. If you have all that faith, my boy, hand it out in little sandwiches that can be taken with a cup of tea. Add a little water-cress, sprinkle it with a pinch of salt, and serve it with a smile. See what will happen then.

Henry, you are no sort of cook at all. You are only up to boiling gruel in your cabin. It's pathetic to see a man satisfied with being as poor an orator as he is a man of letters. This refusal to yield to the ways of the world gets to be irritating after a while. No use for him to want to be a writer; he will never enter the paradise of the literary. He would merely bring to it an absurd respect for his art and the firm intention of pleasing himself before pleasing others. Henry, the lover of good work, takes a workman's pains in perfecting his page.

Thanks to the erasures, this manuscript has become an illegible scrawl, not because in the first draught the writing was so uncertain but because the author is so extremely severe with himself. He has a pitiless blue pencil. No "almosts." Nothing that savours of improvisation. Every word that is not alive, that is merely a word, must disappear. Struggle and toil count for nothing, he must get there. If you could only find me some sort of eraser that would obliterate from this page the exact things that ought to be obliterated: that invention would be even more useful than the best pencil bearing the mark of Thoreau and Son. In everyday life with your neighbours garrulity is irritating enough; in art it is intolerable. The work that comes from Henry's hands is to the point. You can take it and see how firm the texture is. The man who made it wears corduroy clothes because they are durable and take on an exquisite tone with time. Very well. But let me repeat that with these principles you will never be anybody in the literary world. There copy is knitted by the yard for firms that do a thriving trade.

And isn't it just as odd to have such a passionate love for plants, animals, minerals, to study with such fervour all these physical phenomena, and yet to have so little in common with the scientists? Science consists of shells, stuffed animals, glass phials, long names, dissertations in musty books, and what interests Henry is the living animal in all its wildness and freedom, the plant with its sap, the phenomenon seized alive in its natural setting. In spite of his tastes and his gift for exact observation, the poet and the lover in him are too exigent to yield precedence to the naturalist. And besides, there is a strange animal that interests him enormously; namely, himself. This is a very poor sort of recommendation among scientists.

On three occasions, however, he sends Concord fish from Walden to Agassiz, who is preparing his great work on the fishes of America. Agassiz is very grateful and promises to pay a visit to his Concord "colleague." The latter has been appointed a corresponding member of the Society of Natural History in Boston; he has just sent it a goshawk, a rare bird. Even in the village, people have fallen into the way of consulting him as an authority on botanical and ornithological matters. This does not prevent him from being very sarcastic whenever the subject of science and scientists comes up. Just speak to him about the specialists who write a big book on turtles—to amuse a man who knows how turtles live! Or about this or that communication to some learned society. . . He says very little about his own zoölogical or botanical observations; he confides them to his Journal alone, for the benefit of those knowing persons who are going to jeer some day at the amateur naturalist and his discoveries. Go ahead and stuff your birds, pedants. Give them your Latin names. See if you can find one that any tree or quadruped pronounces with its branches or its caperings. In this Journal living animals pass, birds call, fishes glide through the water, the loon flings its laughter over the pond, the sap rises in the plants, the trees quiver to the tips of their branches, juicy bay-bushes scent the air: Hebrew for your Latin. These fancies are enough to show that he doesn't belong to the profession. Leave him to his innocent pastimes.

Besides, this "amateur" places too high a value on ignorance to be taken seriously by the academies. This man who reads Latin and French as well as his mother tongue, Greek fluently, German, Italian, Spanish a little, has a thorough knowledge of old English literature and is more interested than a philologist in the development of the life of a word, as a beautiful plant among plants, runs about the country every day like a school-boy throwing to the winds the knowledge learned from books. The consciousness that he knows so little delights him so much that he is willing to make his ignorance the very apex of knowledge. Absurd Henry, to be so infatuated with his not-knowing.

Sometimes, as seldom as possible, he goes to the city, for now and then he wants to consult some book that interests him. It is a sad business, reading in a big library. Fresh books, vibrant, vagabond, libertine books, how in the world can you stay so still among those rows of shrivelled corpses? The friend who comes to see you at intervals pities your distress.

When he has finished his reading, the villager invariably goes off to consume a dish of boiled apple pudding at some cheap eating-house (he distrusts their accursed stews), then crosses the town without stopping till he reaches the end of Long Wharf, where his grandfather had his store. There he looks at the sea, the ships, the piles of merchandise. Save for a glance at the market on his way, this is all he sees of Boston. The stir of the metropolis means nothing to him whatever; the fronts of the substantial houses and the faces of men seem to shut him out. Everything here, to the very stones, reeks of respectability. The windows full of idlers and the brawling vulgarity of the streets make him ill. The city is a pickpocket who wants to filch from you the most precious possession you have and leave you on the sidewalk dejected and destitute in a vast solitude. This is because you were not born, because you never played as a boy in one of these crowded neighbourhoods, because you grew up on the bank of a river that wanders through the fields, bathing the whole world with its freshness. For others no doubt, among its stones, the city has wondrous gifts; for a boy who is thinking of old Minot's cottage on the hillside it is full of shams and shoddy, and what this boy demands is the real. There is a club in Boston made up of some very sympathetic people who meet on the last Saturday of every month; among them are Emerson, Agassiz and Henry James. But although Henry has been invited he never goes there. Quick, take the train and put twenty miles between yourself and this dismal burden of stone house-fronts. Quick, get back to Concord where the village is merely a shabby excrescence amid the verdure. At Concord there are no steamers, no Long Wharves, no crowds in the streets, no immigrants, no big, bustling shops, no special editions; and you feel as if you were at the heart of the world. In Boston there are no humming and singing telegraph-poles where you can listen to the news from afar. Call it parochialism, if you like, but parish towers answer one another. Concordance is no empty word.

At Concord you have a chance to remain simple. Suppose you were to become a great writer or a fashionable lecturer or a light of science and lose the simplicity of heart that alone permits you to have access to the unknown riches that surround you. That would be a fine advancement! There you would be with the esteem of everybody, with your glory or your hard cash, wondering how in the world you could get rid of all these substantial advantages and recover your boyish ingenuousness, and the keen, inquisitive nose, the gift of marvelling at the commonest object that have always so astonished the good William. You would have taken a false step indeed. You would have been transformed into one of those men who are too sober-minded, too dignified or too intelligent to stop and pick a tempting huckleberry beside their path. Your eyes would be dead to the miracle of every day. You would no longer want to be a sailor and skirt the bays and promontories of "some fair wild island in the ocean," suggested by an oak-leaf. You would lose your elasticity. You would become old before your time, old, respectable and unhappy. You might even pose as a little saint and cease to feel yourself a man complete with his virtues and his vices, no better at bottom than the neighbour he scoffs at and lectures. You would be a success, and you would have lost everything, while at Concord one never becomes a success.

There may have been a moment when Henry wondered if the art of writing could not support the writer; but this moment had passed. He understood the trade and the taste of its customers only too well. Precarious as his other resources might be, they were better than that. As a small boy, running barefoot in the fields and up to all sorts of mischief, and later as an ingenious older boy, he had learned how to dig, plane, paint houses, plant, survey. And now Henry continues to work by the day, as occasion offers. A precious thing, manual labour. It stops babbling tongues and toughens a frail body. It gives a tone to what you write afterwards. Your qualities as a workingman reappear when you come to weigh and balance words. When you have finished a fence of pickets and lattice at $1.50 for every five yards, or built a woodshed by contract for six dollars, it is very pleasant to receive the money; but that is not everything. You must also reckon the pleasure you have had. And add to this the profit you have received in indirect ways, such as the quality of the page on which you relate the impressions of the day. Henry does surveying, and he also helps his father in the workshop. When he is not engaged elsewhere, he gives him his mornings. The family industry is being transformed. The Thoreau pencils are selling fairly well, and a new market has opened for the famous plumbago powder—the secret. It happens to fit exactly the needs of a new invention—electrotyping—and the people give them ten dollars a pound for it. Even though they can sell only a few hundred pounds of it a year, this is not a bad stroke of business for the little family. The pencils have become only a side-issue; they work for the big industry. But Henry makes a trip to New York to dispose of a lot he has made, for he has a large debt to pay.

The poorer you are in Concord, the better you know your true wealth. It is all very clever to create happiness with a thousand costly accessories, but to create happiness out of nothing, to be happiness yourself, is much more interesting, and happiness of this kind has quite a different quality. To have been born poor is a privilege too. In the most authentic great man, no matter how magnificent and complete he is in appearance, never to have worn rags or gone without a meal, never to have been able to toss his dignified respectability to the winds, never to have known what hardship means is a lacuna that can never be filled up. Think of that poor, great Goethe, too well brought up, as he said, to have had any intercourse in his childhood with the boys in the streets. . . . Whatever you may say, the boy who has never set his bare, smarting feet on the hard ground has missed one of the best of gifts. He has not been judged worthy of experiencing the real savour of this world. Henry has no inclination to make a profession of his poverty, to set himself up in the square for the admiration of connoisseurs. He saves it for himself because it keeps him warm, as a sheepskin coat warms a driver in winter. It has a taste that he likes and it helps him to keep up his good spirits. It lives with him like a comrade in the attic he has arranged for himself in the new house, the yellow one, where his parents have been living on Main Street since August, 1850. He is very much at home there and William lives across the way. At the foot of his garden the boat is moored.

There in his den Henry lives like a king among the spoils of his expeditions, his collections of birds' eggs, mosses, plants, arrow-heads, his bedside books, his manuscripts—and always a store of nuts to take the place of pipe and bottle. There he sleeps and works and talks with his comrade, enjoying the tawny shade of the latter's eyes and blessing the fate that has provided for him so generously. Recently his classmates have asked him for an account of himself for the record they are preparing of the class of 1837 at Harvard. Henry's reply is as follows:

Am not married. I don't know whether mine is a profession, or a trade, or what not. It is not yet learned, and in every instance has been practised long before being studied. The mercantile part of it was begun by myself alone. It is not one but legion. I will give you some of the monster's heads. I am a Schoolmaster, a private Tutor, a Surveyor, a Gardener, a Farmer, a Painter (I mean a House Painter), a Carpenter, a Mason, a Day-labourer, a Pencil-maker, a Glass-paper-maker, a Writer, and sometimes a Poetaster. If you will act the part of Iolas, and apply a hot iron to any of these heads, I shall be greatly obliged to you. My present employment is to answer such orders as may be expected from so general an advertisement as the above. That is, if I see fit, which is not always the case, for I have found out a way to live without what is commonly called employment or industry, attractive or otherwise. Indeed, my steadiest employment, if such it can be called, is to keep myself at the top of my condition, and ready for whatever may turn up in heaven or on earth. The last two or three years I lived in Concord woods, alone, something more than a mile from any neighbour, in a house built entirely by myself.

P. S. I beg that the class will not consider me an object of charity, and if any of them are in want of any pecuniary assistance and will make known their case to me, I will engage to give them some advice of more worth than money.

As he sends off this description and thinks of his fellows at college, he sees this poor devil, at the head of a factory, condemned to sweat money out of his machines and his workmen . . . this poor devil, launched in politics or absorbed in business, deep in the auriferous mire . . . this poor devil reduced to working as some high office-holder . . . this poor devil, consenting to spend his life manufacturing counterfeit money stamped with the effigy of Jesus, the enemy of all money . . . a whole list of poor devils, with round shoulders or an air of satisfaction, who have not wasted the money their fathers sacrificed to send them to college. He sees them with their positions, their prestige, their prosperous households, their wives, their children, their mothers-in-law and heaven knows what, and himself beside them, the failure, without position, bank-account or influence, with his workman's clothes, earning a meagre living by the labour of his hands, hands which, like theirs, have thumbed so many books. And how glad and privileged he feels in his attic with his tawny-eyed companion! He would be only too happy to work in their gardens or split the wood for their stoves, offering them his pity in exchange for their dollars. If he met the most fortunate of them all, he would feel like hanging a placard round his neck: "Have pity on a poor rich man"—for some passer-by with a generous heart to slip into his hand a pennyworth of compassion. And if no charitable passer-by appeared, he would gladly give

the poor fellow his own mite. You are magnanimous
when you are a success.

Is it not from the worst that we often get the very
best? Then why not meet ill fortune with a high heart
and refuse, on the dullest day, not to be happy over a
mere nothing, a trembling leaf, a swaying twig, or the
smile of old Minot's house on the hillside—happy, you
don't know why, because you are happy, happy as a
child who plays with his poverty as a comrade, finding
in its eyes the colour of your own real wealth?

When you are a rich man like Henry you want to treat
yourself, now and then, to some little trip. For one
who disposes of his time as he pleases, this is merely a
matter of gathering together a few odds and ends. A
week or so of surveying, a windfall in the shape of a
lecture or a cheque for an article provides you with the
means of surveying good fortune for many hours, a
week, two weeks, not to mention a store of memories.
This is one of the satisfactions of the lot of a man who is
free, as all men ought to be free. It is good to work on
your manuscripts. But you never write a story to be
compared with those that are traced by your feet as you
welcome the surprises of the road.

There are always more surprises in Concord than
anywhere else; but the world is wide and you want to
see how the sun shines in other places. And besides,
you want to give your old notions an airing; no matter
how wide open you keep your window, they are always
in danger of getting a little musty. . . There are those
hills on the horizon towards the West behind which,
at nightfall, from the top of the Cliffs, you see that
blazing reflection. The land of the sunset is a powerful
magnet.

What if you were to explore one of those hills that
rise up, like a challenge and a promise, beyond that

stretch of country over there—climb it, brush your boots on its brow, watch the sun rise from up there and see if you can discover the faraway spot in the valley from which you set out? That ought to do your soul good and expand your lungs. There is that solitary Wachusett, for example, forever crouching there in the distance, as if it were watching over some treasure; you would like to go and ask that brother if he finds his solitude bitter or friendly. His younger brother from Concord is coming to make him a visit. That blue wall is not a fabulous vision; it is a solid reality, in harmony with the woods, the fields, the river. It belongs to the family too. Another time the thirty-seven hundred feet of Monadnoc draw him up. He has to prolong his visit, live with the mountain a while, become familiar with the dawn and the sunset on those heights. The visitor camps for one night, two nights, in the open, on the summit of the vision that holds him aloft with all its mass till a small man, on this pedestal, has the illusion of being a somebody.

On the day before, in the morning, well before dawn, he had set out on foot with a companion. They passed through villages and woods, with staves in their hands like pilgrims. The fields were full of fragrance for the early risers, the farms still asleep in the twilight of dawn; save for one reaper already sharpening his scythe, they were the first that morning to tread the July countryside; they passed through the hop-fields, rested on the fence-rails of a farm from which the sound of music reached them; and in the afternoon in the valley they sought shelter from the broiling heat and bathed their feet in the streams they found there. And at last they arrived together on a grassy plateau, strewn with clumps of huckleberry and raspberry bushes, in time to see the moon rising in this tremendous silence—two little souls,

serious, lost in wonder, half frightened at finding themselves so high above the rest of their fellow-townsmen.
And the dawn, the notes of the birds before the dawn
on these heights, the great waves of the slopes below
rise out of the shadows as if they were at sea—on what
a ship!—as the camp-fire pales and the day breaks and
the landscape unrolls in all its unreality: old Massachusetts, the whole of it, bathed in the sunrise, at their
feet, spreading its panorama before them in the summer
morning! The air of the heights intoxicates them; it
has a quality that is unknown to dwellers on the plain.
It is not so much that it acts upon your lungs: its rarity
has a strange power of exalting the spirit. Henry revels
in it and feels at home on the shoulder of the mountain.
If he did not live in Concord he would be a mountaineer.

And the charm of the mountains persists. Sometimes
he goes still further west, as far as Greylock or Saddle-back
Mountain, to pay a visit to Their Majesties. And then—
wonder of wonders—the mountains he has always seen
towards the sunset rise, in a spirit of contradiction, to
the east! Is he a new man who, without realizing it,
has taken a trip round the world? . . . Before beginning
his climb he stops in this mountain valley at the next
to the last house. It would be fun to spend a week in
that house if they would take him in. The mistress is a
young woman who continues to arrange her hair while
she talks to him in the friendliest way, without any fuss,
thank heaven; she is dark and her eyes are full of fire and
she questions him with as much familiarity as if they had
been children together. She makes him think of his
cousin in Bangor. And they really are cousins in a way.
She has taken him for one of those daredevil students
who often come on trips to the mountain. On the top
he finds bits of newspapers they have left about; it is
strange to read a stray sheet of some old paper alone on

the summit of a mountain by the light of a camp-fire. What wears the best at this altitude is the advertisements and the market prices, for there is a bit of real poetry mixed with them, though the advertisers are quite unaware of it (fortunately); as for the rest, editorials, news, jokes, reviews, heaven save us! And then, after a cold night that he has passed without a blanket, the day dawns over an ocean of fog that covers the three adjoining States as if it were a dream-country rolling off into infinity. . . It is the earth that has become unreal, and you are planted there as if you were the centre of this tremendous glory that rises with the sun. . . And you descend Tabor again, a little drunk with this vision and no longer in the least cold in spite of the night passed without a blanket.

In the other direction from the land of the sunset lies the sea, quite close—another magnet. The peaks are silent and contemplative, but the sea stirs and rustles like a forest of gigantic pines, lulling its old anguish. On an island in the middle of the ocean you might contrive to have a rich existence if you could ever forget Concord. Or in one of those villages about Cape Ann. The whole Atlantic coast and all the width of the continent lie at the ends of the roads that set out from the village square.

Yes, to go off for two, three, four days, according to the occasion and the plumpness of your purse, to leave Main Street and the church-tower and the sidewalks of the grey little town behind you and attempt an unex-plored world . . . that's the thing, Henry . . . the real holidays of life. You must have them complete. The first thought of most poor souls on such occasions is to take the train or the stage. They are poor souls indeed. When you are rich you have the means to travel on foot. Henry has no intention of surrendering to a machine or

animal the pleasure of treading the road and devouring
it for him; this traveller likes the taste of it far too much
to leave it to a mere auxiliary. It is a part of the adventure. When a vagabond journeys on foot, the earth
invites him to her table and lets him roam all over her
domain; those other people are mere stupid tourists who
follow where their baggage leads them. Before they
set out, the latter are sure to worry about where they
will find a lodging; why do they leave home if they begin
a journey with the thought of lodgings?

Henry starts off with a pack on his back. It's a marvel, this knapsack. See if you can find one like it in the
shops! The traveller has manufactured it to suit himself.
It is waterproof and has compartments; a notebook, the
map of the country, his old music-book for pressing
flowers, his change of linen are in no danger of being
injured. If he is going some distance he carries a little
bundle in his hand. It is a package tied up in a handkerchief or a piece of brown paper. He recommends this
to you as preferable to any sort of handbag, first because
it is lighter and swings more merrily in your fist, and
secondly because it causes less trouble. Don't forget
the inevitable accessory of any expedition, a good stout
umbrella. A raincoat or an oilskin might be more
becoming, but they keep you too warm and they are
unwholesome, while under an umbrella you are always
exposed to the air and you have only to shut it up when
the shower is over. And then you have the rare pleasure
of hearing the rain patter on your roof, while you are
perfectly sheltered yourself; you are a householder on
your own threshold, and you take it easy listening to the
rain dripping from the eaves. When you are tired of
carrying the umbrella in your hand, you can carry it on
your shoulder and even hang your bundle on it, or any
other prize you pick up—a bird or a bit of sea-weed.

People may laugh at you. Let them. They will never have so much fun in all their lives.

The clever fellow has thought of everything, down to the sewing-case for mending rips and fastening on buttons that fall off. These accursed leather shoe-strings are always undone and cause endless bother in walking; they really abuse their right to relaxation. Henry and William have often exchanged their views on this grave subject, a theme worthy of philosophers at least who despise the fiddle-faddle of learning. One day Henry finds the knot-that-will-not-come-undone and triumphs. If everyone applied himself to solving such problems, the world would soon stand on a different basis. But above all, do not forget to take along some old newspapers. You will find them providential. If you don't already know to how many uses old news-papers can be put, on a journey or at home, try some experiments. You are leaving your shanty for a week or two or for six months and you are afraid that during this time your kettle will rust. Wrap it up in a news-paper and go your way in peace. Or you want to give your copper basin a good scouring; take a wad of news-paper and polish it up as it should be. Your face will smile at you in the mirror you have brightened so easily. And what a comfort a few old newspapers are on your trip, if you have taken them along: they serve as wrap-pers, as a tablecloth, as a plate, as a means of starting the fire, or as a light, warm chest-protector if it turns cold. And there are still so many fools in the world who believe that newspapers are made to be read, to inform you about accidents and politics. Among the humble truths that might shed a little light on their existence, this is not the least important: in spending your two cents you are making a golden investment if, instead of unfolding the sheet, you place it carefully on a pile of old papers for the approaching day when it will reveal its true use.

The question of provisions also demands a good bit of attention and experience. Henry has weighed this for a long time. He has been armed with certitudes ever since he first took the road. For drinking on a journey nothing equals good strong tea. Because you have seen so many old souls busy over teapots, brewing and stewing, don't imagine that tea is an old woman's beverage. A grave mistake. Winter or summer, it is a powerful and subtle tonic. For solid food, carry with you a good loaf of heavy cake. If it is made by your mother it will be A-number-I. You will thank me for this advice. Add a little cornmeal, enough to make some gruel, a small bag of rice, some salt. With a spoon, a tin quart-measure, and, if you like, a saucepan—not to mention the matches and the knife that a walker must always have— you are the master of circumstance. No longer any need to knock at a door, when the fresh air of the road has given you an appetite, except for the pleasure of a chat or to add a glass of milk to your usual fare if you want to bring back your childhood. You are both the inn and the traveller.

These arrangements are very important for the success of the trip. As for your clothes, they should be durable and old, preferably brown or tan—the colour of the earth. They will show the dust and the mud less, and you will not offend the landscape as the figure of a townsman in the country does with his funereal black. In heaven's name, avoid the "tourist's" get-up. You must slip through the countryside like an old family friend, not like an intruder. One more recommendation. A straw hat is one of those creations in which the inventive genius of man triumphs. Light and as solid as flexible armour, it places between the burning sun and your poor skull just the right amount of space for you to be able to speak of the *good* sun. . . Suppose a shower, a downpour, surprises you on a day when you have left your umbrella behind. If it does not last too long the wide rim of your head-covering will shelter you. If the straw is a little warped after this bath, well, it has seen plenty of others. It will soon get back its proper shape; your oval, square or pointed skull takes care of that gratis. And this invention, you know, costs only a few cents. If some accident befalls it, if it has not been fastened firmly with your handkerchief knotted under your chin, and a gust of wind blows it into the water or some ditch, well, good-bye, old friend. . . I shall regret you because my head breathed its warmest thoughts through you, but I shall find another like you for a mere song at the first shop I reach.

If you travel with this modest outfit, you must not expect to be treated as a rich gentleman travelling for his pleasure. That humiliation will certainly be spared you. Nor must you be too surprised if, along the road, you are taken for a pedlar by the women on the door-steps or the labourers in the fields. That's natural enough, and it will even please you, for nothing could be more creditable. They may ask you if you are able to mend an umbrella (why an umbrella in your hand in this radiant sunlight?) or if you are not a tinker. Or a clock-setter. Or one of those casual labourers who work by the day in the hay-making season. You will certainly not be offended by anything of this kind; indeed you will be flattered, for it will show you that they don't take you for a fool. This is a compliment you don't often receive from your own fellow-townsmen. At home they are not particularly struck by your ability, but out in the world your ten fingers are in constant request. Even if some theft has been committed in the neighbourhood as you are passing through with a friend and they look at you suspiciously and the constable discreetly walks along with you, you are not indignant at the inquisition. How could the police, with their infallible noses, fail to suspect two mischievous-looking young fellows, roaming about the roads without any apparent purpose, instead of the traveller who puts up at the best hotel and orders his dinner in a lofty voice? You and your companion must be the criminals, or good-bye to the constable and the constable's nose.

In case you don't care to sleep out under the stars, ask for a bed in some house along the way. It is so much cosier. You will make the acquaintance of some very good souls. Under their roof, as your wet boots are drying before the fire, you will feel that you are in the very heart of the country. And you will not have to refuse the hotel boy the tip he has failed to deserve, the wretch, because he has polished your famous boots instead of greasing them with a rind of pork.

So, no matter where you go, the world responds to your expectations. It likes to be approached on its own level, and it is for you, the man with the knapsack, that it keeps its finest stories. Finally, you will spend less money than if you stayed at home.

Henry finds the highway tedious, for it is the road of trade and traffic. He has not buckled on his haversack to perform a military march. On the highway the gravel crunches under your feet, the dust gets between your teeth. If his itinerary obliges him to take the road, he at least walks on the bank, stopping from time to time to listen to what the wind has to say on the wires. What's the latest news? As a rule he follows the paths, taking short-cuts across fields, jumping over hedges, clambering up the little hills without slackening his pace. He has a good wind. Once he has made up his mind to reach a point he has marked on his map, all the obstacles in the world, natural and artificial, can get in his way: he makes straight for his object, scaling every one. Obstacles are made to be leapt over—a much quicker way than going round them. He never loses his sense of direction in the woods. He is a walker who can count more years of experience than Christianity can count centuries. A pagan of a walker.

This time the man with the old umbrella is going off alone. To set out in company would certainly be to multiply by two or three the pleasure of the adventure. But where can he find them, the rare birds that share his tastes? He knows one or two perhaps, scarcely three. Most of his friends are simply not to be thought of as travelling companions. People who wear black clothes and are impeccably correct to the very soles of their feet, people who are charming in their own houses but whom you can't imagine eating a bowl of gruel before a camp-fire. They would make you conspicuous on the road. You can't go and ask them to travel like a common tramp, with an old umbrella and a bundle. And besides, you who are an indefatigable walker and as abstemious as a camel would soon leave your companion behind. Half-way along the road you would hear him complaining back there that his boot hurt him or that he was melting with perspiration. He would have to belong to a special type, a Henry number 2 or a brother John. . . Or a William. But William does not dare to start out this time; he is afraid of what might befall him with such an intrepid companion when it is no longer a question of a mere afternoon's ramble to Nine Acre Corner.

Some friends have sent Henry an invitation to lecture over yonder; it is a chance for a little trip. If he sometimes has to be urged a bit, it is only for the stupidest

of reasons. When he goes to see some of his friends or
appears in public, he has to dress up more or less (a
remnant of respect for the conventions, you know). . . .
His old togs, frayed by all the thickets of the wilderness,
have such a beautiful patina and they are so well moulded
to all his movements and so easy at the arm-holes that
it is heart-breaking to be obliged to give them up and
harness himself in a frock-coat in which he feels as
cramped as a best man dressing up for his cousin's
wedding. The mere thought of it almost spoils his
pleasure in advance. He would like to be his everyday
self, not this promenader in his Sunday best.

But Henry is ready for any sacrifice. He is going to
take the train for Worcester and pay his friend Harrison
Blake a visit. The latter is an old Harvard man like
himself whom he met through Emerson when he was
living at Walden. A little too full of starch, this good
man—Henry would like to pinch him now and then to
see if he has blood in his veins—but a firm and faithful
friend. They write to each other regularly. Henry
is a little bored by the correspondence, and he would
be very happy if he could make this excellent Blake,
who absolutely insists upon regarding him as a sage and
a great philosopher, understand how seriously mistaken
he is. No, my friend, you are quite wrong; I am a very
ordinary soul and very much at a loss how to reply to
you, for to me two words exchanged with a carter mean
more than all the moral counsels in the world. You
insist on asking me for all sorts of spiritual directions,
and I am as threadbare in philosophical matters as I
am in the matter of clothes. You are throwing your
respect away, dear fellow. It is very hard for a pagan,
an artist and a savage to make himself intelligible to a
churchman, for he is a churchman, this good, faithful
Blake. It is a safe bet that in fifty years he would never

understand. To appease this keen spiritual hunger, the great "philosopher," in his letters—after ten years of correspondence they are invariably addressed to "Mr. Blake"—copies out for him whole pages from his Journal, carefully selected from those that are the most "moral." Their correspondence and their relations always keep this grave tone. Henry feels the frock-coat that cramps him at the arm-holes. But Mr. Blake is certainly the most loyal of friends.

Henry feels more at home with Daniel Ricketson, who invites him to his house at New Bedford, the whaling port. On the first occasion it is mid-winter, and Ricketson, who is a Quaker, is clearing the snow off his front steps and thinking of his visitor who is very late in arriving. Up the carriage road comes someone who looks like a pedlar, in a long overcoat, carrying a little bag and a big umbrella. But it is the expected personage, and he strolls up imperturbably through the friendly snow; he has had no thought of preparing a sensational appearance; they will receive him cheerfully in this disguise as Santa Claus, for it is Christmas Day. The following year Daniel returns the visit. He is a new friend. There are good years for friendship as there are for trees. It even comes to Henry from across the sea in the person of that tall, fair-haired, distinguished-look-ing young man, the descendant of Anglican bishops, who, on his trip through America, comes to see Emerson who sends him to the Thoreaus' house, where there is always room for a boarder. Rather an odd fish, this Thomas "Cholmley," and a little hard to swallow just at first, but charming at bottom under his English patrician's uniform, fresh from Oriel College. He is just back from New Zealand, where he has had a taste of cattle-raising. They go off on several rambles to-gether about Concord; with William to make up a trio,

they set out for the conquest of that old solitary Wachusett. Henry has very little use for these over-civilized
young blades who respectfully ask him to take them
along on his walks; but he has made an exception of
this tall, fair-haired fellow who has been to New Zealand. Some day he must take him to New Bedford.

There, at least, there is no constraint. On the very
threshold he shakes off his gloom, the melancholy of the
northern pine; he is himself, he is a child. In this congenial atmosphere he is ready for any joke, and he
laughs and sings. He doesn't quite catch the tune, but
who cares?—it sounds just as well. The bathing is
excellent and they get up a boating-party. One afternoon—is it the venerable Alcott's presence that excites
him?—when Mrs. Ricketson is at the piano, the northern pine, seized with a mad gaiety, actually begins to
execute a Zulu dance around the room, taking pains to
tread on the toes of Alcott who smilingly watches his
good colleague's extravagant behaviour. If that blessed
Blake were only in a corner of the parlour too, on this
occasion, ready for a little nip from the dancer's boots!
It would enlighten him better than the longest letter on
the nature of Henry's philosophy. Henry's face is as
long as a night-cap when he is with ceremonious people
who bore him. He writes deep, serious things because
he is not interested solely in trifles. And there he is,
forever pigeon-holed as the most dismal of souls. They
haven't seen him, brimming over with nonsense, acting
a pantomime with his own intimate friends; they have
never heard him singing at the top of his lungs alone in
the woods or surprised him with the children doing some
marvellous trick. No, he is and he will remain the
morose ascetic who went off into the woods one day,
full of hatred for humanity, and pounded out his black
thoughts in a rough-hewn mortar. Rubbish! . . . Let

them talk, Henry, while you go on dancing about the room. And look out for your toes, Alcott!

One day, towards the end of July, 1850, Henry sets out hurriedly on a strange journey. He is not going to spend Sunday this time with a friend who is waiting for him; he has to find the body of a friend who has died. Poor Margaret Fuller, whom he had never known well but who recalled to him the days of the *Dial*, was returning from Italy, married now and a mother, on a ship that had gone ashore in a storm on Fire Island. She was one of the victims, after having watched death approaching for twelve hours till a mightier wave delivered her with her child and her husband. Henry has been commissioned by all the Concord friends—Margaret was William's sister-in-law—to search the scene of the shipwreck and try to recover her pitiful remains and her belongings. He scours the beach, questions everybody, pursues his inquiries. Plunderers of the wreck have been there before him. At first nothing is found but a few papers, some love-letters and the little body of Nino. . . Then, eight days after the shipwreck, Henry, who has got his direction from a lighthouse-keeper, finds on a lonely beach the shapeless remains of a body, ravaged by the rough jaws of the sea—a few bones with a little flesh still adhering to them. . .

Concord enfolds a man very tenderly in the arms of its river and woods when he comes back with roughened skin from such trips as these. But when you are at once a stay-at-home and a nomad, there are few holidays to be compared to a long expedition when your confounded circumstances permit you to think of such a thing. And nothing could be happier than the happiness of the preliminaries when you are making your plans and studying your itinerary, inspecting your knapsack and your boots, and reading the books about the country you are going to explore. Don't talk about recreation or satisfying some asinine taste for the picturesque by following the footsteps of other travellers. Henry sets out from his village to reconnoitre, to get light on some very important matters and bring back something to fill up his chests there in the garret. These are his campaigns.

There is that crooked beak, shaped like a fishhook, which Massachusetts thrusts out into the sea—perhaps in an attempt to catch that big greedy fish Long Island, if the latter, tired of sniffing the unprofitable metropolis, should decide some day to turn to the North for its food. Wouldn't it be a good idea to go and see how the wind blows there and have a look at the old sea-dogs that incrust it like shell-fish? Cape Cod. A long tongue of land curving out like a breakwater into the open Atlantic—an immense organ from which the ocean draws its grandest tones.

This year, with his book out at last, Henry can give himself a little extra treat. William has decided to come too. They set out together at the beginning of October (they are obliged to take the train so as not to spend an eternity on the way) and stumble straight into a shipwreck at Cohasset. The train is crowded with Irishmen who are on their way to identify the bodies—from the beach to the church the farm-wagons come and go, some of them carrying the corpses, others the sea-weed thrown up by the storm. Immigrants from Galway in Ireland, and here they are, livid under their white sheets, arriving, feet first, in the land of their hopes. The flag of the shipwrecked vessel is drying there on the rocks with pebbles on its four corners, still keeping its colours—not dead like the Irish lads. The captain and the other survivors will lead the funeral procession. . . At the base of the fishhook they leave the train and take the stage as far as Orleans, where the tongue of land grows so thin: it is nothing but a sandbar sixty-five miles long by a few miles in width. How good-natured the people in the stage are! Simple and natural as if—O joy!—no blessed social categories existed in their astonishing country and they were all old acquaintances. Does the nearness of the ocean teach people the art of living?

It rains and blows the next day, when they start out on foot. Never mind, they are not going to wait for it to clear. They walk along the shore; the umbrella shields them and the wind drives them on. They are not loaded down like those two little Italians who are walking towards Provincetown with their organs on their backs. It is an entirely new landscape for the lads from Concord. No trees. Here and there a cottage with a red roof. Octagonal windmills, such as they have never seen except in pictures. In the fields heaps of clam-shells; the pigs, they say, are fattened on the clams, those marine acorns. And see there, those stunted apple-trees sheltered in a hollow, those little old toy-like trees from which a child could pick the apples by hand. It would be difficult to creep your way under them, the branches are so low and shrubby. The little Cape Cod horses are as amusing as goats. You great Concord farmers, if you could measure the scantness of the land the people cultivate here—about as much as a miser could hold in his palm! But it yields a little rather meagre corn and the vegetables in the tiny gardens actually seem to be thriving. This is the country of the sea.

The best thing is to leave the road and march along to this roar that you hear uninterruptedly on the right. The companions have come here not to follow a road but to enjoy the ocean. They cut across the fields in the direction of the three Nauset Lights. Then, in the wind and rain, they are lost in an absolutely bare plain, shut in by fog. The smallest object appears immense in this desert and as if suspended between sky and sand. It is just the way one should see this interminable plain. Henry feels so happy that he could sing. He is going to try to keep clear of the villages up to the very end of the Cape so as not to break the powerful charm. At the end of this vast plain, and after crossing a stretch of upland covered with shrub-oak and beech-grass and a strip of bare sand, they suddenly find themselves at the top of a Bluff: at their feet lies everything they have come to seek—the beach and the Atlantic. The ocean is dark under a stormy sky—as Atlantic as possible. Those white lines of foam, some distance out, reveal the sandbars. And beyond that nothing . . . nothing but Europe, and faraway Jersey . . . so people say. It is too beautiful here for you to have any desire to go over and see it. From this point on the two umbrellas set out to skirt the shore, as close to the water as possible where the sand is hardest.

Twenty-five good miles lie before them to the tip. As they sail along under the umbrellas that shelter and aid them, with the wind at their backs, the walk side by side becomes glorious. Two happy souls under their whalebone turtle-shells travel along so close to the water's edge that every now and then they have to leap quickly aside to escape a great wave that has watched them from afar and flung itself upon them: perhaps it is the umbrellas that have provoked it into lashing them with its kelp-weed tails. And when you have played with the waves it is a delight to scramble up the sand-bank that forms the back-bone of the Cape, so as to have a wider view of the ocean and look off into the distance and over to the left, to the desert of sand. The rolling country yonder, covered with autumn-tinted shrubbery, permits them at intervals a glimpse of the bay. Walking now on the ridge, straddling the Cape, now on the fine sand—there are no rocks to break the wonderful monotony of this shore—the wayfarers take their time, resting now and then; for the sand, soft as it is to their feet, makes walking difficult after a while. Not a sail in sight, for the sea is too heavy; not a soul on the beach. It is as if the ocean preferred to see no one about him when he is roused. Days might pass without your encountering two natives of the country, those plunderers of wrecks with faces hard as a stone, a stone that the sea has rolled from the beginning of time and is ready to go on rolling for as many ages as it chooses.

But they do not ask for any distraction. The enormous spectacle fills the scene. It is better even not to talk amid this continual roar that obliges them to shout; and if they do it is only to thunder some Homeric lines to put themselves in tune with this bass voice. Surprises strew their path, marvellous plants, dragged up from the sunken palaces of the sea, all of which they would like to carry away if they could only keep them alive in their flexibility and their lustre. Henry chews a tip of one of them. The beautiful sea-medusas that strew the beach in their tattered finery are as if struck with consternation not to be swinging any longer, delicate and transparent, in the hollow of the waves: dispossessed princesses whose hearts shrivel on this alien strand. In spite of the noise of the sea they hear the piping of a plover. Suppose they have a little lunch? It is noon, time to settle themselves in a hollow of the bank and eat something, as two good boys should who have gone a long way since breakfast in the inn at Orleans and are famished by the salt air. Some dry sticks, a fire, a superb clam cooked over the sand as the principal dish; the meat is a bit rubbery, but with a cracker and sprinkled with the cries of the sea-gulls it is quite edible and even savoury. And look there, the weather is clearing. . . .

By evening the pilgrims have reached Wellfleet. They must think of shelter for the night. In that little house over there, with the gable pierced with those small irregular windows, there will surely be a corner for two fellows who are not hard to please. No one at home. How about the other? An old woman who has had her eye on these two suspicious-looking individuals fastens her fence-gate, then resolutely goes back into the house. Hm. . . We'll see. Knock, knock. An old man opens the door and asks them with a distrustful air where they have come from and what they want. They explain. Of course we might be almanac-vendors, but no, my friend, we're not. We're from the famous Concord where the great battle took place at the time of the Revolution. The old man is eighty-eight, so he was fourteen when that historic event occurred. These pedlars who are not pedlars are too much for him. Well, walk in, since you've come from the country of the Revolution. The old woman relieves the strangers of their bundles and their hats, while the grandfather grumbles: "I am all broken down this year. I am under petticoat government here."

The hospitable family is composed of a daughter who looks as old as her mother, and a brutish-looking, heavy-jawed son who goes out abruptly at the sight of these strangers; there is also a boy of ten. "These women," the old man says to Henry, "are both of them poor good-for-nothing critturs. This one is my wife. I married her sixty-five years ago. She is eighty-four years old, and as deaf as an adder, and the other is not much better." The good soul is an old oysterman who, since sailing the seas in his young days, has had much intercourse with oysters and the Bible. He likes to gossip and they converse in a friendly way about oysters, surveying and apple-raising. The half-witted son returns and begins to mutter, without lifting his head: "Damn book-pedlars—all the time talking about books. Better do something. Damn 'em. I'll shoot 'em". . . . Whereupon, the old man, assuming an air of authority as if he were used to it, says: "John, go sit down, mind your business. Precious little you'll do—your bark is worse than your bite." But the sullen imbecile persists in muttering, goes and sits down at the table, eats up everything that is on it and reaches out for the apples which his mother is paring for her guests' meal. She draws them away and sends him about his business. There are many of these imbeciles in the villages of Massachusetts.

But it is a pleasure to listen to the old oysterman who relates his recollections in a language as salty as the water that you swallow with an oyster. He well remembers seeing Washington, a man with such a fine bearing! And to show how well the great general sat his horse the old fellow strikes an attitude, straightens his shoulders and bows ceremoniously to right and left, sweeping the absent three-cornered hat with a wide gesture. It is just as you see him in the school-books, but in what picture will the general ever have such a grand air as he has in this little house on Cape Cod, evoked by the mimicry of an old oysterman? After this they all go to bed. The boy, who is in the chimney-corner, takes off his shoes and stockings, and as he has a sore leg they rub it with salve before he goes upstairs. The imbecile takes off his old shoes and follows. Then the old man, removing his shoes in turn, without ceasing to discourse on the miseries of the world, exhibits with pride a pair of calves as plump as a baby's.

William and Henry retire to their room. Someone behind them draws the bolt and fastens them in. You can't be too careful. After all, you never know with these clever people who are up to all sorts of tricks. . . (Ah, good people, how right you were to distrust two strangers who had dropped from the clouds. Two days later the Provincetown Bank was robbed and the police were looking for two men who must have done the job. Good heavens, to think you might have had those two scoundrels under your roof. . . Nothing more prophetic than the instinct of an imbecile who wants to execute them out of hand. Put this in your pipe and smoke it, you sham pedlars, even if you are not the thieves. You have been taken for tinkers or almanac-vendors already—it may be pickpockets next. If you had never left your own hole-in-the-ground, how would you have ever known that you had in you the makings of all these characters?)

The door is unlocked before dawn and Henry runs to the beach to watch the sun come out of the sea. They have breakfast. The old man begins to spin his yarns again, forgetting to eat, and says to his wife, who reminds him of this: "Don't hurry me; I have lived too long to be hurried". . . Meanwhile, the two comrades breakfast a little gingerly, not being sure of the exact spots on the hearth sprinkled by the old man's tobacco-juice while the meal was being prepared there. They pay their score and set out. The weather is marvellously clear this morning, swept clean by the wind that howled in the chimney.

They follow the dunes. The tide is coming in. The vessels are skimming like gulls over the ocean; one, a barque, furls her sails and drops anchor a gunshot from the shore. In this miraculous brightness of the ocean how large and strange objects on the sand appear: at a distance a bit of wreckage looks like a cliff. The most absurd little rocking-horse here would have the size of some monstrous steed. And always, under your feet, those gifts of the sea that would go so well in your collection: a wet pebble, gleaming like a jewel, debris, come heaven knows whence, rolled by the waves heaven knows how long, roughly modelled by the ocean, polished or tarnished, a beautiful crab's shell, a sponge, a five-franc piece, bearing the image of Louis XV the Well-beloved. Henry's eyes, with their Concord habits, even find an arrow-head, placed there in his honour. They must bathe in that little basin formed by a sand-bar, then sit down to dry and watch the coots dancing like corks on the waves or the schools of menhaden, with their back fins projecting two or three inches out of the water. In some patches the sea is as purple as a grape. That sail yonder comes from some port of dreams for which you are homesick even without knowing what it is. It speaks mysteriously to a man, naked in the sun after his bath, who hears the pores of his skin murmuring together how marvellous it is to belong to a body that is freed from its braces and buttons.

It will be best not to stop at Truro but to push on to the Highland Light where they will find comfortable quarters. Indeed the keeper receives them without asking them who they are, receives them, in his simple brick dwelling attached to the white lighthouse, with the generosity of a lonely soul. They climb with him up the winding iron stairway to the lantern when he goes up to light his fifteen oil lamps. (What a job keeping them in order! There are the wicks, the oil that congeals in winter, the reflectors, the windows, and on warm summer nights the moths that glue them-

selves there by the million, dimming the lights—and
yet everything is neat and in apple-pie order in the
lantern.) Think what a fine place it would be for a lad
with studious tastes who was too poor to feed his own
lamp! And what a beautiful inn! There you are, all
night, close to the waves, snug in your bed, a part of the
lighthouse, yourself a light towards which the lookout-
men at sea direct their eyes. Wonderful!

The Cape narrows and is soon nothing but a shrunken
tongue of land along which move two insects in holiday
spirits. They are approaching the point of the hook.
Three or four days along the seashore, tramping in the
October wind, and there is Provincetown at last, a mere
dot. A compactly built little town, a barking cur,
people going about their business—all these things cut a
sorry figure before an ocean that swings from one
continent to another. The two hundred schooners of
the mackerel fleet that lie there in the harbour are like
toys scattered on a green carpet. There is a smell of
drying fish along the plank sidewalks of the little town,
which is engulfed in the fine sand that filters into everything, into your shoes, into the houses. To bid farewell
to the Cape they push on across the deserted region to
the North of the port. The wind from the open sea
stings and caresses them and makes their skin smart.
The whole burden of the Atlantic comes to die at their
feet in the whiteness of the foam and a rumbling as of
the end of the world.

It is Sunday. Some sailors are engaged in painting
their boat at Provincetown when a tithing-man comes
along and tells them they are disturbing the Sabbath.
That's all very well for you, my friend. On Sunday you
lounge about the house after church, smoking your pipe
with your family, looking at the picture-papers or getting
drunk if you like; it's easy for you to observe the Sab-

bath without causing any scandal. But from where I sit, peacefully watching the harbour and the sea, I can hear the shouts of a preacher from the meeting-house over there with its windows wide open to the sunlight. (Wouldn't you think he was a drill-sergeant or a boat-swain giving his commands?) Now, tithing-man, why not tell that fellow to stop making a nuisance of himself? Those sailors are not disturbing a soul as they paint their boat, but that fanatic poisons the beautiful Sunday air for everybody.

Monday, the departure. They set off for home by sea, saluted, as they leave the harbour, by some red-shirted men who, from their boats, watch the little steamer passing: a Newfoundland dog, with his paws on the rail of one of the boats, watches them too, watches as a big sailor's dog knows how to watch. In no time at all the Cape and everything over there behind them is a mere pale beak almost level with the sea, and before they know it they are tying up at Long Wharf between two big boats . . . Boston . . . the train for Concord. Oh, to get to Concord quickly enough to bring home before they are gone that scent of codfish and oysters and that drone of the sea in the shell at your ear. . . .

It is so beautiful, this desolate coast, so powerfully appealing, this Atlantic solitude, that Henry returns alone to the Cape the following summer and twice later, alone or with William. Cape Cod has become the first colonial possession of an affluent lover of the wilds. But the danger of these long expeditions is that one becomes insatiable. A rich man always wants more. Having gone to the extremities of Massachusetts, to the mountains and the sea, he has taken it into his head to press on to the boundary of the United States, and beyond. . .

Henry, you are ready to throw your money out of the window. William has agreed to go up to Canada with you, or is he the tempter who has induced you to go? However that may be, the matter is settled between the two accomplices. They are going to take advantage of a special excursion train. It is very disagreeable to travel under such conditions, packed in with those idiotic tourists, but it enables them to go a long way for very little money, and once they are there they can get rid of the other reduced-price gentry soon enough and set out by themselves on a tour of discovery. They will have a week before them.

They leave Concord in the morning, before eight o'clock, and by six in the evening they are on the shore of Lake Champlain, which crosses the frontier . . . on the map. For it crosses nothing on the landscape. But is there a single one of these fifteen hundred excursionists who, at this solemn moment of passing from one country into another, is not looking for some mountain-chain, some gulf, some gigantic gate—heaven knows what—to show that here one nation begins and another ends? A frontier, and the face of the earth goes straight on as if it knew nothing about its own political geography? But they begin to hear people speaking in a different language (is that the looked-for gulf?), and already they feel far away from home—on the "foreign soil" of the romances.

More than anything else, Montreal is the church of Notre Dame. A deep cave like that in the heart of a city deserves a visit. It is very still there. The church can hold ten thousand worshippers, but at the moment it seems to contain only three women who are praying, and the latter do not even lift their eyes to look at two fellows who are softly making the tour of the nave with their hats in their hands. A troop of natives come in, countrymen on a visit to town whose first thought is to kneel before the high altar, with the rather awkward movements—as Henry thinks—of cattle preparing to lie down. The glitter of the altars, the candles and the images do not impress him, but he is touched by this ingenuous respect. The silence is good in this cavern. There reigns here a little of the mystery of the deep woods; it is open every day to all comers, a retreat to which you can come and meditate, away from the crowds, and really feel at peace with yourself. If you were condemned for your sins to live in a town like this, you would certainly come to Notre Dame, with the same respect as these good women, to pray in your own fashion between services. If it were not for the priests and their mummery, this Catholic religion would not be a bad thing at all. It has such beautiful shrines for meditation. Even the holy water in the basins would not disturb you very much if, in the minds of the faithful, it were sacred like the water of a fountain dedicated to a goddess. This Roman religion merely needs to be brushed up a little by a pagan. Notre Dame is certainly an astonishing cave.

In the streets, priests and Sisters of Charity. These latter must have been weeping all their lives long to have such scalded-looking eyes; they have the faces of people who have been buried and dug up. They all go about with lowered eyeballs, as if they had made up their minds never to smile again. The sight of them insults the daylight. There are also a great many soldiers about, mounting guard or drilling. Henry wonders of what use all these puppets are. They are probably to amuse the citizens, like a Punch and Judy show. And there are market-women in the square with beautiful apples, pears and peaches for sale. (It is the end of September.) Henry buys some, hazarding a few words of the language of the country. These honest fruit-sellers at least are flesh-and-blood women, and their apples are apples and not church ornaments. And the old French names that he reads in the town have as much flavour as the apples, or as the chronicles of the navigators who set sail from Saint-Malo in their immense old tubs and landed at Tadousac, at the confluence of the Saguenay. Henry has read those chronicles, and they enchant him.

The zigzag fissures there in the rock are Quebec and its climbing streets. And the citadel—and the barracks and the barracks. High up there on the ramparts he perceives from afar a terrible warrior with an immense cocked hat; he wonders if it is the god of war stuck up there like a scarecrow, or if that horrifying puppet with its gun is preparing to destroy the world. These soldiers are the ornament of Quebec; they are set about everywhere to make it clear that the English are energetic people. In the citadel the Highlanders are drilling. They have the graceful, elastic step of mountaineers: strong, healthy young men, condemned to a humiliating and ridiculous occupation that is stupefying them and turning them into automatons in the service of Her Britannic Majesty. Their movements make a sad impression upon a man who stands there, with his old umbrella and his bundle, staring at the soldiers, as if they were a new species whose habits are unknown to him. He is poorly dressed, as his way is when he travels, with a thin, twenty-five-cent palm-leaf hat on his head and a brown linen sack to conceal the raggedness of his coat. The spectator compares himself mentally with that superb officer there who, without his disguise, would probably look just like anybody else. He would almost like to hand him his own duster out of charity, so that he wouldn't have to look so much like an old bogie.

But he had better climb down again to the town and have a look at the milkmen's dogs, harnessed to the little carts containing a single immense can, and the market by the water-side, and the old women sitting in the open air behind their vegetables and fruit—and the ferry-boats continually going to and fro with their motley, chattering crowds. The cabmen talking in French to their old hacks remind him of the ancient France that still keeps its aroma here. In this restaurant he has just entered what interests Henry is not the bottles and the glasses on the table but a great map of Canada hanging on the wall. This table is made of mahogany, and it would be a pity to scratch it. The guest spreads out his handkerchief, then climbs up on the table and begins to study the map. When he sets foot on the floor again, without having broken any of the dishes, he has had his meal; the food itself will be merely dessert.

But it is to see the country that he has come to this "foreign soil." The two friends set out on foot to explore the Falls of Montmorenci. They promise themselves a good deal of pleasure. There may be less uniforms and nuns along the roads. It will be a great experience to see simple human beings.

The peasant women are working in the fields, buxom, healthy-looking creatures with ruddy cheeks under their broad-brimmed hats, and much more agreeable to look at than the natives of the stronger sex. The villages straggle along with their whitewashed houses. Thank goodness, you no longer feel yourselves strangers as you did at Montreal and Quebec. Isn't it odd? No matter where you wander on the planet, as long as there is a tree of any species, a blade of grass, a glint of running water or a beach where pebbles have been washed up, you are immediately at home; while a score of miles

from your own church-tower you have only to set foot
on the sidewalk of a town to feel yourself an alien, with
all communications cut with the world and your own
kindred. A strange business, this "foreign soil."

Evening falls. They have reached the village of Beauport. It would be much cosier if they could put up with
some of the inhabitants. They are in the heart of the
Canuck country, where you have to speak the language.
Even the little curs bark in a kind of French. Henry
courageously knocks at a door, and when they shout
"Entrez" from within some fine little phrases emerge,
the fruit of his reading since school-days. His accent
may not be very good, but often enough the people
understand it. The only trouble is that he can make
scarcely anything of their voluble replies. And the
blunders are very amusing. These honest Canucks are
full of good will, but unfortunately they are poor people
and have no bed to offer the strangers. So our friends
are compelled to enquire in their best pigeon-French:
"Y a-t-il une maison publique ici?" Who would ever
guess that these two boys are looking for a simple inn?
The Canucks of Beauport have no inn, as they have no
maison publique. But there may be room at the mill or
the grocery. At this other house, where the travellers
sit down for a moment to drink a glass of water, the
people politely excuse themselves by showing them the
loft where the whole family sleep, the only bedroom in
the house. At last, under a less poverty-stricken roof,
they are offered the best room and a bed with coarse,
unbleached linen sheets. But there is no coarseness in
the hospitality of the Binets, who do not lock them
into their room like that funny old oysterman who had
seen Washington; they even ask their guests if they
would like some brandy with their breakfast. No, good
lady, a plain apple will taste better to us than any drink.

The next day they set out for the Falls. The spot from which they can see them best has been appropriated by a mill-owner, who has his mansion and grounds there. Very sorry, dear sir, but we are going to cross your land with as little fuss as if we were in Concord. It appears that you supplanted on this spot a mighty lord of the last generation. But mighty lord or not, there is a great natural spectacle here, and the view belongs to the humblest of walkers who comes from a distance with his bundle to see the Falls. What do we care for your land-title? Sir William and Sir Henry here have a right to enjoy the sight to their hearts' content.

There should still be time to go and see the Falls of Sainte-Anne, a simple matter of thirty miles on foot. On the road they constantly pass wooden crosses and little shrines to the Blessed Virgin with ex-votos. Now and then they meet some villager wearing a cap of red, blue or grey worsted who bids them a polite good-day and lifts his hand to his bonnet. How civil and human they are! Even this fat, friar-like personage in his black, priestly robe—what can these fellows do for a living?—who appears at the door of his parsonage, where they have knocked to ask their way, gives them a friendly greeting. There is no inn at Sainte-Anne any more than at Beauport, but here too there are good souls to put them up. The master of the house, in his red cap, has the true Norman stamp; he talks with his stubby pipe between his teeth, which makes his Canuck French very hard to understand. Just the same, two fellows who have come from New England feel very near home here, very near and very far away at once, much further away in time and space than the excursion-ticket had given them any reason to expect. They are in the heart of old Normandy—Henry has returned for one night to sleep in the cradle of his race. He may not be thinking of this perhaps, but it is very much to his taſte here. The villages, the ſtreams have such charming names: Rivière de la Blondelle, Rivière de la Friponne, Rivière de la Rose, Rivière du Sault a la Puce, Pointe aux Trembles. . . How can he help feeling that he belongs to the race of poets-without-knowing-it who thought of such names as these? All the little houses turn their backs on the road, perhaps the better to preserve the fragrance of the old country.

After the visit to the Falls and a good ſtiff walk along the Saint Lawrence, they ſtop again at nightfall at a farm where they pass a very agreeable evening chattering French in the great kitchen. It is Sunday. William's pipe pays a tribute of incense to the little Canuck gods who have never died on the cross. What they cannot make intelligible because of their accent they write. This little girl knows how to write. Henry amuses them all by drawing a map of the country in chalk on the old oiled table-cloth. They are the beſt of friends in no time. With the few words at their disposal they talk about the soil, for that subjeĉt can be expressed in very simple terms. The good people talk about "senelles," and Henry at firſt supposes that they mean snails till they show him the little red apples of the hawthorn. They also go out for some real apples to give the two ſtrangers, beautiful, firm, glossy apples that have juſt been picked. In the autumn fragrance of ripe apples, Mother Earth says thanks in a universal language.

These poor Canucks, who are so gentle, with their rather humble politeness and an intelligence that seems to have been arreſted in its development, are pitiful creatures in the eyes of you Yankee touriſts, and you make fun of them because you are so clever and so ſtrong. But what would you have been if it had been perpetually rammed down your throat by your father and your father's father that the one great thing in this world is to obey our holy mother the Church? You would have been dunces, and you would have been mean, hard-hearted dunces. You would not have had the openheartedness, the simple courage, the good nature and humanity of these people. (Henry is thinking of the clear, laughing " By gosh " of the wood-chopper from Quebec who had come to see him in his cabin.) A little of the wealth of these "poor souls" would not come amiss in your pockets, shrewd fellows that you are.

But they must rejoin their fellow-excursionists. Quebec. Yes, the soldiers in red, the priests in black, the nuns, the seminarists. . . You have seen enough of them. To Montreal on the boat, and then the train that is to carry you home. In the car the inevitable wag of the party begins to imitate the cry of the cabmen in the streets of Quebec. Among these prosperous Yankees a silent man is thinking of the landscape along that tremendous river, so many miles wide, with its falls, its islands, and the little children who said good-day so politely to the strangers on the road. Reckoning all the expenses, the journey to Canada has amounted to $12. A little more, to be sure, than the net profits of a year of farming at Walden. But he does not regret his money.

Henry has cousins at Bangor, in Maine, the step-sons of his Aunt Elizabeth, one of whom is in the lumber-trade. He has never gone back there since that time in his twenty-first year when he had wanted so much to find a place as a schoolmaster almost anywhere. While he was living at Walden, he was seized with a desire to go up and shake hands with his cousin and do a little exploring with him in the forests up there. Henry lived in the woods, and the woods are cousins of the forest. One special attraction was that mountain which was more than five thousand feet high and in the midst of the wilderness and still almost unknown, Ktaadn. A royal mouthful, with that dense primitive forest he would have to penetrate before reaching the giant and offering it the homage of a very small cousin who had come a very long way with his knapsack to dine with His Mightiness.

On the last day of August, in the second year of his stay in the woods, he left his cabin (no need to bolt the door) and set off with his outfit in his haversack. From Bangor, Henry and his relative, the lumber-merchant, reached by buggy the meeting-point of the two branches of the Penobscot, where two companions were to join them. On an island in the river, where some degenerate Indians were living on their lands, they engaged two of the latter who were to serve as guides. One of them pathetically called himself Louis Neptune. The real journey began here.

Humanity, in this region, already presented the rough, honest features of a wood-cutter in a red flannel shirt. A solitary store stood for trade; it was filled with all kinds of "sweet cakes" upon which the lumberers threw themselves like starving men after their long fast in the woods. They also sold cartridges and toys for the children who were anything but visible. Perhaps these too were to amuse the wood-cutters. The road stopped here; they marched forward in Indian file. The forest had engulfed them; from an elevation they saw, as far as the eye could reach, nothing but its sombre green bosom. Pines, beeches, birches fraternized and struggled over the moss. There was no animal so scarce as man, and what a surprise it was to encounter him in the form of Uncle George, as he was called, living here on his lands so far from everyone, with another man and two women and his beasts, like a pasha! They were to spend the night under his roof, for it was here that the two Indian guides were to join them.

Excellent Uncle George, offering his hospitality with such an open hand to four travellers, and refusing to take any recompense! It was easy enough to see that his ancestors belonged to the good Scotch race. And what hospitality! Henry saw them preparing a royal dinner over an enormous fire with logs as long as an .axle-tree: on the table were ham and eggs, wheat cakes, cheese, salmon, shad, sweet cakes and stewed cranberries, all in profusion. And butter in such quantities that they gave it to you to grease your boots with. Henry felt very much alive in this land of Cockaigne. Henry the sober rejoiced in this munificence, for it was all seasoned after his own heart and everything was so simple, so grand and so beautiful in this forest setting. He dreamed at Uncle George's of that "larger and more populous house, standing in a golden age," where his blessed fellow-townsmen, those dear little provincial souls whom he knew all too well, had died of their stinginess, and the large spirit, the magnificent generosity reigned that he had found here in the remote depths of the woods.

Louis Neptune and the other Indian did not arrive, and Uncle George consented to serve as their guide. They would lose nothing by this. With a neighbouring settler whom they persuaded to join the party, there were six of them in a boat that played in the cleverest fashion with the current, the rapids, the whirlpools and rocks on a level with the water. George and his neighbour Tom were quick and sure-eyed boatmen. Henry was enraptured with the sport, which was all new to him. This was the logging country, where the great felled trunks adventurously jostled their way down the watery road and came to a stop in piles, waiting for the flood to dislodge them. It was a country of lakes too, big and little and strewn with islands. They were now on North Twin Lake; it was evening, and in the moonlight they rowed by turns, singing, pausing now and then to listen to the voices of the solitude. Henry no longer knew where he was nor what adventures lay before them through these interlacing waters and islands. . . .

At the loggers' camp where the expedition halted in the afternoon, they had had some tea and sweet cakes; this was the last human vestige in the direction they were going. And now as evening had come they made camp, cooked their supper, and then, stretching out with their feet to the fire, gossiped a little before going to sleep while they studied the starry sky. By daylight, through the clouds that encircled it, they had already caught a glimpse of the giant's brow. This was a trout country too, and the fish fell upon the bait ravenously, shimmering like flowers as you heaved them out of the water and flung them on the bank. Henry, the veteran fisherman, had a dream about them. He dreamed that he was fishing the whole night long in a miraculous shower of these flower-fishes. The vision was so acute that he was compelled to get up early in the morning and go and see whether it was true or whether he had only dreamed it. He went to the bank, cast his line and in the moonlight caught as many as ever he could want: trout and roach leaped and fluttered just as they had in his dream. They were like flying-fish.

The party was obliged now to leave the boat and turn towards the mountain on foot. Uncle George had never been further than this spot. So now it was Henry, rover of the woods, who took the head of the column. Following his old custom he took the compass and steered straight through the dense forest for the foot of the mountain, without seeing it. By noon they had breasted their way over so many firs and birches that their stomachs were groaning, and they broiled some trout on sharpened sticks, each with his own fish and stick. Gathered about the fire, they were like six sorcerers fishing in the flames. That night they camped within sight of the summit. But the guide was too impatient to wait for the next day; he scrambled up alone, on all fours, hanging by branches, slipping and recovering himself, till at last he reached a rocky plateau where he could reach with his finger the skirt of a cloud. And the next morning, while his companions were still struggling in a chaos of rocks, there he was on the summit, on the last ridge, pressed on all sides by the clouds.

He had hardly expected to find the Giant in such a savage humour. The little man who had come to pay him a visit felt rather overwhelmed; the spirit in him was silent, intimidated. He had hoped for some sort of rugged smile. But no, the Giant sounded as if he were muttering between his granite teeth: "What the devil are you doing here, you little worm? Go back to your mother." The Giant had no invitations for a little man who had made such a long journey and run the risk of breaking his neck to see him. He was a crabbed, secretive Giant who didn't like people to meddle in his affairs. Had this rather cold welcome somewhat disheartened Henry? The country through which he passed on his return, after having tumbled down the mountain by the bed of a torrent, drenching himself to his heart's content, was stamped with an almost menacing severity that chilled him at times. The desolation of these dense, infinite forests, without a suggestion of a path, without the faintest sign of anything akin to this biped who was groping his way and had to scramble up to the top of a fir-tree to get his bearings was so enor-

mous that he felt excluded, baffled, effaced—so utterly
that he wondered, as he touched his own body, if it
was not itself matter without a soul. . . . Had he had
to come all this way then to find the limits of his own
wilderness? Was such a region as this, absolutely devoid
of any relation to humanity, outside his domain? Would
the gods of his own wilderness at home refuse to haunt
the forests of Upper Maine? In that case Walden would
find its master here. Was that so? Strange, anyway—
very strange.

He did not become himself again till he heard the
laughter of running water and found the boat once
more. That was human at least. The Giant no longer
weighed on him, nor the mighty roof of the forest. They
descended the stream; the rapids were terrible. You
should have seen the two men with their spike-poles,
catching hold again of the empty boat after letting it
drop over a fall, leaping into it and allowing themselves
to be whirled down the rapids, cool and collected,
familiar with all the tricks of this crafty water. When
they reached the neighbourhood of Tom's house, whom
should they see but Louis Neptune and his companion,
each in his own canoe! In their old clothes, broad-
brimmed hats, broad capes, they looked like veritable
blackguards. And their explanations were like their
looks. It was not their fault that they had missed the
rendezvous; they had been the victims of a wild jollifica-
tion and had not yet recovered from the effects, poor
devils. It was all right. And they were welcome to
their muskrats too.

A glass of beer at Tom's, a farewell to Uncle George,
whose dogs were mad with joy at the sight of their
master and fairly devoured him; then off for Bangor,
Boston and Concord.

Henry was coming back to see his cousin again. This

mass of virgin forest, with its watery veins, dappled
with lakes as the lakes were dappled with islands,
attracted him as a kind of challenge; and this ursine
wilderness disturbed a little the thought of his own.
Seven years later, the pair were off again, in an open
wagon, on the road from Bangor to Moosehead Lake.
This time the Indian they had engaged as guide and
paddler met them as he had promised. No drunken
Louis Neptunes this time. Joe was a good-looking lad
of twenty-four, short and stout, with small feet, a
broad face, eyes narrow and slanting towards the
temples, wearing the red flannel shirt of the lumberman.
Although he knew all the American slang, he was a full-
blooded Indian.

This time they were not going to disturb a Giant in
his stony meditation. They were setting out by water
for Lake Chesuncook, another solitary majesty but a
less lofty one. After crossing Moosehead Lake on a
little steamboat, they carried their canoe and provisions
over to the Penobscot. It was a joy to Henry to watch
Joe tarring the little boat, which was nineteen and a half
feet long and painted green. They sat in the bottom on
birch-bark mats, and there were two big paddles which
they used by turns; they sat with their legs stretched
out or tailor-wise and sometimes knelt. Whenever a
bird appeared, Joe said its name in the Indian language—
a strange melody, as if the bird were naming itself. You
couldn't help thinking how happy the creatures would
have been at the Creation if that great poet, the Redskin
god, had been there in his paradise to name them.

This was the country of the moose, as big as a bull or
even a powerful horse, with two palm-leaves on his
head for horns and delicate hoofs that divide very far
up and are flexible when he bends over. It was a long
time since Henry had done any hunting, but his curiosity

was too lively for him not to accompany the two others when they pursued the moose, whose tracks they saw on all sides.

Joe, in the silence in which they glided along in the moonlight, imitated the call of the animal by blowing into a birch-bark hunting-horn. No reply this evening: nothing but an occasional dry rushing sound as of the closing of some faraway door in the forest, a falling tree. But later, as they were ascending a little tributary stream, a great head appeared which, when they took good aim, dropped into the water. It was not Henry's shot, needless to say. The animal was as big as a good-sized mare; the long fall from the high shoulders to the receding rump gave it almost the look of a giraffe. Henry watched Joe, skilfully removing the skin, making a fearful butchery of what the moment before had been a clothed and perfect form. Henry was no milksop, but he did not like to see life destroyed. It was true that this evening he did not refuse to eat a moose steak, which tasted rather like pickled veal. It was also true that three comrades eating together fried moose-meat cut directly from the animal and cooked over live coals in the open wind, in a magnificent solitude, while they sat with their backs against the towering fir-trees to the sound of the rippling water that rocked their canoe, was a very different thing from seeing a similar scene pictured in the almanac or in the tales of missionaries. You felt as if you were living a mighty life. And as for savagery, you didn't have to aspire to it any longer; you were eating it, you were partaking of it.

In the moonlight, the fairies had taken possession of the prospect, erected their scenery, arranged their lighting effects, and Henry half thought he was some personage of the forest of Arden in the brain of Shakespeare and not just a little fellow from Concord crouching in a canoe with Joe the Indian and his cousin the lumber-merchant. Henry was sleepy and he fell into a dreamy state: he was floating through prodigious gardens and avenues bordered with fantastic architecture where he heard the sound of Joe's horn calling the moose: *ugh, ugh, ou-ou-ou . . . ou-ou-ou . . .* The venison had gone to Henry's head. The others were hoping for the chance of a second shot. But for him the hunting was finished. One moose was enough. That great despoiled carcass had impressed him too painfully, and he had not digested the moose-steak very well. He had not made the journey with any such intentions as these. And there were enough of these red-shirted woodsmen coming in the pay of employers or a company to massacre trees and animals; the forest should know the face of at least one disinterested friend.

Henry left the others to their pleasure and sat down by the camp-fire to examine the fruits of his own hunt—the botanical specimens he had collected that afternoon. Then he took out his notebook and jotted down his impressions, just as if he had been in his own bedroom at Concord. But his room was vast this evening, and what an evening it was here for a solitary man with that stream of moonlight on the river . . . with those great shafts surrounding him with their sombre profiles . . . friendly shafts destined for the axe, destined for the saw, for the crime of being great and brawny and for holding under their skins the promise of such beautiful timber. The common destiny of trees and men, to be doomed to trade, to be sold in planks or pencils, instead of being understood, loved and glorified. In the dancing light of the flames the little men and the tall trees looked as if they were bending over the shoulder of a boy who was writing instead of joining in the chase.

At Chesuncook, that great log-house belonged to

Ansell Smith, who had cleared a good stretch along the lake. It was enough to see the assembled logs of which it was made, lapping over one another several feet at the corners, enough to see that forester's broad-axe leaning by the door to love the fine, manly air of the place and be happy at the prospect of spending the night there in a beautiful room where the wooden partition creaked with every movement. On the way back to Bangor, they stopped at an island that had been left as a reservation for the Indians. The Governor was a rare old boy whom they found sitting on the edge of his bed, in his shanty, dressed in a frock-coat and well-worn black pantaloons, with a red silk handkerchief about his neck and a straw hat. He was deaf, but he had hardly a grey hair in spite of his eighty-nine years. His corpulent squaws were gathered about him. They were tamed, Christianized, slatternly Indians. They were interested in politics, and were not in agreement on the question of the school which the priest, the sole holder of the Roman candles, wanted to close. Henry stopped for some time by an Indian who was making canoes. He would have liked to spend a whole season there, as an apprentice, and master this fine, primitive art. But he was obliged to take the trail for Concord again.

How was he going to like it after having gorged himself with this wild nature? Very much indeed, you may be sure. It had variety and all sorts of fine shades, and he never wearied of his old domain as he would have wearied after a while of the deep, monotonous forest. These solitudes of Upper Maine were like a strong wine that he liked to have a taste of now and then as a tonic. But they would never have done for every day. Those dear old attaching surroundings at home were . . . how was he to put it? . . . "nature humanized." Exactly. You would never have believed it perhaps:

hu-man-i-zed. A fellow does not come back from
Upper Maine, you see, without a curious little memory
to accompany the indigestibleness of the moose.

Four years later the taste of this strong wine tempted
Henry again. He had made another visit to Cape Cod
early in the season and had scarcely been home a month
when he started for Bangor. This time it was not his
cousin who was going to make the journey with him
but his friend Edward Hoar, the beloved companion of
many a ramble about Concord—including the one when
the two "damned rascals" set fire to the woods. Rambles of long ago, for Edward had been living for eight
years in California. They meant to reach the Allegash
Lakes and return by the East Branch of the Penobscot.
In this way they would encircle Ktaadn, giving it a
sufficiently wide berth not to disturb the Giant.

They could not do this without a guide. The Bangor
cousin recommended one whom he had known from
boyhood. He was another Joe—Joseph Polis; a very
different sort of fellow from the Joe of four years back.
This Joe was a grown-up man, forty-eight years old,
who had spent his childhood exploring the solitudes
around the sources of the St. John. He now lived with
his wife in a pretty house surrounded by a vegetable
garden, just like a New England villager who subscribed
to the county paper. A stoutly built chap, of rather
more than middle height, with a broad face—the true
Indian type. He spoke a passable English, using l's for
r's. He belonged to the aristocracy of his tribe. Joe
was glad to join the expedition and agreed to the price.
He was to carry his own canoe—literally, for he bore
it on his head to the stage, where he installed himself
beside the driver. As an old hand, he brought with
him, along with the great knife that dangled in a sheath
from his belt, nothing but his axe, his gun, a blanket

and a good supply of tobacco. Joe had bought a new pipe. He was very economical with his words; when you spoke to him, he muttered some vague phrase, as if all such things interested him very little. At the tavern, when a tipsy man asked him if he smoked, adding, in reply to a kind of yes: "Won't you lend me your pipe a little while?", Joe looked straight over his head and answered with an absent air: "Me got no pipe." Joe's silence would be the greatest relief after the palaver and smartness of white people.

As there were three of them in the bark canoe, with their baggage, there was no room for them to stretch their legs, but even so it was better than it was in the stage. And in the evening how much better than the inn was the little tent, set up in a dense wood where it was as black as an oven. They were in no need of a lullaby to put them to sleep as they rolled up in their blankets; but Joe, at Henry's request, sang in Indian a slow, rather nasal chant on some well-known themes, obligingly furnished by the missionaries, about the only and sole Almighty, ruler of the world. But there was such a fine simplicity about it that you utterly forgot the flatness of the performance: it was like a child singing his childish thoughts. Henry, who slipped outside the tent some time after midnight, saw a bit of phosphorescent wood. With his knife he shaved off a few chips which, when he placed them in the hollow of his hand, lighted up the lines of the palm. It was the first time he had seen this. He was so entranced by his discovery that he had to go and wake up Edward and show him his magic night-lamp.

In the morning, the piercing *ah, te-te-te, te-te-te, te-te-te* of the white-throated sparrow ringing through the wood sounded the Sunday reveille. Joe wanted to stop for the day. Joe was a good Protestant and he had prin-

251

ciples; at home he never failed to go to church. Of
course if they were absolutely determined to go ahead,
he would have to go with them, but the money he
earned would be the wages of sin. . . Well, perhaps
this could be arranged . . . later.

Joe was exquisitely ingenuous. He was full of admiration for pious people. He said his prayers on his
knees, in a loud voice, in his own language, morning
and evening. If, by inadvertence, he happened to lie
down at night without having said them and remem-
bered it, he immediately scrambled out of his blanket
and said them in double-quick time. You could see
that he had been to a good school. This evening, to
atone for having worked on Sunday, he said a particularly long prayer. But how much more natural a Joe
he revealed when, glued to the bank on his stomach,
he began to talk to the muskrats in their own language,
calling them with a strange squeaking sound with his
lips. . . Or better still, when he named in his own
tongue some incident of the forest life. The Indian
word for echo was *Pockadunkquaywayle:* kindly place
the accent where it belongs and see if you can find anything like it in your own language. Henry was quick
to note every scrap of this music; it enchanted him.
The words of his own tongue had been worn away like
pennies that have been passed from hand to hand for
centuries. Joe's words were like butterflies—he wanted
to catch them without hurting them at a moment when
they were motionless on a leaf, with their wings open
and still beating. How he would have liked to write a
dictionary of all these earthy words, which had the
quality of the pressed leaves he brought home in his old
music-case or those veiny pebbles on the beaches of
Cape Cod.

Two white men and an Indian plunged into the immense forest of fantastically shaped larches, where the mosquitoes poisoned them and made an infernal buzzing din about the fire when they stopped. Sometimes, in the depths of the night, a man rolled up, still awake, in his blanket on his arbor-vitae mattress heard in the dense silence the long-drawn call of the loon, rather like the hallooing of a man on a very high key. They reached Lake Apmoojenegamook, the goal of the excursion, and then Heron Lake, where a procession of sheldrakes passed them.

But no creature could have been odder than this odd fish Joe. As sharp as a weasel, by turns lively and taciturn, sparing of words and gestures, he was always master of himself except when he had made a good shot, when he trembled with emotion like a novice. If you asked him the same question twice, his silence gave you to understand that you had asked him once too often, and if you suggested that he might explain one of the numerous tricks he knew, he would oblige you to swallow this reply: " There are some things a man does not even tell his old woman." And then sometimes, along the trail, or when he was paddling, or, more often, in the evening, after he had said his prayers, when you were not asking him anything he would suddenly begin to tell you some interminable yarn. You should have heard him describe his interview with the famous Daniel Webster whom he had gone to see in Boston. After an endless wait, he was received like a dog by the great man, so rudely that Joe said to himself: " You'd better take care. If you try that I shall know what to do." A humbug, that Webster, a talking-machine. No Indian would ever have received a visitor so bluntly.

Joe had preserved the old Indian custom of leaving a trace of his passing by making an inscription on a tree or hanging up a bit of birchbark. Once all of a sudden he said to Henry: "Me make a bet. We two follow the path. I take canoe and you take the rest. See which gets there first." And he at once pulled off his boots and stockings, tossed the boots to Henry and set out ahead. To make up a bundle of all the utensils, the moose-skin, axe, paddle, gun, frying-pan and the rest, would have taken time for a little white man who merely gathered up everything he could, dashed off in pursuit, overtook the Indian, passed him. . . But he was forced to stop, for the innumerable utensils slipped out of his arms, and Joe overtook him in turn. The obstinate little white man, however, hugging all his traps desperately to his sides, outran the Indian again and saw him no more. When the man-canoe came up with him, both were out of breath. Joe explained that he had cut his feet on the rocks and concluded with a laugh: "Oh, me love to play sometimes."

One night Henry had a bad scare. In a desolate region where a great stretch of the forest had been destroyed by fire, he suddenly noticed that Edward was missing. It was inexplicable. Among the standing or fallen corpses of the trees, he vainly searched for him in the twilight. Near a waterfall that made the earth tremble, Henry camped with Joe, but he could not sleep. From time to time he thought he heard the voice of his friend calling him through the roar of the water. What could have happened to him? He was near-sighted, and he might have fallen over some precipice. On the morning after this terrible night, Edward was found again, smoking his pipe to soothe the cry of his hollow stomach which had been empty since the day before. He thought they were ahead of him when they were behind. After this they could have eaten two moose-steaks each for breakfast.

The great journey was ended. They were back again

among men, or almost. That evening, the new-mown hay on which they were sleeping in an open barn was like a foretaste of the feather beds that awaited them; the hay was full of grasshoppers, but the smell was delicious. Now, from time to time, they met an Indian in a canoe on the river, and Joe would exchange a word with him in his own language. Before reaching the end of the voyage, Joe, who had taught Henry the proper way to paddle, asked: "How you like 'em your pilot?" There was his house at last. The two friends stopped there for an hour to rest after the rough journey. They caught a glimpse of Mrs. Polis, who was wearing a hat and a silver brooch; but the Indian did not introduce his fellow-travellers to his "old woman."

That very evening, two veterans climbed into the train for Bangor, with their battered belongings, back again from the lakes of Finland perhaps or, who knows, from a journey across some *terra incognita* of the map.

What a beautiful trip! Joseph Polis. . . He was just a poor devil of a denatured Indian who said his prayers like a theological student—a fallen sovereign who hired himself out as a guide to strangers. Just the same, it was Joe who had made of this fortnight the richest of the three expeditions to Upper Maine. Henry was full of him. He could talk of nothing else but their guide, mentioned him in his letters to friends, thought of him every time he ate something that Joe had taught him to like. Joe had entered his life for good and all. Poor Joe was going to find himself placed, without knowing it, on a level with heroic and immortal figures; he had earned on this expedition a great deal more than his dollar and a half a day.

Joe had spoken for his whole race, which had always appealed so strongly to Henry's heart. Every time he had found himself in the presence of an Indian—degenerate, catechised, mere shadow as he might be—the blood had spoken in him; not the old Norman blood, nor the Scottish, nor the English, nor the Welsh, but this subtler blood that is mixed, in everybody, with the red blood. There was no romantic passion in this cult; it was like an avowal of a secret kinship. Yes, it was of Joe especially that he would think if he was able to carry out some day the work he dreamed of composing so lovingly on the North American Indian. Joe's coat-of-arms should be a bear paddling a canoe. There were far less proud artists than these to whom America could turn for the designs of its armorial bearings.

So many dreams of childhood, affinities, old desires, found their embodiment in Joe. . . The artist's love of the finest shades of instinct, admired in a descendant of the race that scattered music as it scattered words along the way. The taste for the primeval so ingrained in a man to whom, in spite of college and the classics and his environment, a valueless arrow-head spoke more intimately than a verse of the Bible. The ambition also of a writer to secrete the flint-flakes under his phrases, so that other vagabonds, finding them there some day, might make a collection of them and keep them in their dens. All this found something in Joe.

VII

At the end of October, 1856, Henry was asked to go down and survey an estate in New Jersey, giving some lectures at the same time. Alcott persuaded him to go. The two friends took the boat at Norwich, Connecticut, so as to reach New York by way of the Sound. Norwich was on the Thames: breezes blew there that seemed to come from afar.

Henry was leading a very dissipated life these days: visits to friends, expeditions, lectures. For here and there, outside of Concord, people were inviting him to come and utter those obscure or unpleasant truths that fell on the fallow ground of their understandings. It was all the same to him: he sowed as chance directed him, and the sower for his pains gathered in a little cash that had a more genuine ring in his ear than the applause of the audience.

Just two years before, during a brief trip to New York, Philadelphia and back to New York, he had had another glimpse of Horace Greeley who had taken him to the new Opera House to hear Grisi. (It was like a dream when you went to the theatre with a man as well-known as Greeley; you didn't pay for your seat, and you even had a little usher to conduct you to your place as if you were the Ambassador from Brobdingnag.) He could offer as an excuse the long, long period of vegetation from which he was just emerging and the natural desire, as soon as he felt less limp, to get out and see a little of the world. And yet he reproached himself for this dissolute life. You see what it means to have a few dollars in your pocket at last; you squander them as fast as you can, just like the "fortunate ones of this world." It's a foolish business, and you will soon deserve to end your days at the Poor Farm with those half-witted souls whom one sees planted about the fields like boundary-posts at the foot of Brister's Hill.

Surveying. . . For he was not just treating himself to these delightful outings. He was obliged to earn his daily bread, even if he no longer baked it in the open air in the woods where its fragrance mingled so well with the aroma of the pines. Of all the various little manual trades that Henry had practised since his youth, surveying had turned out to be the most substantial and profitable. When they spoke of Henry in the village they now said: "Oh, yes, the surveyor. . . " You were free to suppose that there was a touch of malice in these words and that the good people really meant: "That fool who goes off every afternoon to survey the waste lands instead of making pencils with his father. . ." Well, perhaps they did mean this—not that it mattered to Henry. As for lecturing, that was just another way of surveying the waste lands, the swamps, property, propriety and the improprieties. It was even a preferable way, for it was much less trying to spin words than to drag the geometer's chain.

A surveyor: not everybody can boast of becoming that at thirty-five, after having tried many other trades without any dazzling success. Henry was decidedly unjust in accusing his fellow-townsmen of not finding any use for his talents. The people of the village were very glad to turn to him when occasion arose, for they knew he was scrupulously exact in his measurements. To draw up a plan of other people's land was to remain free to gather there what seemed good to himself, without the knowledge of the owner, whose only desire was to keep within his own little bounds. With his

instruments, made to suit himself and partly with his
own hands, the compass, the staff and the chain, Henry
was ready to make surveys for anyone who asked him,
whenever he had the time. It was often in the winter,
the slack season on the farms, and then, when he was
aiming at the staff, he could no longer distinguish so
clearly against the snow the white trunks of the birches
which were usually so useful. But the work occurred also
at the season when he took off his coat for greater comfort. Sometimes it was a matter of a few days, sometimes an operation that required a week or two weeks
of brisk work (a loafer turned then into a model workman . . .). There were times, of course, when, in the
face of this landscape that flouted them, he consigned
all these boundaries, and all this business of fixing them,
to the devil; naturally, but no layman could guess all
the pleasure this work brought with it, aside from the
routine and the wages.

In the first place, you must have a companion to carry
the chain, set up the staff, etc. You shout something to
your helper over there, and the echo joyously replies as
if some practical joker had hidden himself to play a trick
on you; whereupon you feel like shouting at the top of
your lungs till the rascal shows his mug. And then, no
matter how seriously you apply yourself to your work
it cannot completely absorb you. You are out of doors
and there are two of you; the helper is not always as
stupid as a surveying-staff. Sometimes the work lies in
the woods, where you are most at home; sometimes
through a swamp where you sink in up to your knees.
Then at noon you fish out of your pocket a bit of bread
and cheese and have your lunch there on the ground.
Or you happen to have a meal at your employer's table
with the farm-hands. If your employer is a fool, there is
nothing for it but to hold your tongue and enjoy his

vulgarity on a bit of bread for your dessert. If he is a really decent farmer, as some of them about here are after all, it is a pleasure to share his simple meal after these hours in the open. In the evening you are certainly tired, after having tramped about all day with your mind fixed on your work; you are much more tired than if you had come back from a long walk. But there is another self within you who is grateful for your rested nerves and head and who suddenly appears, after the day is over, refreshed and keen, ready to catch any sound and gather in any shade of beauty that is entirely free from toil and wages. No, no, you haven't the slightest idea how light the surveyor's chain is or how pleasant to carry through the woods or over the wet fields, compared with all those chains that I see you dragging about after you, my friends, condemned as you are to the "liberal professions". . . You don't know how valuable it is for a writer to survey other people's lands in this fashion; you don't know how much else a man measures as he goes about, without the aid of the compass and the staff.

In the mid-winter of 1852-3, Henry had even given himself a stronger dose of surveying than he could have wished. In his finances the debits and credits were usually in a sound equilibrium, but at this time he found himself confronted with a large debt. He had to settle with the publisher for his book.

The matter was quite simple. They had printed a thousand copies and in three years had sold some two hundred. Since the cost of publishing had not been covered, the author remained in debt for the balance, according to the contract. It was all as smooth as silk. The method of publishing "at the author's risk" is just as simple a bit of machinery as the "royalty" method: the only difference is that instead of receiving

money you spend it. You see? There's nothing com-
plicated about that. Two hundred-odd copies sold of a
work of which at least three reviews (in the *Athenæum*,
the *Tribune* and the *Massachusetts Quarterly*, all well-
established publications) on all the press copies that had
been sent out had served to launch it, was a very impressive result for an author who was making his debut
before the public. But the summer before, after various
disappointments in regard to articles on which he had
built some reasonable hopes, the happy author, in
order to meet a note that was falling due, had been
obliged to borrow eighty dollars from his friend Horace
Greeley—merely a small advance which he had expected
to be able to repay shortly. A responsible magazine
had just accepted his *Yankee in Canada*. And then, lo
and behold, after printing the first part of it, without his
name (houses like this are so discreet, you know), and
adorned with fearful misprints, the magazine proposed,
for the remainder, to exercise its right to make cuts—
owing to certain bold statements that were too shocking
for a respectable review. The author would not hear of
this and simply demanded that his article should be
returned to him, neither more nor less: in this way the
sensibilities of the readers of *Putnam's Magazine* would
not suffer and Henry would keep his manuscript intact
for better days. As you please, dear editors. Literature
was decidedly a paying business. Henry was sailing
before the wind. Just one more little effort and he
would get there.

But what was the use of cultivating sarcasm? The
thing to do was to pay his debts. He didn't owe Horace
the whole State of California, but just the same the sum
was large enough for a man who as a rule owned nothing
in the world but his own joy in living, a stout pair of
corduroy trousers and a boat. When you have hands

you use them to pay your debts, instead of attempting, like a mere government, to make a new loan in order to pay off the first one. A man has more decency than a government. Manual labour is quite willing to pay for the loving labour of the soul.

With a will he set to work surveying in mid-winter for sixty, eighty days without intermission, at a dollar a day. To pay for that *Week on the Concord* he spent fort-nights tramping over the snow-covered ground, measuring and calculating, forgetting all about his reading, his Journal, everything. It was all in the day's work. Penal servitude, if you like. But you take it in good part if you are a man. Deprivations like this toughen your hide. They are like a long journey into the land of trivialities—from which you never return empty-handed if you have the eye of a good huntsman; on your return, you have a better perception of some things, including your own naked self. Besides, if literature fed its servitors too well, wouldn't it be setting a premium on obesity, on growing fat and flabby? That thought soon lightens the snow-clogged steps of a man who, while he spends a winter day surveying, is thinking all the time of the evening when he will relight his little stove in the attic and find himself alone once more with his abandoned meditations. . . For the rest, these months of intensive geometry were only a stage along the road he would have to survey to be quits with the publisher. Two years before, to pay off a former instalment, he had had to set to work with all his might making pencils, grosses and grosses of them, which were worth hundreds of dollars. And then, unable to dispose of all this merchandise quickly enough, he found himself reduced to carting it to New York and selling the lot for a hundred dollars. A bad stroke of business, but what are you to do when you have to get hold of money at any price? . . . At the time he had even considered speculating on his friends the cranberries in order to meet that confounded debt. A vile thought, as vain as it was impious, for after looking up the market price in both Boston and New York he had quickly perceived that it was the same with cranberries as it was with pencils: those mean souls would only take them at the meanest price. And now, after these bouts of surveying, he had still to make up the full sum that was due to Munroe. It was costing him $290, that precious book.

But after all these troubles he had a substantial reward. For more than a year Munroe had been asking him what he should do with the unsold copies that were encumbering his basement. Space comes high in Boston, as you know. And Henry, who had nothing but his attic, had at last taken pity on his poor over-burdened publisher and told him to send all the unsold copies to Concord. So one fine day the express-wagon unloaded all this merchandise on the Thoreaus' doorstep, like riches fallen from the skies. They kept pouring out of the wagon as if there were enough of these poor *Weeks* to fill a century. Take them all, Henry; they are your property. They are like the waste lands; no one will dispute them with you. In the end the work returns to the worker. Isn't that fair? Don't despise your work. It is a weighty book. You will have the best proof of this presently when you lug these bundles up to the third floor. See, there's the receipt—seven hundred and six copies—most of them in sheets. This Munroe is certainly an honest man.

And how imposing these piles are in your attic! Towering there, they humiliate your few beloved old odd volumes. The latter are quite taken aback at finding themselves all of a sudden the property of a rich man. An army of comrades, free and equal companions, has

joined forces with them, and over them all you will
henceforth reign, a sceptical and tolerant sovereign.
They bear on their brows the stamp of fidelity, these
newcomers. You can safely wager that they will be
your companions for life. See how firmly their feet
rest on the floor. Of course if some of them now and
then are seized with a desire to travel you are not the
man to hold them back; they are free. For now to his
former trades Henry has added that of a bookseller.
He will sell his book directly to admirers who send a
small sum of money with their order. All he has to do
is to tie up the package. There is no commission to be
paid to any agent. This simplifies things so much.
And the work acquires all the more value, coming
straight from the writer without an intermediary. It is
wrapped up and addressed by the author of the book in
person, and thus you have an autograph in addition for
the price of the volume. Purchasers, book-lovers with
a real flair, what more do you want? You should order
Weeks by the dozen, ten, twenty copies at a time. . .
Stupid bibliophiles.

Two years went by before another surprise comparable to this befell the master of the library in the attic.
It was another enormous bundle of books, but this time
it came from across the sea. It smelt not of Munroe's
basement but of the hold of a transatlantic liner. A
surprise from that English friend, the tall, fair-haired
fellow with the silky beard who had boarded with the
Thoreaus the year before and accompanied Henry on
his walks. And what books! "Cholmley," knowing
Henry's taste for the beautiful things of Asia, had sent
him all the most famous Oriental books that he had been
able to find. Good heavens, what an Arabian Nights'
dream! . . . The great sacred books of India, translated into English, French, Latin and Greek, and even

some in Sanscrit. . . This procession entered the house
like the three Magi with their retinue, bearers of gifts
for heaven knew what new-born being . . . forty-four
rare volumes, most of them not to be found on a continent that was prodigal in corn and wheat but not in
fruits of this kind . . . things of which you had dreamed
and that appealed to you so powerfully, and now here
they were, right under your hand, day and night. . .
The Hindu side by side with the Indian, your nearest
kindred touching one another! Precious stones flash-
ing their fire about your den, lighting up the pale
arrow-heads. I can laugh at you now, pretentious
libraries!

At first Henry was simply astounded by this patrician
generosity, which had gathered together all these treasures for him; astounded by all these illustrious personages who surrounded him, who had come from the other
end of the world as friends, come with their veiled faces,
great black eyes, wide with dreams, their dark skins,
strange faces, slow gestures, to offer the son of a pencil-
maker the flower of their wisdom so that he might place
it among the flowers of his own country. But the sages
of the Orient smiled at the seven hundred *Weeks* and
did not seem to be in the least offended by the pile of
nuts in the corner of the little room. Henry soon felt
quite at home beside them, and all these presences, the
new and the old, mingled in one friendship in the warmth
of the old stove.

But when you have distinguished visitors who have
made a long voyage in the belly of an ocean liner, you
must offer them lodgings that are worthy of them.
Henry had some well-seasoned wood, gathered along
the river, and he had tools. For these beautiful books
he was going to make a new bookcase, a bookcase of
honour that would be a sort of Asiatic province royally

accommodated on the third floor of the house on Main Street.

There could never be any question of repaying the magnificent Thomas such a debt of gratitude as this. Whole seasons of surveying would not be enough. But he did send him a few American books, among them a novelty—not a rarity, for nobody bought it—that scandalized its few readers, a bewildering book, powerful as a buffalo, multitudinous as a seaport, torrential, insolent, shameless. Henry regarded it as a work of the grandest kind. Emerson also. Thomas would see. A purely American product and, what was astonishing, something that made you think of the Orient. It was written in Biblical verse, like the Song of Songs or the Rig-Veda, and it had the strange title, *Leaves of Grass*. The book was not signed. A very slender present, you see, friend "Cholmley." You must tell me what you think of my buffalo.

In a den where stones, birds' eggs and plants had long swamped the books there was now almost an affluence of tops and backs. Among the newcomers there was one which had arrived all alone, quite modestly, the year between the two surprises. It had not come as a surprise, however; it was an expected visitor. It entered there familiarly, as if it had come back from a journey and knew the ways of the house and the fellow who lived there. Its name was Walden. But it was not a pond. It was Henry's latest born. A responsible publisher had taken charge of it; and this time there was no need to run into debt or do surveying for the sake of a book which the author was the only one to love. The name of Ticknor covered it like a flag.

To be sure, there was no wild scramble to buy it. But it sold a little. And responses came to the unknown author; new friends rose out of the ground along his path. You write a book for your own pleasure, without thought of any good or harm it may do, and lo and behold, it sets out alone, in its own right, and makes conquests for you all over the world. Is it possible that you wrote a book in order to discover your friends? It is as if the book were grateful to you for having brought it to light and courteously wished to show its gratitude.

It bears under its title a picture of the cabin (the poor cabin that will never again be able to gossip with the pines—it is doing penance now in the bean-field). It is a book that carries a cabin across the world and invites you to enter and inspect it and inhale the resinous fragrance. It will not carry you off to dance for a week on the water in a nut-shell. It requests your company on a ramble around a transparent pond where you can contemplate your own image in water that is clearer than your mirror. It is not Narcissus that you will see there, returning your own smile to you, but the face of a man who is studying the curious effect of his big nose in the water.

Between Henry's two offspring there have been more than five years of growth. Although they have both been nourished on the same sap that has been accumulating for fifteen years in the Journal, *Walden* is the book of a writer who has reached his full stride—a little too full, if you like—with the same unpardonable waywardness in his composition. You will never turn a pate like that into the saw-mill of a *littérateur*. Well then, call him a liberator instead. That is the way Henry himself expresses it.

To return, then, towards the end of October, 1856, the surveyor set out with all his paraphernalia for Perth Amboy, New Jersey. He didn't want to pass through

New York without seeing that good Greeley, but not finding him at his newspaper office he walked up Broadway, meeting a friend, and then went and settled himself in the Astor Library. You can't study these great brawling cities as you can study a book in a sanctuary of silence; coming from Concord, you are deafened by the 'busses and the trampling crowds. Whither are all those feet rushing? Who is waiting for them at their appointed meeting-places? That is, unless these people are not all simply out of their heads. Here is a blissful refuge! Let's go and sit down for a while and read.

Perth Amboy, on Raritan Bay, faces the island, shaped like a bunch of grapes, that recalls to Henry the rather melancholy days when he was a tutor. A mile and a quarter from the town a friend of Margaret Fuller's, Marcus Spring, whom he had seen on his journey to find the poor woman's remains, owned some property: the estate was situated on the edge of the bay and was called Eagleswood. They had tried to start a phalanstery there, and now the eagles had gathered to establish a "colony."

The question was one of drawing up plans for the future village, a very proper task for a surveyor who had come expressly from Concord. When you happen to know a good surveyor, nothing can be more natural than to have recourse to his compass. Henry's friends had not forgotten him—for instance, there was Marston Watson, who had asked him two years before to come and survey his park on the hillside above Plymouth (no need of a helper that time, for Alcott himself, with his tall frame, platonically carried the chain, assisted by the owner in person). Henry assuredly had very noble friends who not only appreciated his talents but loaded him down with little gifts: in the space of a few days had he not received from Marston, who had presented him with those magnificent big glow-worms the previous summer, some pear-trees the very name of which was like a juicy fruit that melted in your mouth, and a hummingbird's nest from Blake, and a box of mayflowers from somebody else? Quite apart from the Christmas season, the express-company evidently had permanent agencies in fairyland.

The surveyor set to work, plunged into the woods and salt marshes, regardless of rips and tears; before each meal it took him fifteen minutes to pick off the burs that clung to him. These are the little pleasures of the trade. While it awaits the promised village, Eagleswood contains an old farmhouse and a big stone building, together with Marcus Spring's private residence, and it glories in some shops and offices and a school where the teaching is done by various dignified greybeards. Rather too many people and rather too much dignity to suit the taste of Henry, who prefers the informality of the burs; and creditable as the work may be, he longs to have done with it and get home again. There is an accursed woodpigeon that begins to coo every night at the slightest sound from the house. Perhaps it is the former janitor of the phalanstery.

Yes, the work begins to drag, and he cannot drop it because it has been entrusted to him. Nor does the society of these worthy greybeards, the atmosphere of the "colony," offer any great attraction. The big city, where Alcott has stayed behind, is close at hand, and Henry feels like a molecule subject to the law of gravitation. He longs to make a trip to New York and go and see his friend and have a little vacation from these old fossils. Just for one little week-end. On Friday, November 7th, he enters Alcott's room and finds a guest there, to whom he is introduced, John Swinton. This young man, a delightful fellow, full of fire and

269

revolutionary instinct, is a good friend of the author of *Leaves of Grass*. Do tell us something about your friend. Alcott has already seen this Walt Whitman who sounds his barbaric yawp over the roofs of the world. Henry is most anxious to meet him.

To-day he is invited to go with Alcott to a certain lady's house, but he means to let his friend go alone: a drawing-room and a lady in New York must be very much like a lady and a drawing-room anywhere else. He knows all about such things even at Concord, in a small way, and he has very little desire to see them in a large.

The next day they meet Horace Greeley at the station and go and spend the day at his farm at Chappaqua. For every Saturday the editor-in-chief of the *Tribune* shakes the dust of the city and his editorial office off his feet and hurries out to look after his little farm, of which he is very proud (his turnips have taken the prize at the County Fair). A friend, the poetess Alice Cary, is also one of the party. For some ten years Horace has more than once shown his friendship for Henry; he would have liked very much to keep him in his family as a tutor for his children. (Horace is a great man who has already had a big book written about him in his own lifetime, and Henry is fond of him and grateful for all the attention he shows a little village scribbler, but . . . but to give up once more that precious independence, to leave Concord where there are so many friends, from Easterbrook to Nine Acre Corner, who have only himself to count upon . . . no, never, Horace must excuse him. . . .) At Chappaqua the guests admire the crops and the farm-buildings, but when he sees how much trouble and expense it has cost the owner to transform swamp-land into fertile ground, Henry remarks to himself how much more attractive a beautiful swamp is than a model farm. And they come back to town for the night.

It is Sunday, and they cannot begin the Lord's Day better than by going to hear an astonishing man who is preaching at Plymouth Church in Brooklyn. There are crowds to listen to him, crowds that have come there to be thrilled by this magician who makes them turn pale, laugh, weep or exult as he wills, as if he were developing and unfolding before them the most moving drama. But it is not the art of an actor, even the greatest actor, that makes such an impression here; it is an elemental force. It is such a beautiful spectacle in that pulpit that you forget you are in the presence of a churchman. He is something better than that—a man, Henry Ward Beecher, the brother of Harriet, author of *Uncle Tom's Cabin*. Henry thinks this other Henry deserves to be called a pagan; the whole ghastly race of preachers is forgotten, the setting of the church disappears, a great wind has passed over these people to purify and uplift them, like a rush of autumn leaves. Henry is thoroughly delighted.

Such a capital Sunday must have a worthy finish. Suppose they go and see Walt Whitman, since he lives in Brooklyn? So, after lunching with a lady who knows Alcott, the two companions set out for his house. Here's Portland Avenue, where the buffalo lives, and here is his number. Disillusionment; he has gone out. The mother, with her kind face, tells them this and asks them to come in. Henry has a mother too over yonder, a lively mother who would be only too happy to talk to two visitors who had come to see her son; and she too would be unlikely to say anything unkind to them about her boy. He thinks of her as he listens to this smiling woman of sixty, as simply dressed as a farmer's wife, uttering a maternal eulogy on her son Walter.

These gentlemen have come to see him because he is the author of a book; and she, who is the author of the author of the book, can only tell them how proud she is of this son, and how much he means to his brothers and sisters, and what a blessing his presence is to them all at home. "If you can come back to-morrow morning, not too late, you will be sure to find him, for he will be very sorry to have missed you to-day." All right, Mother Whitman, we shall be back to-morrow, and thank you for your welcome. We have not seen your Walter, but in the little wrinkles about your eyes and lips there is something that seems to foretell what he is like.

On Monday morning there are three of them to take the ferry and make their way to Portland Avenue, through streets that sound like a country town after the jam they have left; a lady from Philadelphia has asked to go with them. They knock at the door and are invited to come in just as they were the day before. Walter is at home, expecting them. Presently the three visitors are sitting face to face with a great hairy, ruddy animal, who has nothing sinister about him at all. Strange, this fellow is simplicity itself and everything in the room is quite ordinary, but from the very first instant, seeing him planted there, you think of a great sailing ship at sea or of a beautiful tall tree in summer. You would think you were out of doors. Henry feels quite at home in a house where you drink in the fresh air as freely as you do the friendly glass on the table.

It is a house like many other houses that has gathered under its roof to-day Walt and Henry, the Manhattanese and the Concordian. . . But the walls of the house still stand, they bear up bravely under the shock. It is roomy, the Whitmans' house, and built by the hand of a clever workman, as strong as if the father, who died

laſt year, had set up the frame himself. But that muffled
sound which echoes and rolls away, very far away, is
the detonation of these mingling spirits, though no one
hears anything in the house or the neighbourhood but
the sounds of a quiet ſtreet.

Four persons are talking together as friends in the
innocence of Monday morning, three of them observing
and the other, without the leaſt embarrassment, allowing himself to be observed. The appointments of the
room, the old, worn furniture which has known so
many dwellings are swallowed up in this masculine
figure, which is enigmatic because of its very nonchalance and abundant ease. There are so many questions one might address to the high vault of that pronounced eyebrow, the right one. The visitors ask him
this and that, seeking to penetrate beneath the brick-
coloured skin of the enigma, tanned by all the suns of
Long Island; all conſtraint has vanished, so complete
is the absence of ceremony in the man they have come
to see, so ſtrong his expression of virile goodness. In a
rich, musical voice, in direct, everyday words, he speaks
of what he loves—the ever-changing crowds of his city,
the ebb and flow at the foot of those cliffs with their
myriad windows, the human flood rolling through the
ferry-boats, the ſtages, the popular thèatres, the squares.
The enigma does not give up its secret, but it becomes
more and more attractive. Henry also has loves that he
might confess, but he only asks the lover of the poetry
of the ſtreets if he has read the great Oriental poems.
"No, tell me about them . . ." It is an encounter in
which each puts out these verbal feelers. Their words
are less clear perhaps than their attitudes and the expressions of their faces. But the visitors do not dream of
going away.

How had Henry pictured to himself the Manhattanese,

"eating, drinking and breeding," of the *Leaves*—"one of the roughs"? Perhaps he had not pictured him at all. Perhaps he had thought that this rude sketch was only the fantasy of a poet who was enamoured of bright colours and had no prototype in reality. However this may have been, there was the "rough" before him. And he was beautiful, a little coarse, but beautiful. With that whole person, in its radiance of life and vigour, Walt signed his book, signed it with a far more striking truthfulness than the portrait he had used as a frontispiece. Here was the flesh and the blood and the colour. Henry looked and looked again, seeking to fathom the nature of the radiance that passed over him in the presence of the phenomenon. He did not challenge this thing that bathed him and seemed to make him float; he noted his reactions, that was all. This fellow had too much blood in him, perhaps. Perched on a stage beside the driver, amid the hubbub of Broadway, did he not shout out verses as if he were alone on some beach! A wild man indeed!—but with a wildness that did not intimidate Henry's, like that sullen summit of Ktaadn, but stirred his curiosity, provoked him. That strong aroma of masculine health, which he smelled, did not tell him very much. But how did it happen that with this luxuriance of the flesh, which was brutal enough to be offensive, there mingled an exquisite perfume that utterly defied your power to define it? With a disconcerting naturalness this big fellow spoke or listened (he was a most astonishing listener) as this invitation emanated from his ruddy body to the three others—the tall fellow, the little fellow and the lady sitting opposite: "Do take as much of my health as you like. You can see I shall always have enough. Call this irritating, if you like, but it's quite real; and mine is a presence that does not wait for your consent to warm you."

274

HENRY THOREAU

Henry, with his habit of absorbing phenomena, sits there, all eyes—with those eyes that know how to look—seeking to understand, to pierce to the bottom. Henry, the dry little animal, all nerves and tendons, with his drooping shoulders and his narrow chest (look at that great thorax over there, ready for any fist to strike it, where the weariest head might lie without covering it . . .); Henry, with his receding chin, lost in the little apish beard which he is allowing to grow just now, his pursed lips, his big, contemptuous nose, his absorbed, reflective, alert air, his whole life gazing with implacable seriousness out of the blue-grey windows of those eyes that are so round, sagacious, keen, vigilant, shining with perpetual use like a spade; Henry whose lean body refuses to speak for his soul, with his frail health and his tempered will, crouching behind his own glance like a hunter on his knees in some thicket, face to face with this demi-god beaming with nonchalance and carnal opulence; Henry, saturated with the woodland life of his village, beside this other whose soul is peopled with his own Broadway. . . And each is trying to catch the scent of the other.

With his rather sluggish glance, the big animal absorbs the little as he absorbs everything—tranquilly. He accepts without any mental reservations these friendly people who have come to see him—the tall man, the short man and the lady; there is room for them too in his universe. The Leaves exclude no one from their shadow; they spread out as far as Concord and Philadelphia. He is happy to welcome them, though he sees nothing in them that particularly surprises him. He lets them talk, as his way is, draws his own profit from what the speakers say and replies without opening himself particularly or abandoning his reserve. These two birds have come from the land of phantoms. They are

intellectuals, bred in the colleges. Not much of a recommendation in his eyes. It would never occur to you to
say to this lanky New Englander: "Henry, let's go and
have a drink." He's not cut out for a comrade. Just the
same, these fellows are friends of the man to whom he
owes enough to call him "master" and who has written,
thanking him for his book, that unforgettable letter
which he always carries there in his pocket, like a patent
of nobility. They are two Yankees, one of whom has
begun to sing for himself, who have come on a pilgrimage
to greet the boys of Manhattan.

The great animal is not insensible to such an homage
and he accepts it cordially, in the name of his own
people, as a wholesome response. But Walt's interest
is not aroused. Henry, on his part, would have dearly
liked to be alone with this extraordinary fellow so that
the two of them might start one of those talks like his old
talks in the cabin, when some full-minded friend came
to see him and not a syllable that was not sonorous
echoed between the plank walls. But there are four of
them and the conversation begins to wander. They
don't get hold of one another, and what a pity it is!
For surely they have things to say to one another that
are worth saying, points of contact they might establish
together. Henry's big grey-blue eyes express this wish
and this regret. For isn't it vexatious to be face to face
with such a huge puzzle and not be able to grasp it and
turn it round so as to discover in the end, as likely as not,
that the same flame burns in that big chest and under
that narrow, grouse-like throat? Isn't it? *Isn't* it? .

(Ah, my two friends, the future opens out, furrowed
with very different paths from this hour that brings you
together here . . . You have decades to live still,
Walt. . . You are to pass through the horrors of the
great war; you are to see it lying on beds of torture and

to be tortured yourself. Will you then be the man who stood for a fight to the finish? In your great ripe heart, a comradeship as ardent as love will have seized upon you, so painful that you will flee from the world, you will take flight with your sorrow by paths untrodden to the shores of pond waters, to gather the fragrant calamus root—(it grows also on the shores of Walden Pond)—and partake of it mystically with your known and unknown friends. . . And then, when you are past the age for stormy passions, you will find one day the Passage to India: that little chap found it long ago, you big simpleton. . . And many other discoveries are reserved for the consolation of your mellow age: after so many other things have lost their lustre, the trees, the seasons and the skies will offer you their balm and you will voluptuously anoint yourself with it, bathing in the mud of Timber Creek to ease your aching body. Then you will take more pleasure in a squirrel's play than in the shuffling feet of crowds. And how well you will understand the thought of that old chap who said that he was seldom less alone than when alone! Yes, and then, as you approach your sixtieth year, you will seek by a little pond what men refuse you, and you will find it, and you will be stirred through and through with gratitude, my friend. . . And the day will come when, as an old gaffer leaning on a stick, you will visit Concord and receive a whole-hearted welcome in the land of phantoms at a time when the land of the living rejects you, and you will step down from your friend's carriage and add your stone to the cairn that marks the spot of Henry's cabin. . . You will have your florid complexion still, set off by the bushy, snow-white beard that adorns it. . . And you will still be the same Walt, enjoying this miraculous life and rejecting nothing. You will simply have come to understand certain things. . .

The future opens out, and in the distant perspective paths take shape where your feet, my friends, have left their prints. . . Is it possible that lovers like you should never, never meet there? Listen. . . How strange it is! . . . You might think you were listening to words that cross one another. . . Does it not sound like an intermittent dialogue in which two voices reply back and forth over some field that catches their harmony?

HENRY:— *He would be a poet who . . . nailed words to their primitive senses, as farmers drive down stakes in the spring, which the frost has heaved . . . whose words were so true and fresh and natural that they would appear to expand like the buds at the approach of spring, though they lay half-smothered between two musty leaves in a library,—ay, to bloom and bear fruit there, after their kind, for the faithful reader . . .*

WALT:— *Roots and leaves themselves alone are these. . . Frost-mellow'd berries and Third-month twigs offer'd fresh to young persons wandering out in the fields when the winter breaks up, Love-buds put before you and within you whoever you are, Buds to be unfolded on the old terms. If you bring the warmth of the sun to them they will open and bring form, colour, perfume, to you, If you become the aliment and the wet they will become flowers, fruits, tall branches and trees.*

HENRY:— *True verses come toward us indistinctly, as the very breath of all friendliness, and envelop us in their spirit and fragrance. . . There are two classes of men called poets. The one cultivates life, the other art—one seeks food for nutri-ment, the other for flavour. . . The true poem is not that which the public reads. There is always a poem not printed on paper. . .*

WALT:— Whoever you are, now I place my hand upon you, that you be my poem. . .

HENRY:— It is no small recommendation when a book will stand the test of mere unobstructed sunshine and daylight.

WALT:— Read these leaves to myself in the open air, tried them by trees, stars, rivers. . .

HENRY:— I would have my thoughts, like wild apples, to be food for walkers, and will not warrant them to be palatable if tasted in the house.

WALT:— I swear I will never again mention love or death inside a house. . .
If you would understand me go to the heights or watershore. . .

HENRY:— When I stand in a library. . . Alas! that so soon the work of a true poet should be swept into such a dust-hole!

WALT:— . . . in libraries I lie as one dumb, a gawk, or unborn, or dead. . .

HENRY:— The very names of the commodities . . . poetic, and as suggestive as if they had been inserted in a pleasing poem—Lumber, Cotton, Sugar, Hides, Guano, Logwood.

WALT:— Land of coal and iron! land of gold! land of cotton, sugar, rice!
Land of wheat, beef, pork! land of wool and hemp! . . .

HENRY:— I trust that we shall be more imaginative, that our thoughts will be clearer, fresher, and more ethereal, as our sky—our understanding more comprehensive and broader, like our plains—

our intellect generally on a grander scale, like . . . our rivers and mountains and forests —and our hearts shall even correspond in breadth and depth and grandeur to our inland seas.

WALT:— *. . . a bard is to be commensurate with a people . . . he incarnates its geography and natural life and rivers and lakes. Mississippi with annual freshets and changing chutes, Missouri and Columbia and Ohio and St. Lawrence with the Falls and beautiful masculine Hudson, do not embouchure where they spend themselves more than they embouchure into him. . .*

HENRY:— *There are poets of all kinds and degrees, little known to each other . . . I meet these gods of the river and woods with sparkling faces (like Apollo's), late from the House of Correction, it may be. . . What care I to see galleries full of representations of heathen gods, when I can see actual living ones by an infinitely superior artist?*

WALT:— *Accepting the rough deific sketches. . .*
Discovering as much or more in a framer framing a house,
Putting higher claims for him there with his roll'd-up sleeves driving the mallet and chisel. . .
Lads . . . no less to me than the gods of the antique wars. . .

HENRY:— *There is this moment proposed to me every kind of life that men lead anywhere. . . By another spring I may be a mail-carrier in Peru, or a South African planter, or a Siberian exile, or a Greenland whaler, or a settler on the Columbia*

River, or a Canton merchant, or a soldier in Florida, or a mackerel fisher off Cape Sable, or a Robinson Crusoe in the Pacific, or a silent navigator of any sea...These are but few of my chances, and how many more things may I do with which there are none to be compared!

WALT:— *I am a real Parisian...*
I am a habitan of Vienna...
I am of Adelaide...
I am of London...
I am of Madrid...
I belong in Moscow ... or in some street in Iceland...

HENRY:— *Whatever is, and is not ashamed to be, is good.*

WALT:— *I am enamour'd of growing outdoors...*

HENRY:— *When I look at the stars, nothing which the astronomers have said attaches to them, they are so simple and remote.*

WALT:— *When I heard the learn'd astronomer...*
How soon unaccountable I became tired and sick,
Till rising and gliding out I wander'd off by myself...
Look'd up in perfect silence at the stars.

HENRY:— *A name pronounced is the recognition of the individual to whom it belongs. He who can pronounce my name aright, he can call me, and is entitled to my love and service.*

WALT:— *What am I after all but a child, pleas'd with the sound of my own name? repeating it over and over...*

HENRY:— *You may have the extraordinary for your province, if you will; let me have the ordinary.*

WALT:— *The Commonplace I sing...*

And the rest of the dialogue is lost in the distance like the path on which the two drinkers of space have walked a little of the way together, before taking their separate roads, one in this direction, the other in that.

Yes, there are these lost paths that both have trodden, paths where they have only never met because one has followed them a few hours, a few seasons before the other. It is a thousand pities, my friends. If you had encountered each other once, not under the roof of a house in Brooklyn, during a call, but in the fields, while you, Henry, were surveying, or on a beach after the two of you had been bathing in the sea, how much the sand and the tufts of grass would have helped you to the beautiful understanding that is impossible for you now, Henry, withdrawn as you are in your shell, and for you, Walt, great unconscious animal that you are.

But after all, these dreams do not cover an atom of the reality that is in you. How much better it is that the future should close again, that you, Walt, should be there in the house on Portland Avenue with your mother and your family (cherish them, they are so dear to you), ruddy and strong, and that the roar of Broadway should murmur in your ears! How much better it is that you should be there, good soul that you are, the youngest of the three, with your thirty-seven years and your perfect health, your intransigence, your youthful, inordinate faith, and that this little creature should not interest you too much. These are not imaginary beings here but four very ordinary persons of solid flesh and blood, and how much better it is that they are!)

In the course of the conversation, Walt, speaking of his friends, the young fellows of the capital, to whom he owes even more than he owes to Emerson, and of the place they hold in his poems, expresses his conviction that they are America, Democracy, the key of the politics of the New World. At this the tight-lipped Henry discharges a cutting remark. They are the mob, and the mob is like peat. It may give out any amount of heat, but it smokes, it reeks, it goes to your head. A fellow who can make a fire of stumps in a clearing doesn't care to warm himself at any such blaze as that. The mob, universal suffrage, the rabble marching in procession over the pavements of a big city or wallowing like pigs to keep warm in the litter of a stable. . . Can you see that clamorous rout of human insects crowding into the porch of those great W's that rise at the threshold of your name, Walt Whitman? Don't you want to close the portal?

And the son of Manhattan says to himself: "That fellow certainly comes from the land of mummies. Those New England people have plenty of brains—if only the gods had given them a little more guts. That clever little devil will never be bowled over by the music of the bugles that grips your very vitals, or the pride of belonging to such a brawny country. He's too skinny, the poor little chap."

Walt, though he conceals it, has been wounded to the quick in his affections. The America of his poems is not looking for the homage of apostles like this: it is a lively, warm-blooded America that responds to the passion of males. Walt calmly faces the cold disdain expressed by this little shrimp for a Person whom he loves with a terrible love, not separating the good from the evil. "You don't understand me," he says simply. From that moment he is enlightened. They can go on talking amicably enough. Henry can say anything he likes, black or white; Walt has taken his measure. The "no" has worked. A thunderbolt has suddenly dissipated the fog that veiled a gulf between them immensely wider than the East River which the visitors have crossed.

Would you imagine that such a chasm could yawn between two beings who are talking quietly there in a house on Portland Avenue—an apparently impassable chasm, in spite of all the foot-bridges that reach from one to the other? . . . Between two poets who are united in a sovereign contempt for the literature of the literati—two plebeians, each in his own way—two children who go forth every day, one of whom could no more do without his daily walk on the populous pavements where, from their glances, he gathers in the affection of men and women, than the other could do without his ramble among the people of the trees, the plants and the waters of Concord, with the track of the railroad for his Broadway between trains—two loafers who have remained free and unmarried for "reasons"—both of them drawing as it were from a spring of elemental joy—both passionate idealists who, with equal cheerfulness, might so easily "go and live with animals"—both mystics, with a great appetite for the concrete—both affirming to the point of arrogance their quality as individuals—both equally secretive and reticent—both great friends of the Indian—both poor in money and refusing to earn the bread of galley-slaves—both having to record the practical failure of their first books, printed at their own expense (lucky Henry has disposed of more than two hundred copies of his, while as for that big fellow, his sales can be counted on his ten fingers . . .)? Yet there they are, looking at each other, from opposite banks, while the tumultuous tide rushes down between them, scouting the frail bridges they have attempted to fling across its violence. And what an uproar fills the Narrows, as if to affirm that for all time the continent

284

and the island shall remain as they are, two separate
worlds!

On the continent there are men with whom you feast
on friendship, crowds of comrades, day and night, never
too numerous for a hearty fellow who is hungry for the
presence of other hearty fellows like yourself. There
are those who call you by your first name as you pass
or with whom you walk with your arm about their
shoulders; they are as thick as the trees along the rivers
and the Great Lakes. They are the mass to which you
give of yourself with immense confidence, well knowing
what will be the return from this investment. Here
reigns the "beautiful, curious, breathing, laughing
flesh" that absorbs the radiance of your own strong,
sensual, loving masculinity and sends it back to you in
the flash of the eyes that turn towards you. Where can
one find such delights, richer food for the soul? What
should I do in your blessed retreat, where the golden
days pass with one companion? I should be devoured
by homesickness in a moment—for the streets and faces
of Manhattan, their sounds and their vibrating movement.

Frown as much as you like at these delights, little
man on your island who hold men and women at a
distance as if you were afraid of touching pitch. You,
brother of the live-oak that joyously spreads its branches,
alone in the fields, with no companion near it. You to
whom the company of your own dear thoughts suffices.
You who crouch in the midst of your own distrust, with
your fists clenched, bitter, satisfied, sarcastic, devoid of
magnetism, without any indulgence for your neighbour.
You whom no one would ever think of calling by a nick-
name. You who have no more friendship for your own
body than for those of others. You for whom no
woman waits.

Make your wry face, Henry, but throw out your narrow chest, just the same! For you have no particular reason to feel humiliated. The contrast with that great animal may overwhelm your puny frame. Your head barely reaches to his shoulder, but in that head, little Henry, burns the flame of a spirit that assures you at least this superiority: you have felt his grandeur, while he has not been able to see anything in you. He is not very discerning, the great animal. Go back to Concord with your head high.

They parted indeed after two hours of conversation, with a promise to see each other again the next morning. Matters could not rest there. Walt was going to return the visit of the two Yankees at their hotel. But at the appointed hour, the loafer, the dawdler, had either forgotten the meeting or thought it best to be somewhere else: there was no big ruddy fellow to be seen. They could not resume the conversation.

And on November 24th, Amos and Henry returned to the fold, the one to Concord, the other to northern Connecticut where he was living at the moment, full of memories of their call in Brooklyn—still under the charm of a presence that was vastly more impressive even than the voice of Beecher at Plymouth Church.

Friendship! This had been the torment of Henry's life also, a torment revealed to one confidant alone, the Journal, as the great lover confided it to his Leaves to be spread abroad. . . Always with this vast difference between their two aches: Walt was tormented because he could never be sufficiently intoxicated with it, while Henry suffered from a virtual powerlessness to express it at all.

A sad, sad story and so secret. To whom could this shy soul confide what was concealed behind the mask of his fierce reserve? The trees could not understand it, and they were his closest friends. So there remained only a white page that would receive the confession without blanching.

That the mean interests and commonplace cares of ordinary people should disgust and bore him was natural enough. Should he fall on his knees, beat his breast and bewail the demands of a stomach that cannot endure smugness and vulgarity? He is a mighty walker, he can roll off an infinite number of miles, splash about in a swamp or shovel snow for hours, weed in the blazing sun for a whole morning, split stumps as hard as iron: but your accursed society is utterly beyond him. Protest as you like. He is a lucky chap when he can afford to digest anything or anybody.

But with the few who are dear to him why is there so little real intimacy? As a rule, he finds nothing but disappointment in their company. He does not get into touch with them. He feels this too keenly not to suffer from it. Complete friendship, the only sort worthy of the name, is not the commonplace gossip of good neighbours; it asks to be able to go freely at all hours into your friend's house, without even the need of knocking. Give me the freedom of your friendship if you do not wish to make me unhappy.

With those whom, in spite of all, he calls his friends, Henry always has this feeling of painful dissatisfaction. His constraint paralyses him. He leaves their company still hungry for what he came to seek; so great is his discomfiture that he carries home with their strings untied the packages he had meant to open before them. They were things before which it would have been such a pleasure to marvel together. Is there any disenchantment equal to this? Instead of communing together and admiring one another, it is as if they had put each other out or wounded each other. It is a collision where it ought to have been a jubilee.

So he cares more for his friends at a distance where their image recovers its shape and petty things are forgotten. He is an over-exacting man: he refuses to have the most beautiful thing in the world profaned by being decked out in false ornaments. He insists that it must be absolutely naked, and thus he has only fleeting glimpses of it.

Why is this? Why this lack of sympathetic understanding between true friends? Is it their fault? Do they lack naturalness or sincerity? Do they encumber friendship with compliments, manners or shallow words? Or is it his fault, this fault he imputes to others? Would his friends, by any chance, like him to be a little different?

They have often complained that he is stiff, abrupt, that he remains silent when they expect him to say something. They are not over-fond of his rather crabbed way of speaking the truth and demanding it in return. Perhaps they are not entirely in the wrong. But does all the trouble, all his pain, come from these differences? They have known him for a long time, they know what a firm friend he is, and they are as willing to pardon his singularities as he is to forgive their habit of excessive sociability. Is he asking too much of them—a nobility that is impossible to human clay? Possibly; but even so there must be something else that he has forgotten in scrutinizing his conscience.

Come, my friend, what is it you complain of to your confidant in the evening? That your friends are this or that instead of being their own natural selves, that they answer so incompletely to what you expect of them? You are wounded, you are hurt because they seem to turn up their noses at the good things you were bringing them, and it is not a wound to your pride, it is not just a question of wretched vanity. It is much more serious than that—you are wounded in your affections, poor Henry. . .

Well, but how about yourself? Are you so sure that you respond to their expectations? Suppose, instead of withdrawing into your shell, at the least discord, you were simply to accept what they have to offer you? Suppose you were to show them a little indulgence? Instead, you roughly pull away. Must it always necessarily be they who take the first step? You insist that they should come and seek you out in the depths of your den, after opening as many locks as if it were an enchanted palace. And suppose they haven't the key, suppose they don't know the open sesame? You expect your friends to be magicians, seers who can divine the warmth hidden far down beneath that icy exterior. All very well, no doubt; but tell us, you who left the door of your cabin at Walden open to all comers, why you lock yourself up in this fashion. What robbers do you fear? You can see for yourself that this is no philistine who stands before you, that his face is the face of a friend. You can be frank, you can speak out that desire you have in you—which is going to cause you pain later just because you have obliged it to remain silent and it has its own way of protesting. To no indifferent person, rest assured, will you be showing your gifts.

There you are, so unhappy, with your affectionate impulses shattered, leaving your friend with the feeling that you have been simply an intruder. Are you so sure he would have disappointed you so if you had taken out your specimens, mystery-maker—if you had merely offered him what you brought, offered it simply, directly? You refuse to explain yourself because it is humiliating. Friends don't explain, they understand. No doubt; but suppose your attitude took the place of an explanation, made it unnecessary, dissipated the cloud? Instead of looking for reasons and fining them down like a casuist, suppose you tried to give a little of yourself? Just a little, why not?

You stand there, frozen, waiting—waiting for what?—with that bashfulness, that infernal bashfulness that makes you shrink back from your chin to your fingers instead of making the gesture the other may be waiting for—whatever it may be, a touch on the shoulder, a glance from those eyes that you keep lowered as if you were planning some dreadful deed, a handclasp long enough to establish the contact, long enough for the current to begin to flow. . . Don't you realize, subtle as you are, fool that you have suddenly become, the importance of a little familiar gesture that will set you both free? Come, you who are so brave, so resolute in attack, you who profess to be liberating men who are prisoners of their own sordid existence, confess that you lack the courage. . . .

You should live your friendship a little, you should put into practice the principles of that exalted affection which you say cannot be satisfied among men, live it instead of singing its praises, you infernal New England prude! Your hands are skilful enough for anything, except when it comes to friendship—hands that are so delicate when they pick a frail little flower and so clumsy when they lift this plant that thrusts its pale roots into you. You can't stick this in the lining of your hat where you carry your most fragile discoveries. . . .

Yes, they may have their faults, your friends. They may be too intelligent to understand. They have a gift for whetting your spirit of contradiction, which is so destructive of friendship. But don't you see that you, with your antagonism, are most to blame? You who do not lay aside at the outset, like an objectless accessory in a friendly house, the mask of that provoking, that insupportable chilliness? If you are not "incapable of expansion and generosity," why do you keep all these treasures hidden for your own morose delectation, why are you so absurdly timorous, so savagely bashful? When you have given your hand, why do you withdraw it so quickly, as if your precious ego were in danger of dissolving in the warmth of another palm? Suspicious! Distrustful! Infernal idiot! Barbarian, barbarian, barbarian, who suffer and triumph in being what you are! . . . Don't accuse others till you have accused yourself.

Whether the fault is his or theirs, it is very sad in any case. At times this man who is so rich feels very poor indeed, and all the joy of the river, all the friendship of the woods does not suffice to fill the void in this imploring heart.

What a tragedy, for instance, in his relations with his oldest, his greatest friend, lies behind the appearance of the most harmonious understanding. . . The one man in all the world to whom he is bound by the brightest hours of his life . . . the light of his youth . . . not to be able to love him as he would like to love him, completely, because . . . because . . . Waldo and Henry cannot quite mingle, as the names of Eden and Waldo mingle in Walden.

Because Waldo—the flower of a long line of ministers, so rich a flower in the garland which the established order wears on its brow—is offended by inelegances that clash with his philosophical decorum, a decorum full of grace and suave respect for the venerable conventions. Because a dry, unalterable "no," rebellion carried even into the smallest details, the frank assumption of the character of a bad citizen, revolutionary language ruffle his serenity. And because Henry, on his side, is irritated, cannot approve of that timidity, that spirit of com- promise, and will never believe that instead of showing your disgust for what is disgusting you should cover it up with cream sauce and ask people to taste it.

Because, as an illustrious Sage, the elder, with his delightful smile, slightly—oh! so slightly—patronizes his junior, this dear, crabbed, odd, aggressive Henry, this cool iconoclast in whom he recognizes a force superior to his own that he would like to mollify, bring into line, civilize. This dear Henry who does not want to have the smile that would comfort his friend Waldo and, like the latter's, electrify an audience instead of petrifying it. This dear Henry who is galled by any touch of protectiveness, faint as it may be, and con- ceives of friendship as the region of equals. This dear Henry who had not waited till a great Sage came to illuminate Concord in order to exist himself, who is not the sort to allow himself to be worked up like all those visionaries whom the dazzling Star attracts. Make no mistake, dear Waldo. Yet there is nothing to prevent us from being very fond of each other, even if we do wound each other.

Because almost insensibly Henry feels each day a little further from Waldo, further from his tastes, his habits and the people who surround him, the more pro- nounced his own personality becomes, the more it reacts and frees itself from the influences of his twentieth year . . . till he refuses to write an article on his great friend which Greeley has been asking him to write for years and has accepted in advance . . . till he at last realizes the uselessness of those conversations from which each comes away disappointed with the other . . . till there are longer and longer intervals between those visits to the little white house that merely waste

his time and cause him pain . . . till the day comes
when the distance is so great that Henry confesses it is
dead, the beautiful friendship, that it lies there, motionless as a corpse, on a bed of twenty years. . . .

For years he had seen this moment coming, but when
it was there, in all the harshness of the confession, what
a rent it made! The face of the dead on that couch
spoke of happy hours passed by the fireside, of those
trees and that garden he had cared for . . . spoke of
those walks together, that confidence, that life side by
side. Henry felt an intense pain in his head, in his chest,
which prevented him from working and grew worse
towards evening. In the confusion, the infinite desolation of that black hour, all the friendship of all men
seemed to crumble. And yet at the very moment when
this affection was vanishing and he was bidding it farewell, why did he feel so strangely *near* the dead friend,
yes, in spite of everything, so near, with that pain in his
chest, that it was as if the friendship contained a touch
of the love that eludes death?

But all should not be lost for a man disappointed in
relations that intellectual tastes shared in common cannot
save from ruin. There remain his friends the simple
folk, whom he relishes with a natural sympathy, without any philosophical seasoning. With them, at least,
Henry feels at ease. No more than himself do they enjoy the consideration of the world. They are untainted
by manners. With them he can visit freely back and
forth. Here he can go straight ahead. And look at
him. . . He watches them, in silent satisfaction—from
a distance. What a good sort that fellow is, how close
akin to him you feel. . . At a distance Henry admires
them, they go straight to his heart; but does he take a
step towards them? Never. And why? What is it that
restrains him from following his inclination and seeing

whither it leads? Among these people are familiar and friendly faces to whom he has never addressed a word in his whole life, whose very names are unknown to him. The rover who respects neither wall nor hedge but walks directly to his goal remains obstinately on the borders of a land—beautiful, as it seems to him—where he does not dare to venture.

Strange reserve! Why deprive yourself of the offered feast, epicure of huckleberries, epicure of a humanity that you are content to eat with your eyes? One might think you were afraid of all contact, afraid that everything would be spoiled if you rubbed shoulders with anyone else. Where are those senses of yours that are so fine, so alert, so eager to possess things? Do they hold prisoner among them the sense of attachment? Well, there are so many beautiful things that your intellect grasps but that you do not know how to untie, strange man who watch men and women whom you would like go by, and remain apart, with your tenderness under lock and key.

Strange or not, it is so, and when you are a Stoic, you stifle your secret and your grief and go on your way as if everything in the world were just right. If there are no friends to visit, give them up. You can visit them in thought, and they will come in the same way and join you in your walks: only so can you feel really close to them. If they do not understand that for some people friendship is as serious a passion as love, if they find you cold, nature at least will welcome you without vain words. With her you do not feel an intruder; you and she do not irritate each other; she never disappoints you or provokes a "no"; she never sends you away with your enthusiasms crushed. And so you exaggerate your stiffness, you swagger, you carry your head high, even when you are alone with yourself. You are a happy mortal who has rid yourself of men; you feast on solitude; it has a taste of nuts and sour apples; you laud it to the skies. It is a heroic remedy. You may not always succeed in deceiving yourself. You are not always the dupe of these pathetic boasts. But this makes no difference. You are a savage who leaves these idiots of civilized people to eat the dust of the highway. It is beautiful, this wild life, and you are proud of it, even if it sometimes makes a shy, silent fellow suffer. You are that happy man, made in the image of Walden Pond, self-sufficient, having no communication with the impure waters about it, smooth and serene—yet dreaming perhaps, now and again in the evening, dreaming in its depths of the running, singing waters with which it would be so good to run and sing, thinking how sad it is to be unable to mingle its life with that of the neighbouring ponds, its brothers. You are as rigid and as pure as the ice that encloses it in winter.

And so, because of that impotence from which you suffer, you are regarded as a misanthrope—just as a deaf man is thought to be unsociable. Hear that without laughing, enemy of the human race, you who can laugh, at your own times, so heartily.

To carry every day, over all the paths of the waste lands, like a burden you could not do without, your anxious care for men. To return from your ramble, with the thought sticking to you like a bur. To cherish Nature in your heart and consecrate to her your best hours because there is no friend in the world who, like this companion, gives you the savour of your own humanity, yours and that of all your kind. Not to despair of others or of this world, even in the moments when you are bitterest in your scorn—though it would be so easy to send it to the devil and go your way whistling, with your hands in your pockets. To feel yourself strong enough to build a tower on a little fragment of love, ever so precarious and disillusioned but so hardy. To carry with you that longing for a land where these people who irritate you would have become a society after your own heart. (Does not a mere bonfire of dead leaves in the country bring you the news from that land?) To try your very best to find new words to make your neighbour understand that he should open his window and let in a breath of the out-of-doors while he is working. To have planned for the title-page of your book a cock waking up the neighbours before dawn and dragging them out of the slumber they call their existence. Yes, and then to find yourself described as a cynical egoist, to figure among your kind as the perfect skulker . . . Henry, the echo of your laugh sounds at last on the shore of the encircled pond—sounds and salutes this disguise in which you see yourself decked!

And this is your portrait. What can you expect? So it is, so you have willed it. It is a beautiful portrait. The only objection is that it is so unlike you. Perhaps they are going to use it as the frontispiece of your book. You are the enemy of men when you have much to give and do not know how to give it—when you seek your brothers and do not find them, or find them so rarely, on such false terms. The enemy of men, with these yearnings repressed (oh, so stoically repressed!), this secret hunger which you would not confess for the whole empire of the Indies—with that need of love crowded into your meagre chest, and finding vent at times in spite of you.

VIII

A special session at the Boston Court-house, where the Supreme Court is sitting under the protection of the militia. Free men are judging a man-tool, the property of another man. Perhaps, under his black skin and his woolly hair, the tool has a kind of soul—you never can tell: but since he has run away, the tribunal ordains, in its sovereign independence, that he shall be returned to the hands of his master. If, weary of digging up your ground, a hoe for which you have paid with your good money should take it into its head one fine evening to scamper off, what would you say? The article that has vanished should be restored to its rightful owner. The law is sacred and the judges are there to apply it without flinching. There is no joking with these respectable judges of the Boston Court-house. They have very grave faces with white skins and not the least suggestion of wool on their skulls. They represent His Majesty the Right and His Holiness the Moral.

Are you surprised? Then where do you come from? Don't you know how little it matters before the law whether you are innocent or guilty? The important thing is not you but respect for the law. The judge is there to grind out his judgments, the notes are printed in the record, and at the end of the month the fees fall with all the precision of music. And you fail to take this way of administering justice seriously? You feel no respect for this machine?

Henry's chief feeling was one of humiliation. He had never cherished any great illusions about judges and justice, and in a similar case three years before he had

297

received a painful shock. But this judgment was beyond anything. *Walden* was appearing at this moment, and the book was utterly forgotten in the thought of this negro whom they were cold-bloodedly sending back to his master, like a package. The solemnity of the judgment added to this redelivery of the stolen article a sort of diabolical pomp. In any case, another theft had been committed, for Henry perceived that they had taken from him an essential part of himself. In vain had he tried to find among the friendly fields forgetfulness of these unclean human beings; they had lost their charm for him, for the baseness of men had blighted them. The "enemy of the human race" came back from his walks utterly unable to regain his serenity. He was haunted by the thought of those men who were in prison for having tried to mob the court and snatch the "package" out of its hands. He almost envied those fellows. An honest man belonged in prison in these times of ignominy: at large, he felt almost an accomplice in the legal crime. As he thought of it, Henry's hand went through the motions of touching off a bomb that would send the machine and the machinists to the devil.

You strange fellow, what concern is it of yours—one negro more or less from the plantations of the South? Are you mad? He is just as much merchandise as a barrel of molasses; he can be sold and used up, but he has got to stay in the shop of the man who has paid his good money for him. Besides, all this business is going on a long way from your village: leave Boston and that good Virginia to their own affairs. Can't you see that, after a passing flutter, the people around you go on with their own little concerns? There is nothing so momentous in this affair to interfere with the thoughts of a solitary walker.

To write a few pages in his Journal, in the privacy of

his own soul, is no relief. Faces, not white pages, are what he needs to have before him in order to express his emotion. On the Fourth of July Henry goes to Framingham, where the friends of the cause are holding a meeting, and delivers there the most vigorous speech he has ever written (he never speaks *ex tempore*), the richest in blood and fire. The Chief Justice and the Governor of the State take part in the ceremony: the orator has not failed to bring these puppets along in his bag to produce them in his Punch and Judy show. The honourable Governor is playing dummy. Bang! A good rousing whack on his ear. That will teach him what it means to let the August Work of Justice follow its course. The honourable Governor refuses to hand in his resignation. A good smack in the face will root him out of his chair. The puppet catches it for being Governor; there is very little of him left. He gets all the raps on the nose that are intended for the slave-masters whose interests His Nothingness serves. And to crown the festival, they publicly burn the Constitution of the United States. The organizer of the meeting is William Lloyd Garrison, the veteran abolitionist, whom once the mob dragged through the streets of Boston at the end of a rope. This brave man, who is ready for anything, asks Henry for the text of the famous discourse so that he can publish it in his magazine, the *Liberator*.

Always that fierceness in resistance. Friends who entirely approve of Henry's purposes regard this violence, this extremism, as very unfortunate. Destroy, if you think it good to do so, but don't bring into it that savage conviction, as if you wanted to uproot the old tree of the earth. Keep at least a touch of scepticism. You make no effort to settle things by arrangement. Always this unsmiling gracelessness. See what an accomodating smile your old friend Waldo keeps. . . It's just like the time when you refused to pay your poll-tax and let them put you in jail, and your friends said it was "mean and in bad taste." Is not tolerance the proper thing in a philosopher? He should accept frauds, great and small, magnanimously, as one tolerates the faults of old friends. One shouldn't be so anti-Philistine as to scout all the respectabilities. One shouldn't declare, in this virulent way, one's utter contempt for the Church and the State. One shouldn't go about insisting that the State is the enemy of free, proud men and the natural protector of the basest elements of a people: officials, capitalists, flunkies, policemen, speculators, shop-keepers, money-makers, gospel-mongers. There are charming people in all these groups who are offended by this wholesale censure. And suppose you do consider this court-room—judges, lawyers, public, jury and all—just as criminal as the accused, is that any reason for calling down thunder on its head?

Do you never read the presidential messages in the newspapers? Perhaps you despise the newspapers too? Of course those who produce them are more interested in cultivating their subscribers than the truth, but is that any reason to lump them all together, the liberal ones included, as the "filthy press?" From your point of view, those sensational events which our friend the saloon-keeper confounds under the one name of "politics" are simply ridiculous beside a sunset watched from Fairhaven Cliffs where you go to get your evening paper and the latest news.

Just look at this pitiful specimen of a citizen who has nothing but a ridiculous "no" for his country in time of war! A war that brings the conqueror all sorts of booty is, he tells you bluntly, nothing but an expedition of brigands, sufficiently well armed to impose their will. A poor, silly isolated thief steals something and is put under lock and key, but if he swells to the proportions of an army he comes back, with flags flying and a band at the head of the procession, bombarded with flowers and hurrahs by respectable men and women. An evil deed, you see, becomes a great deed if it is conceived on a large enough scale: the enthusiasm excited by a war is the rapture of a childish people before this stupendous metamorphosis.

As for soldiers, Henry has no flowers for an idiot who, whether he is victor or vanquished, has allowed himself to be seduced by fine feathers and high pay. He has nothing but a glance to give him, enough to divine, under the automaton who fires to the right or left at command and would shoot his brother just as readily, a vestige of a man who is rather ashamed of the work he is made to do and would be only too happy to desert if he dared. The instruction which they give a soldier should logically lead him to distinguish his natural enemy, the instructor. But this professional brave man is a coward. For the sake of dressing up in a fine uniform, he has allowed himself to be stripped of his dignity as a man, just as some young fellows throw their pride to the winds for a foolish girl. Weak souls, unhappy souls. But in spite of all this there is less contempt than pity in the look he gives these fools, yes, even this masquerade of the militia with their puppets' gestures. Little as one may sympathise with their stupidity, everything that debases man is a menace that touches you in your own person.

You see how far a village good-for-nothing can carry his sarcasm—a lover of wild flowers and beautiful trees and the unknown things that might be equally beautiful. He is not responsible for his country, this "land of liberty" which is subject to the omnipotences of money and morality; he despises the majority and the ballot. He is no pistareen-patriot. He ought to take a lesson from his friend Walt Whitman, whom he has seen in Brooklyn and admires—Walt who stands whole-heartedly for the flag and for war to a finish, brigand war or holy war. . . Henry has not read his articles in that wretched Brooklyn sheet, for he never reads the papers at all. It's a great pity. Walt is not the man to belittle the National Honour and cynically ask to see this interesting creature of which they are talking in the newspapers.

Henry had never met this famous bird on his walks, or that other chanticleer, National Sentiment. Among his own people, among those whom he would like to regard as his compatriots, even among those who are nearest to him, he often feels as lost as among strangers. The prejudices of colour and the flag do not correspond with anything in his geography. Whether you are an American or a South Sea Islander, whether you wear a cap or a turban, whether your hair is in a queue or parted on the side is all one to him. All he asks is, Are you a man, and what can you do? Play me a little of your music, and I shall know. A man, you under-stand; that comes first, first. You can tell me later what kind of dessert you like or what your nationality is, if you have a moment to spare: those things are very inter-esting, of course, but begin with essentials. Talk music.

You see? . . . How can anybody hit it off with a fellow who defends his ideas in this revolutionary way? Henry has only one excuse. If there is in his sarcasms something more than the pride of a solitary man and the revolt of the individual, it is because he feels and speaks as a man whose hands know certain things that philos-ophers do not know. He has not allowed himself to be caught up in the machinery of the workaday world, but he has had to drudge just the same. He knows better than by hearsay what it means to be exploited. Of all those lies that other people complacently accept, sweetening them with the honey of a lofty philosophy, he has felt the effects in his own person ever since he left college. A man who works with his hands for wages has definite and personal reasons for criticising these lies a little more sharply than a humanist in his study or a journalist at his editorial desk. The elements and materials he has touched have given him a sensibility of a subtler kind. "*The callous palms of the labourer are conversant with finer tissues of self-respect and heroism, whose touch thrills the heart, than the languid fingers of idleness.*" This quality, whether he wills it or not, gives him the more fraternal accent of the comrade of the poor. Is it a mere philosopher who, as he follows the railroad that skirts Walden, can ask, as he places his foot on a sleeper, if it is not going to rise up, if every sleeper is not going to take the form of one of those hard-working Irishmen who have placed it there and over whom the train passes at fixed hours, filled with people who roll comfortably along while the others are rolled over?

The older he grows the more sensitive Henry becomes to the injuries which, with the precision of a rite, the armed man inflicts upon the unarmed. The experience of life avails nothing; instead of blunting, it sharpens his susceptibility. That nameless one whom the Supreme Court in Boston has just sent off like a package is an intolerable humiliation—it is enough to blot out the five continents. It is the State burying its fangs in the flesh of a fugitive. The victim may not be a great philosopher, but he has nerves—like the distinguished Governor himself. His thick lips cannot afford to keep smiling.

In an age swollen with the sense of its own importance, this negro slavery was the most brutal form of the exploitation of man by man. Since Uncle Tom had

brought all the lovers of sentimental scenes and tears-in-
the-eyes flocking about his Cabin, the abolitionist prop-
aganda had made headway. Henry had joined in it
from afar, in his own way. To further the desertion of
the blacks, it had developed a whole secret organization,
the Underground Railroad, with its system, its branches,
switches, waiting-rooms, regulating station. Henry had
his share in the administration. He was station-master
at one of those little halting-places in the country where
only a few trains stop from time to time but that are all
the safer in the transit of smuggled goods. Concord
was only a middling-sized village, but it was one that
counted in no small way in the scheme of anti-slavery
sympathies. At the very dawn of the movement, when
Henry was just preparing to enter college, a society of
women had been founded there for the abolition of
slavery, and several particular friends of the family were
members of it. Ten years later, Wendell Phillips came
there, three winters in succession, and aroused the most
violent excitement in the village frog-pond by denouncing a Constitution that openly supported the ignominy.
If the old people were outraged and scandalised by this
audacity, the young were enraptured by it; Henry, at
that time secretary of the Lyceum, sent the *Liberator*
a paper on the first lecture. On August 1st, 1844, an
abolitionist meeting was held in the Court-house at
which Waldo had spoken. William Lloyd Garrison
was there, and Henry rang the bell to fling to the winds
the good news and the challenge.

The friends of the cause did not forget Concord in
their rounds. One of them, whom a friend introduced
to him in March, 1857, made a profound impression on
Henry. A big fellow in his fifties, round-shouldered,
grizzled, rough-hewn, with the rugosity that went with
the frontier type; he came from Kansas, in fact, where

with his sons he led, in those hazardous regions, the far from rose-coloured existence of a defender of the cause. And what a face he had. . . That mouth like a sabre-cut, the metal of those eyes, that stiff, projecting hair planted thick on the low, determined brow, those perpendicular wrinkles between the eyebrows, how much they told. . . You could imagine unforgettable figures like this in old times on a rowers' bench, chained by the feet. . . That astonishing face, hard as steel, stood out so magnificently from the crowd of weak masks—the face of a pirate, a condottiere or a martyr. Another one who did not smile.

Henry felt at once that he was in the presence of a member of his own family. They talked. But he did not need to be convinced by the arguments or the stories of what was going on out there on the frontier. This presence was enough for him: it carried conviction with it. What did it matter if the man talked like an illiterate, narrow-minded, old sanctimonious Puritan pietist? Henry looked at that face, that naked grandeur, that pure force of heroism and self-sacrifice. He drank in the wind that had swept that brow from its childhood, saw all that the horizon of the prairie had left in that glance. It was arranged that the man should come back to Concord and give a lecture. His name was John Brown—in other words, he was as good as nameless. You felt like saying simply the man, for short.

The little station-master acquitted himself of his duties with the decision and the punctuality which, as a ne'er-do-well, he always put into his work. They signalled to you that someone was on the way; you had to be there to receive the "package," before dawn or at nightfall, put him up if necessary, and in great mystery (the whole family was in the conspiracy and protected the fugitive, but evil tongues and spies were not lacking at

Concord any more than elsewhere), then quietly ship
him off again, to a safe place over the Canadian border.
Pass the ball. One more Southern planter would have
to make the best of his loss. Henry, a veteran with a
sure eye, had the qualities of a smuggler. You had
charge of a man with the police on his tracks, stimulated
by a "good reward," and while you were on the way
to get a ticket for him at the station you would notice a
man with a gallows-face roaming about, looking very
much like a sleuth from Boston; so you would decide to
wait for the next train. The runaway could stay a little
longer at the house, where he was in good hands. While
he was living at Walden, Henry had put one of them up
in his cabin. There were certainly risks in this smuggling
business. But when did risks ever weaken the resolution of an honest man? They strengthen it.

For the rest, Henry was an abolitionist of an altogether special kind, very far from orthodox. If the
exploitation of the negroes was the most patent form of
slavery, how many other slaves there were beyond the
horizon of the cotton-fields, everywhere, to infinity,
whom he would have liked to free. . . The views of the
Boston friends were limited by the famous Cabin. They
didn't see them increasing among the people of the
North, those white-skinned, thin-lipped, fair or chestnut-
haired slaves with heads anything but woolly! Henry
saw them all around him, innumerable and more brutal-
ized than he would have been able to say. He reckoned
fully a million of them in Massachusetts, without the
least suspicion of their state, poor souls—which was the
saddest part of the whole business.

When are you going to start a campaign to enable all
these white negroes to escape, these slaves who are so
busy under the eye of their overseers growing the evil
cotton from which the web of our days is woven? To

make them want to bid farewell for good and all to their servile habits and gestures? If people would listen to you, Henry, Canada would be so full that there would be no place to house them.

One morning such a big piece of news spread abroad that a man who never read the newspapers could not help glancing at it. It was the paper for October 18th, 1859. Henry read it. A handful of men, almost unarmed, had seized the Federal Arsenal at Harper's Ferry in Virginia during the night and intrenched themselves there, after making a prisoner of a colonel, the great-grand-nephew of George Washington; they had held it for twenty-four hours. A regular siege had been necessary to get the better of the rebels, or rather the survivors, for more than half of them had been killed. It was his friend John Brown's work. . . That morning and for days to come, Henry could devour more newspapers than his good father had nibbled in a whole lifetime.

But if John Brown had struck, it was not solely to enable his friend Thoreau to give at last the full measure of his egoism. Old Brown had more substantial reasons than that.

Henry saw again the face of the old peasant or galley-slave, the expression of the bluish eyes that brightened up when the man spoke of the cause. It was not six months since he had seen him the last time, and his image was as fresh as yesterday. Old Brown was wearing now a long white beard that gave him a patriarchal look. They had dined together at Henry's. Waldo had come over and the three had found themselves there together. In the evening Old Brown had spoken at the Town Hall; and as he told them how his son had been made prisoner by the Border Ruffians, he had even shown them the chain which the latter had made him wear. The effect was a little crude, but this man so excluded the idea of anything theatrical that you couldn't look at this gesture ironically. As for his plans, Henry had no anxiety at the time; you could have entire faith in such a figure as that.

Old Brown's plans. . . That was what had been suddenly revealed by the incident of the Arsenal, the long, long story of which that low brow and those inexorable eyes had spoken. Born in Connecticut, of good English and Dutch stock, he had found himself, a boy of five, cast in the middle of Ohio, whither his father, a penniless tanner, had come from New England to seek his fortune. A boy who grew up in buckskin trousers, among the animals and the friendly Indians; a sensitive boy who remained inconsolable after losing the only marble he had ever possessed; a boy who, at twelve, was already conducting cattle long distances and had learned just enough to read and reckon a little.

As a big lad of twenty, strong and serious, working in a tannery with his father, he appeared very shy and rather haughty. The Bible and the Church absorbed him, together with an anxious fear for the salvation of his soul, even suggesting to him for a while the idea of becoming a preacher. He married, moved his tannery to Pennsylvania, where he had no very brilliant success, ran into debt, remarried, returned to Ohio and set up in business with a partner. Another failure. He threw himself into land-speculation, went into bankruptcy, then, a poor, uncertain soul, tried any and every means of conjuring away his ill fortune. Long journeys took him across country, buying and selling cattle and sheep. In spite of everything, divine Providence did not assist John the Shepherd and his thirteen children—whom, as a brutally fierce believer, he ruled with a rod of iron:

little matter whether they had any education or not as long as they feared the Lord and his representative, their father. The wholesale sheep-trade which he followed for ten years with a partner ſtill failed to bring him prosperity, and at the end of their enterprise left him the same poor John as before. In incessant litigation with his creditors, always clumsy in business, he found himself loſt in a maze of speculations, plans, combines, and was not entirely free from those barely honeſt little trickeries to which the perfeĉt devotee does not refuse to ſtoop in order to save his worldly goods along with his soul.

It was in the midſt of these vicissitudes, as he was approaching his fortieth year, that an idea took possession of him, an idea that he revealed to his family, one evening, in the kitchen of the old farm in Ohio—to "break the jaws of the wicked and pluck the spoil out of his teeth." What he meant in his pietiſtic jargon was to free the blacks from slavery, and to free them by violence. From that moment John the Shepherd underwent a gradual transformation into Old Brown, Partisan and Freebooter. In Springfield, Massachusetts, he rented a little wooden house where he ſtored his wool; his principal objeĉt in coming there was to place himself in touch with the militants of Boſton, whose debating societies and philosophic views, for the reſt, intereſted him very little. Words, nothing but words. The sheep-raiser explained his programme to them. Brother Brown was going to ſtrike with a vengeance, rise openly againſt the authorities and crush those who resiſted. The direĉt route this time, no more Underground Railroads. It was in the South, on its own ground, that the slave-power muſt be attacked. Towards the time of his firſt visit to Concord, Old Brown, without taking anybody into his confidence, was already thinking, among

the important points he had in view, of that Arsenal
which was so well situated at the intersection of the
three States of Maryland, Pennsylvania and Virginia.
After this, he pondered his plan, perfected it, minutely
prepared to carry it out. But in the meantime, as he had
to live, and the market-price of wool had fallen because
of the war, he embarked for Europe, where he hoped to
make an advantageous sale. London—Paris—Brus-
sels—Hamburg: it was a very fine journey for a
Westerner, but the traveller had carried his old bad luck
along with him in his bag; he was obliged to sell his
bales of wool at ridiculous prices. From Europe he
returned with a loss of $40,000 for his partner and him-
self and the still more firmly fixed reputation of a man
who had no understanding of business.

Then, one fine day, he bade farewell to trade and
went off and established his family in the midst of the
solitude of the Adirondacks, at North Elba. He would
go and see them up there when he had the time, for he
was almost always in Kansas, where three of his older
sons were settled and his mission claimed him. The
Border was his sphere; he was at the front there, in
contact with the enemy—the slaver. Business, litigation,
cattle, the price of wool, all these things counted for
nothing now in Old Brown's mind: it was as if the
victim of eternal combines, the old veteran upon whom
earthly fortune had been unwilling to smile, was meditating a last stroke of business, a supreme speculation,
in which he would risk everything, even his skin, without regret, for the triumph of a great cause—would
sacrifice as a visionary the rest of his mortal life, the rest
of this rough, storm-tossed, agitated life, for a beautiful
share of eternity. . .

Thanks to all this travelling about, managing men and
animals and hides and wool and pushing his famous

plan, he was clothed with a kind of authority that impressed people. He was going to find this useful enough in holding his own with the Border Ruffians who roamed about the country, well-armed, in their red or blue flannel shirts, with a dagger boldly thrust through their leather belts, with an unspeakably villainous air— cut-throats in the pay of the planters, who were determined to remain the masters in their own house and protect the free disposal of their black work-hands. To earn his living, he did surveying, a trade that permitted him to study the ground in more ways than one. Between whiles, there were surprises—hangings, lynchings, tar-and-featherings, raids, cold-blooded butcheries with the sabre—all work for a soldier.

Old Brown was appropriately free from sentimentality. For instance, to avenge the abominable sacking of Lawrence, when the partisans of a Free Kansas had allowed themselves to be trampled upon like cowards by their enemies, he arranged a little party of his own. With a sort of company of which he was captain and cook, he intended to show these swine that they were not always going to triumph with impunity and spread among the band a wholesome terror. In the old man's camp, they sharpened the cutlasses on the grindstone and got ready for business. A list had been drawn up of the condemned persons who were to pay for all the rabble. While he was getting ready, one of his companions who was a little anxious came and recommended caution to the chief. The latter replied: "Caution, caution, sir. I am eternally tired of hearing that word caution. It is nothing but the word of cowardice." The chief was greatly excited and ready for anything. Forward, men; let the cowards stay behind.

They were soon there; the little troop collected for a moment not far from Pottawatomie, where the birds they were going to catch had their nest. There were three brothers here, Germans by birth, known for their pro-slavery sympathies—big brutes with whom he had already had a bone to pick as a neighbour, together with a family of poor devils from Tennessee, a father and his two grown sons, who had followed the lead of the Germans. There was also a member of that pseudo-Legislative Assembly which claimed to rule the State in the name of the slave-holders. At ten o'clock in the evening the little troop got under way, taking all precautions. They knocked at the door of the Tennesseeans, made the father and his two sons come out, conducted them two hundred yards from the house and cold-bloodedly put them to the sword. A bullet in the father to finish the business and make it surer. One of the two brothers who had offered resistance had his arms cut off, his body mangled, his skull torn open, a hole in the jaw. All this made less noise than a musket volley; it was a thorough job, swift and stimulating. A little further away, at midnight, at the " Representative's" house, a similar scene. The wife was ill with measles; the condemned man asked to be allowed to stay with her till they found someone to look after her. "It matters not," said Old Brown; "you have neighbours." And he did not even allow the man to pull on his boots. Off with him. Shortly afterwards the "Representative" lay in a thicket, with his head and side run through; they had sent him to represent his friends the slave-holders in the Legislative Assembly on high. There remained the three Germans, one of whom turned out to be spending the night with neighbours. The same ceremonial. The next day he was found in the ravine, with his skull split in two places and half emptied, a hole in his chest, his right hand cut off, hanging to the wrist by a rag of skin. The work finished, they went off

and washed their sabres in the river and the butchers
started for home, rather disgusted. They needed some
good hot coffee to settle their nerves. But it was all in
the day's work and Old Brown regretted nothing.

The hand of the Lord had smitten these infidels a
little roughly. These were the ways of the frontier,
where sober notions of good and evil were not in vogue.
But one of the sons of Old Brown who took part in
the expedition lacked the iron nerves of the old man,
although his Christian name was John also. The night
after the deed, returning half out of his wits to the
house of an uncle, he cried to his brother Owen, who had
joined him: "Out with you, you filthy murderer. . ."
and then wandered off into the brush, his poor mind
gone. . . With Jason, another of his brothers, the
demented man was soon captured by the Ruffians, who
had hurried out in search of them. Jason saw the rope
that was about to encircle his neck hanging from a tree
over his head. But for days and days, both of them,
chained together by their ankles, their hands tied like
convicts, were led about the roads, while John, who had
not recovered his right mind, imagined that he was the
officer in charge of the troop, shouted his commands and
told his keepers how they ought to kill his brother, the
stammerer. And the Ruffians of the guard bullied and
tortured their prisoners with all the more zest because
they thought the poor madman was pretending. During
all this time they were scouring the region to dislodge
Old Brown, who was actually not far away. He was
roaming about in the neighbourhood, waiting for an
opportunity to free his two boys. But it was impossible
to lay hands on him. With four of his other sons and a
few faithful followers, he had gained the brush. He had
also gained the reputation of a bird whose feathers it
was not good to stroke and who could not be safely

approached without plenty of precautions. Be sufficiently energetic and people will respect you. When
they shouted in the fields: "Look out! There's Old
Brown!" well-armed people whom you would have
supposed were brave, if only because of their numbers,
ran as if the devil were coming out of the bushes. Old
Brown had become a bugbear. And years followed,
full of guerilla warfare, raids and forays, and through
them passed a man on horseback or marching along
with bent shoulders beside a wagon, who was now here,
now there, but never where you expected to catch him.
You could burn, destroy the village where he had his
headquarters, but to catch the Old Man was another
pair of breeches.

A new stage in the march towards the goal which Old
Brown had fixed. He published a tract in which he urged
the army to disobey orders, "respectfully and amicably
offered to the Officers and Soldiers of the American
Army in Kansas." He summed up his argument in these
words: "It is as much the duty of the common soldier
of the U. S. Army, according to his ability and opportunity, to be informed upon all subjects in any way
affecting the political or general welfare of his country,
and to watch with jealous vigilance the course and
management of all public functionaries both civil and
military; and to govern his actions as a citizen soldier
accordingly: as though he were President of the United
States." This appeal, signed "A Soldier," did not win
the approval of the friends in Boston; but the Old Man
could get along without their approval. The Old Man
was collecting his wits for a still more serious action.
He set to work, quietly, to instruct a little troop of
voluntary followers. His war budget was not very
heavy, and often he had not enough to eat. Then, on
a brief raid in Missouri, he entered a planter's house,

revolver in hand, killed another man, freed the slaves, ransacked the dwelling, took two prisoners. All this just to keep his hand in. In mid-winter, with a single companion, the Old Man travelled more than six hundred miles escorting to Canada a wagon full of negro women and children; his fingers and his ears were frozen, but his skin was tough and he could stand it. There was a constant reward of $3000 for anyone who arrested him. It was worth the effort, but no one interfered with him, even when on one occasion Old Brown calmly entered a town, made a speech, and calmly went off again, after a glance at the handbills in big letters in which his admirers were invited to capture him. Didn't anyone want $3000?

Much later, on the night of October 16th–17th, a wagon descended the hill which, on the Maryland side, leads to the peninsula where Harper's Ferry rises, formed by the confluence of the two rivers. The horse stiffened its legs, for the wagon was full of pikes and ammunition. A round-shouldered old man with a white beard and eighteen other men accompanied the convoy. The plan, matured through long years, was being executed. It had definitely ceased to be a question of Uncle Tom and his Cabin; it was a question now of bayonets and bullets. Do you understand, Boston friends?

The plan was to surprise and carry the place, cost what it might. And then, who could say? . . . Once masters of this important point, they could fortify themselves in the mountains, the blacks would rise, they would run from all the cotton fields; they would arm (they had pikes—a thousand of them, specially made), and there would be a general conflagration, the war carried into Africa. They would establish a provisional government, of which the constitution was already drawn up on paper and the principal parts were assigned. There was $600 in the treasury.

Meanwhile, the little troop advanced, made a prisoner of the watchman on the bridge, who thought it was a joke, a few passers-by, and then the janitor of the armory, which they entered with the game all in their own hands. John Brown's company were masters of the Arsenal, in the dead of night. The hardest part was over; from this point they could strike out. Five miles off, on the heights of Bolivar, there lived a landed proprietor, a slave-holder who was no other than Colonel Lewis Washington, a descendant of the great man. He had in his possession the pistol given by Lafayette and the sword presented by Frederick the Great to the Liberator. At midnight, by the flickering light of a torch, the colonel saw, outlined against the door of his bedroom, four armed men who informed him that he was their prisoner and ordered him to hand to one of them—a black—the sword of the Great Frederick. Then they courteously conducted the colonel away in his own carriage, made the slaves climb into a big wagon, and the procession turned towards the Arsenal. They stopped on the way at a neighbour's, where the scene was repeated. The latter was also treated to a ride, with his six blacks. At the Arsenal Old Brown distributed the pikes to the negroes, placed them in charge of their former masters and thus addressed the colonel: "I shall be very attentive to you, sir, for I may get the worst of it in my first encounter, and if so, your life is worth as much as mine." Then the Old Man calmly girded himself with the sword of Frederick the Great. The trains were stopped on the bridge where he had placed a guard. The alarm was given. The fire-bell rang. The good citizens of the little town took down their shot-guns, since the more formidable weapons were in the hands of the rebels. The Old Man, very much master of himself, ordered breakfast for forty-five persons at the hotel nearby. And the day rose on this astonishing victory, as clean as the Liberator's sword.

Twenty-four hours later, in the engine-room, Old Brown, his body torn with bayonet thrusts, his head gashed, his hair matted and his face stained with blood, was stretched out with his son Oliver, who had ceased to beg them to kill him, motionless at his side, and his other son Watson dying. Of the twenty-one men involved in the raid only four remained who were alive. Seven had escaped, including those who had remained at the farm to guard the stock of arms and two of those who had occupied the Arsenal, who had succeeded in getting away during the night. And on a rock, in the middle of the Potomac, was the huddled body of the youngest of the company, a boy of eighteen who, while he was attempting to escape by swimming, had been overtaken and riddled with bullets. There his body was, perched in mid-stream, a fine target for the troops that had passed in the afternoon. It was altogether too tempting for everybody not to take a shot at it before dropping in for a drink at the hotel, which had made a lot of money to-day. In the bed of the river lay another corpse, and as it was not very deep in that spot they could see it clearly, with its face drawn in death and seeming to move with the water. Another fine target for the clever sharpshooters: this man too was one of the companions of the raid.

In the Arsenal they were waiting for the Governor of Virginia. Already officers, reporters, congressmen, curiosity-seekers were filing past the Rebel, lying there on his mattress. Old Brown did not look at all like a man who had been beaten; he spoke calmly, weighing his words, as if he were at home on his old farm. Meanwhile, the town began to be filled with shouts, brawls and a general fanfaronade in preparation for the saturnalia when the militia and the brave population would be fraternizing in an orgy of victory.

Henry was agitated to the depths of his soul, depths that one might have supposed were better sheltered from squalls. Agitated at the thought of the gallows-rope strangling the tough neck of his friend Old Brown. Agitated by the cowardice of the worthy disciples with all their good intentions who, since the raid, the crime against the safety of the State, had run for cover, desperately disavowing the rebel. . . No, gentlemen, no, gentlemen, we hadn't the faintest suspicion of it; you can see we are as white as snow. . . It was a stampede of runaways, a chorus of denials. Even the *Liberator* treated the raid as an act of madness. Not one of these people was capable of seeing how beautiful it was, just because it was mad—with a madness that purged the world of its reasonable reason! The Knight of the Umbrella and the Bundle had always been for madnesses like this against the niggardly prudence of the sham humanitarians. That obstinate, that furious old lunatic, with his hobby of carrying the war into Africa, had actually carried it there. That old Trojan who continued to believe, with a belief as tough as a stump, in other realities than the price of wool, who was ready to sacrifice himself for an idea. . . He himself had staked his fortune on a folly. John Brown, murderer or madman, was a brother. And that brother was going to be hanged.

In Henry's innermost sanctuary there was no security left—the gods were tottering on their socles. It was no longer possible to think of anything else, to resume the thread of one's dear old thoughts. Nothing but a few passages from the greateſt poems corresponded with the obsession of this hour and seemed to meet the circumſtances. When he went out his ramble was finished before it had begun: what was waiting for him at the end of his solitary walk rose up, from the moment he set out, to demand its due. His eyes no longer saw what they had seen; when he lifted his head, he saw rising againſt the woods a face with a low brow and bluish grey eyes, the hard face of the old cattle-driver, the driver of a whole people towards the Promised Land, the face of the martyr, imposing silence on all nature. The sun set behind a gibbet. Wachusett, over there, was like a judge delivering a sentence. The beauty of the world could no longer vie with this beauty of the man who was dying for a mad cause.

Henry was unable to sleep. At night, he would relight his candle, seize a scrap of paper within reach of his hand and cover it with lines. No event, near or far, had ever inflamed him to this degree. He was another Henry, unknown to himself. Old Brown, what have you done to a man who had such a beautiful equanimity and such a disdain for the affairs of the world? What power is this within you that can arouse such a mad passion? You have thrown him into a pitiable ſtate. He is much less ſtrong than another fellow who lives in Brooklyn and whom your fate does not prevent from eating and sleeping. For this latter at leaſt a man who is going to be hanged for his crime does not blot out the universe; luckily for him, he remains the maſter of his serenity. He is not like Henry, aſtonished at the sight of all these villagers, these good citizens who have the heart to go about their little affairs, as if nothing were burning their vitals. For him the whole life of the world seems to be in abeyance, as on the eve of a cataclysm. Will it not rise in one mass to free this upright man and avenge his defeat? The wildness in Henry's soul is boiling up, boiling over with rebellion; it runs to Harper's Ferry and bars the exits of the Arsenal.

He must speak, and at once, dissociate himself from these wavering souls, these cowards, utter all his admiration for the criminal, while the latter is still alive. For they have condemned him hastily, in all the heat of public indignation, as an altogether special criminal. They have actually had to carry him into court on a stretcher because of his wounds, of which those in his head have made him half deaf. And they are waiting, from one day to another, to pronounce the sentence. It is vain to tell Henry that he is mad, that he is almost alone in his opinion, for a man who, alone, rushes to the defence of a friend, marches surrounded by a whole army. To counsels of caution he replies as Old Brown replied at Pottawatomie. To hell with your caution, you skulkers.

Henry announced that he would speak the following Sunday, October 30th, in the vestry of the parish church. At the last moment, when some advisers still tried to stop him, he replied roughly: "I did not send to you for advice, but to announce that I am to speak." And he spoke. The defence had succeeded in causing a postponement of the sentence, but there was no doubt what it would be. Henry's object, however, was not to save Old Brown's neck; it was merely to celebrate the beauty of his character and his act. Henry Thoreau, fool of nature and the beauty in man, as Hokusai in his Japan was the fool of drawing, was ready to maintain against the whole world that John Brown, his friend, convicted of high treason, was right, and this to the very foot of the gallows if they judged him worthy of being hanged also. That is what beauty means, that is what friend-

ship means. It does not consist in lending you half a
dollar in case of need or an umbrella if it happens to
rain. It consists in accepting blows of your own free
will and bearing witness at any risk. In not letting go
of your own kind if he has fallen into the hands of the
enemy. Henry spoke. His listeners were all ears. It
was no philosophical lecture this time. There may have
been a few stifled growls in certain corners of the hall.
But no one protested. It was as if his conviction had
stirred that soft dough. When it was over, the few
rabid people were no longer talking of the gallows
for John Brown: they held their peace. The general impression was excellent. One good mark for
Concord.

Henry was very anxious to repeat his "plea" at
Worcester, where his friend Blake lived. He would
have liked to repeat it without remuneration in every
county in New England. Meanwhile, he spoke in
Boston, two days after Concord. It was November
1st; the sentence had not yet been pronounced. Perhaps
it would be to-morrow. Half an hour before the moment
set for the lecture, the hall was full. For an hour and a
half the people listened religiously to this fervent little
man who, far from attempting to excuse the crime,
celebrated it. Henry had more expression and enthusiasm than usual. He was no longer a man bored with
the necessity of uttering fine-spun sarcasms and over-
concise aphorisms before rows and rows of eyes that
could not make him out at all: he was an embattled
soul, stirred by friendship and emotion. There was
electricity in the air and in the applause. Even in his
casual remarks before and after the lecture it was as if he
had lost all his old savage shyness and discovered how
to communicate with men. Henry spoke fluently, in a
tone of exaltation, thundered against the Union, the

President, the State. It was as if there were no more barriers left.

As for Old Brown, in his prison at Charlestown, nothing remained for him, after the sittings of the court, but to lend himself to the little ceremony that was being arranged in his honour. He was preparing for it with no ill grace; was it not the final touch of the great plan that bore his signature? He had formally refused to countenance any attempt of his followers to enable him to escape. If they left the prison door wide open he would not go out; he had made this statement to the warden, who was a very kind man. John Brown was an obstinate old soul. Even his wife, who had come down from North Elba and was in the neighbourhood, was obliged, the first time, to go away without seeing him, broken-hearted but well aware that nothing could avail against the will of the Old Man; this will might have weakened at the farewell scene. He had only consented to see her yesterday, at the last extremity. The warden had invited them both to his own family table. When the time came to part, after these too happy moments, the Old Man would have liked to keep her longer. But they had had to bid each other good-bye, agreeing to meet again at Harper's Ferry; she was going to wait there for his body, which was to be turned over to her. The condemned man had spent his time, since the sentence, writing letters in his peasant hand to his friends. "Yesterday Nov. 2nd I was sentenced to be hanged on Dec. 2nd next. Do not grieve on my account. I am still quite cheerful. God bless you all." It was a whole month now since he had been condemned to death; his wounds were healed, and it would have been good not to be lying idle in prison. A true old stager is bored by this inactivity.

On December 2nd, in the morning, he left his cell,

surrounded by uniforms. It was a clear dawn and mild enough for the season. As far as he could see, on all sides, there were massed troops as if for the arrival of some great personage. Old Brown was a little surprised; he had had no idea he was so important. A van was waiting for him. He was only fifty-nine years old, but as he climbed into the wagon he had the air of a very old man; his white beard, which he had clipped a little for the raid, completed his patriarchal appearance. That box there in the ·van was quite long enough to serve as a bench for three persons, and he sat down between his friend the warden and the sheriff on his coffin.

The man they had come for was as calm as a traveller who had come out to see the country after having kept in his room for six weeks. Perhaps he was thinking that his laſt great combine was not ending so badly for him, on the whole, since, at the coſt of a few seconds of fluttering at the end of a rope, he could see as far as the eye could reach fields golden as glory. But nothing actually lay before him save the winter landscape of the valley. "What a beautiful country this is," he said. "I have never been down this way before." The journey was not long. They were there at laſt. Old Brown climbed down, more briskly than he had climbed up, and ascended the ſteps of the scaffold, from which he descried the Blue Ridge Mountains. It was a spectacle to fill eyes that had taken in many horizons during their lifetime. When he became once more aware of the scaffold, he shook hands with the warden and the sheriff. Then they pulled the cap over his head, tied his arms behind his back and passed the noose around his neck, taking care not to let it catch in his beard. In his old trousers, in his old slippers, Old Brown ſtood upright there, as if he were in command of the three parade companies who were taking ten minutes to find their places. Perhaps he was counting these minutes, but nothing appeared from under his cap. In a natural voice, he merely said: "Be quick," and stood there, without a tremor, awaiting his reward. A signal, the floor gaped, and at the end of the rope a great body hung, oscillated a moment and was still.

But Old Brown had come out of his prison that morning with the prospect of a much longer journey than those few hundred yards to the scaffold. His wife was waiting for him at Harper's Ferry. Fifteen men escorted his remains, which were not unpunctual at the rendezvous. And then the pine coffin set out, accompanied by the widow and a few friends. In the towns where the train stopped, the crowds surged about the station, the bells rang, the reception committees stepped forward, a guard of honour watched the corpse all night in the court-house. The body of the condemned man seemed to be armed with an even more formidable strength than that of the Old Man when his head had had a price on it out there in Kansas. At last there remained only twenty-five miles to be covered, feet foremost, by the Old Man who had so often travelled them with his great peasant strides. And then he was at home, after his five days' pilgrimage, at the family farm, under a great rock opposite White Face Mountain, and very calm as the hymns that he had loved, sung about the grave by the blacks of the neighbourhood, faded away in the silence of the mountains.

Since December 2nd, Henry had been haunted by the feeling that his friend was the only living man in New England. The others did not need to have a rope passed round their necks in order to die; they did not exist. In a number of towns, to celebrate this living man, they fired a salute of a hundred shots at the hour when he at last received his full reward—towns where enormous crowds gathered in the church to pray in memory of him. Concord was a village, but Henry had been chosen by a few people to request the Selectmen to allow the parish bell to be rung at the hour of the execution. Did not Concord owe this attention to John Brown, who had twice been a visitor there? But the authorities refused for fear of compromising themselves; these people were among those million slaves who carried Virginia into the very heart of Massachusetts. So they met in the afternoon at the Town Hall, among themselves, Waldo, Alcott, William, Sanborn and those of the Concordians who were not dead, in solemn commemoration of the condemned man who had already judged his judges. Some words were spoken by Henry and Waldo, and they all sang a funeral hymn. After the ceremony, William and Henry vanished into the fields, their minds full of a figure that would go so well in a triptych, as Henry sometimes thought, between those of ruddy Walt in Brooklyn and Joe the Indian.

That same evening, on his return, Henry found his good friend Sanborn waiting at the house with a word for him: "To-morrow morning, Emerson's covered wagon and mare will be hitched up at sunrise. Will you call for it, pick up a traveller at my door, take him to the station at South Acton and put him on the first train for Canada? He is a friend, but he's a queer chap. Pay no attention to what he says to you." Henry did not inquire further. It froze hard that night, but at the hour mentioned he was at Sanborn's with the rig, and was soon on his way with the queer fellow, who was quite a young lad. He had put him on the back seat of the wagon as a precaution. Starting so early, the poor fellow had not had time to brush his teeth, and this made him feel ill. In short, this brother seemed to be a little cracked. He rambled on in a steady stream. He absolutely insisted that his driver was Mr. Emerson; and on the way he suddenly flung himself out of the wagon insisting that he was going back to Concord. Henry, who was bent upon carrying out his mission, was obliged to place his hand on his shoulder and force him, with the little arts one uses with a man who is not in his right mind, to get back into the wagon. Hastening the mare, they at last reached the station, which was only three or four miles away. There was scarcely anyone about, the train arrived and the traveller started off. Then Henry returned the wagon and the mare to the stable, and before going home for breakfast stopped at his friend's house to tell him that everything had gone well. There was no need for either of them to know more. If someone asked you to do a friendly service and you were employed in the system of the Underground Railroad, what difference did it make to you to know whether you had taken to the station on a December morning someone who had escaped in a raid with a price on his head or a mere traveller who thought you were Mr. Emerson? Henry said nothing whatever at home about his early morning drive, and everything passed quietly, as it should. There would be plenty of time to tell about these things some day.

Three months later, his friend Sanborn himself was obliged to decamp to Canada. Summoned to appear before the committee of the Senate charged with investigating the great conspiracy, he had not presented himself and was threatened with arrest as a defaulting witness. As he refused to testify, there was nothing for him to do but to disappear. After a short absence he returned, and one fine day in April a police-sergeant with five men came out from Boston to arrest him at his house in Concord. The fire-alarm rang and the village was instantly up in arms; they were not going to allow Sanborn to be kidnapped. The helpless sergeant and his men were obliged to leave their prisoner in the custody of a guard of citizens. Another good mark for Concord.

The following day, he appeared before the court in Boston. The friends were there, ready for anything, to save Frank Sanborn if the case went against him. And look over there, by the door, at that big bearded fellow with a greenish coat: what a florid complexion he has, and how attentively he is following the discussion! In the name of all the gods, it's Walt! Happening to be in Boston, to see through the press the third edition of his *Leaves*, which Thayer and Eldridge are going to bring out (these Boston guys are beginning to swallow the satyr whole), he has turned up to give his comrades a strong hand if there is any need for it. But there is no occasion to intervene, for the court declares the arrest of Sanborn illegal, and he returns home in triumph. It was through his friend Sanborn, who had once been introduced to Henry by Waldo and who kept a little school in the village, as Henry himself had done at twenty, that the latter had met Old Brown at the time of his first visit to Concord. But all the "confederates" in the plot, or those at least who were accused of having aided it, were not of the same stripe as Sanborn. Seized with panic, some of them had placed the frontier between themselves and their responsibility, real or supposed. There was even one of them, an old friend of John Brown, whose constitution had been so little able to endure the uproar of the raid and the fear of being compromised that he had had to be shut up as a lunatic.

And a year and a half after the raid—scarcely ten months after the commemoration of the Fourth of

July at North Elba, before the rock under which the tough carcass of the Old Man rested in the solitude of the Adirondacks (Henry, who was invited, was unable to go, but he had sent a few pages that were read)—the same Governor of Virginia who had come to see the traitor and conspirator lying, a prisoner, on his mattress at the Arsenal seized the same Arsenal himself, and the next day, April 10th, 1861, the decree of Secession was voted. War was on. The troops of Massachusetts, defiling through the streets of Boston, sang the song of John Brown, the song of the soldiers. The dead of Antietam were strewn over the earth on the outskirts of the town which the Old Man had entered with his eighteen companions, armed with pikes.

It was war, and thousands of young fellows were going to kill one another for . . . for . . . for . . . You, Walt, you know what it's all about, don't you? . . . And you, Henry? . . . Mark you, this is no war of conquest: it is civil war, holy war.

IX

Early in the month it was delightfully warm: one saw the little yellow butterflies fluttering about, encouraged by this smiling Indian Summer. And then it turned cold after the middle of November; it was necessary to pull up the last turnips in the garden to save them from the frost. What joyous walks one had during the days when the first crust of ice resisted the sun! But it was December now. The winter was driving down as brutally as a wedge. Over the fields the crows flocked together in vast protesting flocks. A heavy snow covered the countryside. It was a beautiful soft mantle that you trampled down in silence, carrying the feathers on your boots and leaving behind you a long chain of footprints.

Just one year, day for day, after he had taken that young lunatic to the station, Henry had gone out for his walk and stopped for a long time before some old stumps, to count the concentric rings that marked their age. He liked to know how old his friends the trees were, even when they were no more. Was it there he caught his cold, in spite of his overcoat? No one will ever know. That same day, as the day before had been the anniversary of John Brown's death, he was talking about the old man with two fellows who maintained that he had no right to risk his life. But how about Jesus then? Would he have hesitated if he had foreseen Calvary? That is what people always say when a man has made such a simple sacrifice of his life. . . But this evil cough persisted. Henry had certainly made a mistake in paying no attention to his bronchitis and

going off to deliver a promised lecture in the neighbourhood. He was taking some care of himself, but without
any great results. There was nothing to do but to let
the illness wear itself out. He had had bad times before
and pulled through.

Henry had never been a colossus. In his youth he had
had to interrupt his studies at Harvard for a year because
of his health; since then it had been toughened by the
open air of his great farm but it had always been liable
to relapses. A serious attack of bronchitis had kept him
for weeks at home when he was twenty-four. Then, at
the time of the hermitage, he had received a kick from a
horse which stretched him on the earth, and he had felt
the effects of this in his chest for years. His frame had
held out well, however, and whenever he needed to be
repaired, well, the cabinet-maker had plenty of odds and
ends of wood in a corner of his workshop.

Even as an invalid, kept in the house, he was able to
profit by his days and find a good flavour in life. But
now and then, especially at the hour when he ought to
be setting out for his walk, it was all he could do to
resist a flood of black thoughts as he dreamed of the
daily appointments he was missing again. At such
moments as these, sunk in a chair or flattening his nose
against the window, he was a very sad little soul whose
life had been turned into prose and who, in a fit of
depression, could easily understand how, in some circumstances, Tom, Dick or Harry would commit suicide.
When that accursed frame won't go any more, what are
we good for, great gods! He would have liked to pull
down the blinds so that the daylight could not offend
him any more with its sneering remarks and slumber
away the hours waiting for the end like a mortally
wounded animal that has resigned itself. But these
moments quickly passed, for if the daylight defied him,

his guest, the imagination, marched in and defied the daylight in turn; it had plenty of ways of making game of that blockhead. And then he had sometimes undergone those phases when, though he was not actually ill and was even out for adventure, nothing spoke to him in the spectacle that had always had such a powerful attraction for his senses; the dulled body remained cold and refused to touch the offered nourishment. Inspiration deserted him, as if his friend found the lodging decidedly too narrow, as if this frame were too puny for him to hang his pictures there.

As he approached his fortieth year this discord had taken the proportions of a long-standing quarrel. Since the spring of 1855, Henry had been feeling rather limp without knowing exactly why. A great languor spread through him, condemning him to inactivity as he awaited the end of the crisis. Spoiled were the beautiful plans he had cherished for this summer, a new trip to the Maine woods. He was good for nothing but to drag his reluctant carcass along under the elms of the village, like an invalid. The excursion he had determined to attempt, in July, to Cape Cod, had not remedied this strange weakness to any great extent; he had his ups and downs but always the same debility in the end. Autumn wandered by. And then, towards the end of the year, the strength came back to his legs and the spirit returned to the soul of a powerless wretch; perhaps the arrival of the magnificent Oriental books sent by his friend "Cholmley" had something to do with it. So he could go out this winter and not lose all his pleasure. When the first fine days came, Henry could not pretend that he was absolutely fit for a long excursion, but there was no doubt that spring had come back to his limbs as well as to the world, and he was seized with a sudden hunger for the open, for work, for adventures, the more he felt his strength returning—excursions, visits, the trip to New York, with those two hours spent in Brooklyn face to face with that mass of ruddy health. And this continued the following summer, when he went off to revisit the beaches of the Cape and Upper Maine; didn't he have to give himself a thorough cleansing for those seasons when he had been shut up? His fortieth year had just struck. And this year can give a good sound if the bell is not cracked. Yes, even if one's oldest friendship is broken, like a branch that has had to bear too much snow.

You too no doubt have gone off on these adventurous excursions, when you were young, set out for discovery and slept out of doors with one, two, three companions. But the cooling of the years has relaxed your ardour, and the comrades of yesterday are too busy to fritter away their precious time; you only make journeys now by your own fireside, or by train, very comfortably, and you put up at the best hotel with your wife. You have become sedate and sober, sparing of your legs and your enthusiasm. Your beautiful youth has been left behind you, loitering in some glade. But this fellow has too generous a heart to leave such a charming companion on the road; he still wants to go off on a jaunt with him, even if he himself is past forty. This is just the age when his presence is most dear. So he carries him off for a fortnight, in July, 1858, to the White Mountains in New Hampshire, which he has not seen since the famous week when he went off boating with his brother.

But to tell the truth, this was not at all the same story. The suggestion of the journey came from Edward Hoar, the companion of his last expedition to Maine; and with his friend Edward he had to travel in a hired wagon like a pasha, stop at inns where he was devoured by flies and put up at tiresome hotels, crowded with people he would much rather not have seen. The real moment came when, leaving the wagon behind, they set out with their knapsacks on their backs to explore a wild ravine on Mount Washington. But then, in leaping over the rocks, Henry sprained his ankle and was obliged to rest for several days under the tent in the bottom of the ravine before he was able to take the trail again. On returning from this expedition, the companions who had joined them and who had worn their good clothes looked as ragged as runaway thieves while Henry, who had set out with old clothes suitable for the road and the season, looked almost dressed up beside them; and yet it was he, prudent soul, who provided the needle and thread to repair their rips. He had more liberty and pleasure on his excursion with William, the following summer, to Monadnoc. Not that William was always charmed with his old crony who upbraided him when William, tired to death, felt his head buzzing and wanted to stop. So much the worse for him: he should have known what to expect when he started out for discovery with the intrepid Henry. You don't go to Monadnoc to have the fidgets. But they had camped five nights on the summit under a fragrant shelter of spruce branches; Henry had brought his hatchet with him. Then the whole world vanished out of their minds, including the hotels with their orchestras and dancing. They were alone with the mountain, which did not offer the same welcome to strangers as to intimates. William could growl as much as he pleased because he did not have all his precious comforts, but Henry was rich enough in enthusiasm to sow the whole mountain-top with it.

Scarcely had the son regained his old strength when another invalid took his place in a chair at home; it was the father's turn not to feel quite himself. Past seventy now, he had begun to cough, like his own father, and he fell into a rapid decline, so rapid that since the middle of the winter of 1859 there remained no great hope of saving this good father Thoreau who, in spite of all, after the bad luck that had pursued him at the outset, had succeeded with his pencils in sketching for his family a kind of existence that was not too unprosperous. With this excellent father, who was so self-effacing and who read his newspaper so devotedly and did not contain an ounce of anything that remotely resembled pride and revolt, his boy may never have had very much in common so far as aspirations were concerned, but he loved him dearly. And now, seeing him old and ill and more silent than ever, less and less able to attend to his business and his garden, he could not do enough for him. His mother was touched by this; well as she knew the fund of tenderness that was buried in the heart of her son—deep enough down to be protected from the frost— she was continually surprised to see him expressing it to the old man with all the little shades she would have thought peculiarly feminine. Then, at the beginning of February, fully conscious, after saying good-bye to his family (he had only been in bed for a week, and on Sunday he had been up again for a little while), as modestly as he had lived the little man quietly went out—as a candle of good wax bids you farewell, after shining for its hour, with no glitter that fatigues the eyes, leaving behind it only a fragment of sunken wick. So the circle in the little house, where once there had been half a dozen, was now reduced to a mother of seventy-two, who had also had her troubles, and her son and daughter—for the aunts did not live under the same roof.

Since the last months of his father's illness, the weight of the business that kept the family alive had fallen on

Henry. He assumed it without any discussion, since from now on they had only one man in the family to count upon. An annual income of $1200 to $1500 was not to be found in a blackbird's nest. Sophia, his sister, took charge of the book-keeping and the correspondence, but he had the work of overseeing the mill at Acton, where Warren Miles did the grinding for the Thoreau concern, together with the packing and boxing in the workshop adjoining the house. The plumbago was ground so fine at the mill that, in spite of every care, it leaked from the workshop into the house, where they breathed it in every room; you might not have noticed it perhaps, but your lungs, like a miller's, had to get used to it and put up with it. Perhaps too the manual labour amounted to less than it had been in the days of the pencil-making, but Henry had to devote himself to the routine of the business and be on hand. And so during the whole year when his father died he was scarcely able to go out; to steal a moment, to escape and go huckleberrying was a rare victory. And this caused him even more suffering than the plumbago caused his lungs. With his always absorbing personal occupations, the tasks in the workshop composed a very full existence. Never had the days appeared so short, so precious. His friends must not insist upon his writing to them often.

So Henry carried into the new year this infernal cough that would not hear of the desires of a rambler who wanted to breathe the fragrance of winter in his own haunts, on the Cliffs skirting the meadows where the flocks of crows were lighting. But why worry? With the fine days all the good things would return. His spirits remained, shut up as he was, his spirits and his taste for a good, solid book that warmed his heart. There was nothing to do, in his confinement, but to recall, by noting it in his Journal, with what skill, what astounding celerity, the squirrel attacks a pine-cone, crunching the seeds, holding it between his paws upside down, turning it over like a top as he tears off the scales where they are soft and nibbles at their base: the vivid recollection was enough for one who kept coughing to make him feel once more that he had the soul of a wood-sprite.

The winter came quickly to a close. The prisoner profited by every afternoon when the air was less harsh to make an expedition to the post-office, Great was his desire to go and tell his friends and acquaintances in the swamps that a cheerful soul who was doing penance for sins of which he was unaware had not forgotten them, in spite of appearances, and was only waiting for the sky to brighten to resume his walks. At the end of February the bluebirds were already spreading the good news along the roads. He had heard them, one fine day, on his way to old Minot's who was now quite alone with his eighty years in the little house on the hillside, for his old companion, his sister Mary, had just died of pneumonia. But Henry could not walk far without having to sit down on the first stump he came to. He had difficulty now in keeping warm. At the end of March the snow fell in such abundance that the trains could not run any more; and it had driven so since yesterday that this morning one side of the houses was covered with a white mattress that choked the windows; the people were almost prisoners behind their own doors. Just the time, when he couldn't think of stepping outside, to finish that letter to Ricketson he had begun: let his thought at least escape to New Bedford and the fishing-boats, since it was utterly impossible for him to put on his best pair of boots and go and spend a Sunday with his friends. The other day,

Blake, with a companion, arrived in Concord, where they spent the night; they had walked from Worcester and went back the same way, the lucky devils. . .

William dropped in to see the prisoner and would have liked so much to be able to pull him through this tight place. Since his strength was not coming back, in spite of all the little strolls they took together, stopping constantly (it was no longer the intrepid Henry who dragged William on), why not try a change of air, a long journey? William had lived in the West and extolled its tonic quality; this would be a thousand times better than the climate of the West Indies which the doctor recommended. They could set out together for two or three months. You'll see, Henry, what a gay blade you will be when you come back.

Henry agreed, not that he had any particular desire for such a grand tour as that, but because he had a very particular desire to be a man again, to lose that perpetual cough, lose it far, far away, so that it would never find its way back. Let's go. Then, at the last moment—from caprice or lack of money—William changed his mind; and Henry, who now wanted to go, had to find another travelling companion. A son of Horace Mann, who was also called Horace Mann and had dedicated himself to the natural sciences, offered to join him. He was a very sober young fellow and not much of a talker; he didn't have a particle of that liveliness of William's which would have been such a great resource in stirring up a tottering companion.

The itinerary was drawn up and the date of departure fixed for the middle of May. They were going to make several stops *en route*, for the veteran walker no longer felt that he had the strength to accomplish in one stage such a journey as this to Saint Paul in Minnesota, the land of wheat. The two travellers set out, reached

Niagara, the first stage, then Detroit, Chicago, and finally East Dubuque on the Mississippi, which they ascended by boat for two days between the high bluffs of the river to Saint Paul, where they found one of the Thatcher cousins from Bangor. This was the main stopping-place. They stayed there three weeks, in the course of which Henry went on an expedition with a naturalist he had met; he made a new acquaintance, the prairie squirrel, an odd little customer with his cope of six light and dark stripes, feet like a marmot's and an air that was anything but shy, sitting bolt upright before his burrow. Then they embarked on the Mississippi as far as Redwood, where there was a Sioux Agency; there were also said to be buffalo in these regions, but they failed to catch a glimpse of one. It was the annual pay-day, and the Indians had come in on their ponies; they offered the travellers a performance of dancing and music and feasted on an ox. Not bad; but all this was a little stagey and not worth an hour of Joe Polis's company. On the return, a stop of a few days at Red Wing on the Mississippi; Henry wrote "Concord" on the envelopes instead of decorating his letter-paper with these two dear syllables. The ray no longer shone from the centre; no, the ray turned back towards the centre. And then, by railroad or boat, Prairie du Chien, Milwaukee, Mackinaw, with another stop. It was July, but it was rather cold, and a man who had become shivery appreciated the chimney-corner in the hotel. At last Toronto, the long sail across blue Ontario, the Thousand Islands, the Saint Lawrence and, stop of stops, old Concord at the end of the long, long railroad. Henry was tired.

It was very fine, assuredly, the Mississippi, the prairie, and all those images he had seen filing past. All the same, he had taken few notes on the way, and they were dry and often very trivial; the points of interest were dispersed over such a vast distance and unrolled so quickly that he had hardly had the time to absorb them. And then his senses no longer took hold of things. This journey had nothing in common with the other beautiful journeys, when he had carried his belongings in a handkerchief tied by the four corners; there was the wearisomeness of the hotels and the cars, not to speak of those vile medicines the invalid had taken along in his bag. Henry's hope in this air-cure had not been great when he started; and in fact, he would have covered his two thousand miles and spent his hundred and fifty dollars for nothing if he had not had the joy of seeing at last with his own eyes the aboriginal crab-apple, that tree which refuses to be grafted, with its terribly acid fruit, of which he had often dreamed and which was no longer a myth now that he had touched its branches with his hands and brought back a flower in his herbarium.

The sad thing was that he had also brought back his cough and his weakness. The change of air, the movement, the distraction had roused him a little, invigorated him in appearance, but at bottom it was still the same story: Helplessness and Co. He was thinner than ever, he who had so little flesh to lose, and remained incapable of resuming his occupations. For a long time he had not been able to walk like a real walker, dig with any vigour in his garden, manage a boat on the river or even write to any effect, till health seemed to him a human attribute that was visible only in dreams.

But he still wanted to make the most of the summer and go and see that good Ricketson. Five days stolen from the wretchedness of his monotonous existence, five good days of intimacy, sea air and relived memories were a conquest for a weak man who scarcely had the strength to go to the post-office any longer. His friend took him out driving and carried him to a photographer in New Bedford, who turned his camera on a full-bearded Henry, just back from Minnesota, with a rather wandering eye. Then Ricketson returned his visit, spent three days at Concord, where they even went bathing together once in Walden, the water of which ought to have paid off an old debt of gratitude and friendship by delivering from his cough the unfortunate fellow who had so often placed on its banks the figure of a lean but infernally tough young man.

At Minneapolis Henry had seen some volunteers drilling and a detachment of others leaving for the front. For war, the call to arms was rising all about the sick man, who remained sufficiently himself, however, to keep clear of the collective madness. Insults to the national flag, the election of Old Abe to the presidency, the whole jingo phraseology was for him nothing but newspaper talk, and he would not have given two cents for a hundred yards of it; he did not read the papers any more willingly, in spite of the upheaval, and the *Tribune* was much less timely in his eyes than a book he was reading at the moment: *Six Years in the Desert of North America*. During the two months of his journey, he had hardly looked at one of those sheets the people were devouring. Abolition, yes, that was his cause; but who knew whether the other interests involved in this war had not brought greater weight to bear upon it than the question of the four million men to be liberated? You admire the regiments that march across Manhattan in their brand-new uniforms—but how about that old ironsides in his seedy trousers and his old slippers whom they strung up on a gibbet? He did not call the newspapers and Old Abe and the uniforms to his aid; he simply made a gift of his own life to the cause, and that was all.

But this was war, nevertheless, that immense, stupid horror from which you couldn't withdraw your mind. How could a sick man get better in this atmosphere of a people who were entirely absorbed in the business of killing one another?

As the struggle grew graver and graver, as the piles of victims rose, the reality of the war penetrated him more and more; even in the village, even for one who despised the newspapers and the bulletins, it floated into the house, like the plumbago powder. After Bull Run and the panic, confusion and stupor, Concord was plunged in the blackest gloom. Henry, who had just come back from Minnesota, seemed full of interest and even enthusiasm. A good defeat, there would be nothing like it for putting these people into their right minds again: all these hare-brained souls who have been assuring you with a smile that it would be over in the turn of a hand, that they would soon see the famous warriors of the North coming back again leading by the nose the little swaggering Southerners. . . How this good drubbing would wake them up!

Then autumn came and this beastly bronchitis had not gone; it seemed to have settled down to live with him and, finding the house to its liking, refused to leave. Henry was unwilling to try the experiment of another climate a second time. And he hadn't the hundredth of an ounce of confidence in medicine and doctors.

The only remedy was to make the most of these last beautiful days. His walks were at an end; every five yards he had to stop. Mr. Hoar, who was away, had placed his horse and carriage at the sick man's disposal, and he made use of them almost every day. September and October were very pleasant, and Henry drove out in the carriage like a man of substance, escorted by Mr. Hoar's dog preceding his friend the horse. These

drives brought back his appetite and a semblance of
strength. He made a trip to the causeway, his old
boulevard; he noticed there the curious hatchings which
the storm of the preceding night had made by whipping
the sand of the road. Often Sophia accompanied him,
and for her he did the honours of some of his favourite
haunts. Together they went and spent an hour at
Walden one inviting September afternoon; while his
sister sat down to make a sketch, Henry very gently
picked some wild grapes that were growing on the edge
of the pond. These wild grapes that he picked and ate,
for the last time perhaps before the great winter buried
everything, were not as sour as one might have supposed. And this little trip of the brother and sister to
Walden, in the ripeness of September, had itself the
taste of grapes.

Soon the cold spread over the earth, and the damp-
ness: it was no longer possible for such a fragile body to
brave the open air. Henry accepted this humiliation
which his body inflicted on him. This body, of which he
had demanded so much, would have no more of it and
turned a deaf ear. It had reached its limit.

Too long had the master expected it to be a thing of
steel and obedient to him, as a sharp plane eats its way
jerkily into a piece of tough wood. He had always
treated it without consideration as a bond-servant that
had to march at his beck and call and be silent. Nothing
was too hard for this unhappy retainer: dragging immense logs out of the river, clambering up trees, remaining for hours buried in the snow or in the mud of a
swamp, climbing the steepest mountain-sides without
resting, sleeping out of doors in the thinnest of clothes,
enduring hunger without relaxing its muscular effort,
leaving behind it all the walkers, climbers, skaters and
surveyors in Christendom. It even seemed as if the

master were wreaking his spite on it a little, as if the
overseer took a perverse pleasure in overstraining the
strength of his negro, without tolerating the slightest
complaint from him. He had trained him to make up
for the massive strength that his narrow frame rendered
impossible by an incomparable dexterity, by the strength
beyond strength that says "I will" and does it. The
drudge had never demurred: at most, on two or three
occasions, it had stopped for breath in spite of all gee-ups
and blows of the whip, like a cart-horse that comes to a
halt, determined not to take another step. But then its
whim would pass and the animal would set off again,
resigned to its tasks like the submissive old servant that
it was. Sometimes, as you saw it working itself to
death, you were stirred to an immense feeling of pity for
its lot. But who could make a tyrant like that listen to
reason!

Now at last the body no longer wearied with re-
proaches the master who had persecuted it with his
demands. It was foundering, it was leaving him, without a complaint, without any bitterness at having had
so few holidays. You must get yourself out of your fix
as best you can, master, and good luck to you. It was
going away very quietly, young in years but spent with
fatigue, to the bourne of workers that can work no
more. And as it went, with little breathless steps, it
was going to pay the toll-gatherer a debt of its master.
John and Helen had paid it very early, that sum owed
by the line of Thoreaus in America, though the father,
never very brilliant in his business, had not settled it
till seventy years had passed. Sometimes Henry had
felt so happy that he had wondered if some day the
debt would not have to be settled for good and all.
Well, pay it, my servant, since the debt is due, and make
an end of it.

What is the use of complaining when an old servant leaves you, even if you are unable to replace him? Henry did not lament over his failing body. As he had endured without frowning the sunlight that had roasted his bare arms and the cold that had nibbled his fingers and toes, why not endure this lethargy with the same equanimity? You never heard him speak of what he had parted from and left down there without news of himself, his friends the trees, the ponds, the little coves of the river, his boat. All these things lay as if in a corner, wrapped up in the silk of a great reserve. The invalid slept now on the ground floor, in the parlour opening on Main Street; through the open door he could see in a corner of the dining-room the garden of green plants that Sophia lovingly cared for. His good friends would drop in for a little chat and bring him the scents of the out-of-doors. Sometimes they read a deep sadness in his emaciated features, for a child-man who had gone out every day could not help feeling a little dismal to be lolling here in a chair while others were taking part in the play. His shoulders drooped more and more, as if they were melting, his lean body wasted away, his bony nose shrank, there was a little vagueness in the big eyes. But Sanborn dropped in, or William, or Alcott, and they gossiped as gaily as in old times— better than ever now that gossiping had become the sole form of activity and companionship that was permitted him. An invalid does not speak of his illness, since it is understood. One doesn't keep repeating what is plain enough; when it rains all day, are you one of those people who are perpetually saying that the weather is beastly? Just once, standing by the window, he said to William: " I cannot see on the outside at all. We thought ourselves great philosophers in those wet days when he used to go and sit down by the wall-sides."

344

And as William, who had lost his walking companion, was down in the dumps, the prisoner continued: "It is better some things should end." One didn't feel grief in Henry's company. One left him with the impression that life goes on and that a man can easily attach an exaggerated importance to his own disappearance.

And isn't existence still beautiful when you can read, write, dream? Once Henry would have thought that if he had been deprived of his life in the open it would not have been life any longer. What a mistake! See how well you can get along without your body. Another discovery. Go and take your holiday, my body, if you can't hold out any longer; I shall go on my way alone. The mind can get along perfectly well without its servant.

Henry made haste to place some of his papers in order and put one or two of his projects on foot; he worked on his manuscripts whenever his strength permitted him to do so. This was the heart of his life now, since he could no longer cling to branches to reach a mountain-top. He had not learned to indulge himself; on the contrary, he was harder than ever on himself and more punctilious. You have to dust every corner with the greatest care when you don't know what great person-age you are going to receive. Three years before the *Atlantic Monthly* had published one of his essays and mutilated it, and the author had instantly demanded the rest of his manuscript back again, for he was unwilling to leave it in the hands of such vandals. Now the review, under a new editor, asked him to contribute again. He could give them such pieces as *Walking* and *Wild Apples*, in which he had put as much of himself as words were able to contain. It was on these especially that he was working. He also wanted to complete his pages on the Maine Woods, of which the two first parts had already been published, so that they might form a whole. If he could only leave behind him something besides fragments, apart from those two still-born books. . . These were great plans for a man whose strength was ebbing, but the will to carry them out as well as he could gave a singular value to the rather insipid scrap of life that was melting in his mouth like a gumdrop.

In the warmth of the rooms, sitting in his rocking-chair, the prisoner dreamed—for his mind in the breakdown of his body remained quite clear—dreamed, as he watched the cat playing or the plants in the dining-room that accepted their imprisonment with all that greenness. He dreamed of many things, things behind and things before him. Regrets, old Henry, under that calm surface? Why? When forty years of a full life have left you with this pleasant taste. . . What better taste could life leave in the mouth of one who is about to quit it? The taste of a shop, of cosmetics, of rare roast beef, of incense, of loving lips, of rum, of medicine, of an old book, of a mother's tenderness? For him, as he thought it over, it had the taste of huckleberries. Regrets would have been inconsistent with this feeling that he had spent his existence well. To have preserved the brightness of that marvellous gift. Not to have allowed it to tarnish. Not to have let it grow mouldy. Not to have spoilt it. To have remained an artist who, behind his varied occupations, behind his apparent idleness, behind his very savagery, had firmly practised an art, trained himself in it, perfected it unceasingly. Was not that worth the sacrifice of some of the little things to which men seem to cling so desperately? One cannot have everything, and as he reckoned it all up he did not repent his choice. He saw especially what advantages he had had. Certainly they were very appreciable.

For inftance, in remaining a bachelor, had he not escaped the drudgery that usually falls to newly-married couples in the country? He had not been a hog-reeve, charged by the town with running after wandering pigs that go about grubbing in the fields of honeft farmers. But during this time he had been able to run after a good many other animals. . . .

Henry weighs the results of an experiment that is finished and finds them of fterling quality. See, you can turn them over in your hand; there is nothing unsubftantial about them. To have remained poor. To have left to others who care for such things the burden of possessions in order to savour the free pleasure of the world. Never to have been tempted to sacrifice for a little ease the moft succulent part of life, like those who reach their end without knowing that they have lived. Yes, to have been this fool who is handling now the returns of wisdom: how does the reckoning ftrike you? And not to be any the prouder because of it. Not even to offer yourself as an example for other people's children. To have succeeded in not being for a moment one of the people who count. Not even a failure. Absolutely nothing at all, at the age of forty-five. No more a man of letters than a shopkeeper. Simply H. D. T. A man whose sole desire has been to live, who has looked forward to nothing but the satisfaction of being alive. To have dared to live againft the grain of one's whole merchant line and to find oneself at the end so comfortable. In short, *to have succeeded in one's business*, and with such a tiny capital. . . Isn't that luck, isn't it almoft fantaftic? Is it not as if, from the paradise of merchants above, the sailor of Saint-Helier who made his money in a shop on Long Wharf were sending you his grand-paternal congratulations? (We accept them, grandfather, you who are recalled to the memory of your descendants in this germ you have left them with your blood.) There are some people who have no right to die, because they have never lived; but Henry fancies that he deserves it, really deserves this reward and this proof.

In a box within reach of the hand of the dreamer, a box that he had carpentered himself, the silent notebooks confirm him. There they are, thirty or forty irrefutable witnesses. Whoever wishes to question them will hear convincing words.

They contain the biography of a man. Through the jungle of their thousands and thousands of pages, paths wander in every direction leading towards other perspectives than a pond where you look at yourself. They enclose all the wildness of the brush, the swamps, meadows, running waters that a Saunterer can trace again and again without coming to the end of them— with vistas over the sea and over the hills and beyond. From the country of the Rising Sun to the country of the Setting Sun the whole space is filled with surprises that will invite him to pause. He will find there fruits to refresh him on the way—inspirations at many a turning of the path—guide-posts leading him to precious discoveries—if only the discovery of himself. And as he walks along he will stoop down from time to time to pick up an arrow-head, dropped there as if on purpose; he will soon have a whole pile of flint-flakes in a corner of his attic. This jungle is a present which the mysterious Henry in his turn wishes to make, a surprise for his own kindred. Of all he has received he has kept nothing back. It was given him in trust, it seems. Henry has never believed in private property; if he has seemed to be collecting and treasuring things during his lifetime, it has always been with this legacy in view, always to enrich the common good.

Especially he owes something to his own parish. To this little town with its church-tower which has regarded him as a ne'er-do-well he will show how generous he can be. It is a beautiful thing, a church-tower, so beautiful that it hides the universe from many of the village folk who creep confusedly in its shadow. It would never occur to them to use it as an antenna, set up there to catch communications from the larger world. A church-tower is a beautiful tower that does not merely sound at church-time. The tower has a soul that speaks in its own language to the souls of men and sings because it is beautiful to be a tower ſtirred by the messenger winds. When this Concord with its woods and waters and dewy fields grouped about the tower vibrates and dances with joy at the great news come from below the horizon and falling from the tower, the spirit of the tower becomes the maſter-spirit of time and space. The bell sounds for the world; it has a sound that is caught from afar. Yes, the bell of the parish ought to be of a rare metal when, in these note-books here, its vibration extends to the remoteſt village where men dream in the shadow of their own church-towers: it is as if it were the voice of their own wonder, their own revolt and their own love of life. . . .

The dreamer does not weigh very much as he sits there in his rocking-chair. But all this is so evident, so plain, so full of comfort that even if he is torn by this cough he can rock very happily in his chair and regard himself with a certain detachment in his decay as if he were contemplating a tree that has been ſtripped of its leaves or as if he were someone else than himself.

So the winter flows by for a man whose voice is dying, is nothing now but a murmur (those rolling r's of old are only a memory now). To finish the year he has had pleurisy, and he has scarcely been out since November.

Even the post-office has faded away in the withdrawal of the old world. What remains of Henry is buried in his manuscripts. The spirit is bent upon proving that, without this miserable servant who has given it the slip, it can carry on just the same, for a man who has been dogged so long does not so easily give up his old delight in contradiction. As for living at this slackened pace, it is, truth to tell, hardly worth the trouble; his only regret is for those two women, for whom his departure is perhaps going to make things rather difficult. But aside from this, it doesn't mean the end of the world because a fellow named Henry is going away. You might as well tell us that the lilacs and the bluebirds are not coming back with the spring. Rubbish! . . . See, there it is already. That comrade is quite capable of getting along without an invalid who once would have run to meet it, hailing it joyously from afar even before he had seen it. And then, for a man who is stealing away at forty-five with his fortune made, what a good thing it is to be thus escaping extreme old age, when you grow fat if you don't ridiculously shrivel. Say what you like, Henry has surely been a lucky dog all along the line.

From behind the parlour window that comprises his universe, he sees the children passing on their way to school. Many of them are comrades who have indefeasible rights over the heart of their old friend. When they do not come in to greet him as they pass, he complains that they are not exercising these rights, a custom that is so sweet to him. Since he cannot go huckleberrying with them any more, they should come and tell their old friend what they are thinking of him in the outskirts of Concord, among the little people whose habits the children know. It is well known, however, that behind this window lies a prisoner whose soul is hungry for this love that is silent because it prefers to remain anonymous. It is known, for people stop in to see him whose charitable words, alas, are so far from being as precious as the simple presence of three little scraps just out of school. To-day it is the Rev. Mr. Reynolds, a neighbour, who is astonished to find a sick man working so assiduously. "You know," Henry explains, "it's respectable to leave an estate to one's friends." The following day it is that blockhead who thinks it is his duty to say to you by way of consolation: "Well, Mr. Thoreau, we must all go." To him this departing soul replies: "When I was a very little boy, I learned that I must die. . . So of course I am not disappointed now. Death is as near to you as it is to me." Or it is Sam, the old innkeeper, still jailor and tax-collector, and on his way to becoming one of the bigwigs of Concord, who does not find him greatly changed since the night when he had him as a boarder; he is as cool as ever and almost contemptuous in his calm strength. This time it is not the poll-tax the collector has come for but the ground-tax, and to-day he will not meet with a "no." The tax-payer knows perfectly well what he owes, he has made his provisions. He has even jotted down on a paper the names of friends to whom he wishes to have one of his books or some knick-knack given in memory of their mad Henry. To William, the Chronicles of Froissart, to Eddy, Waldo's son, his microscope, and the shells to his sister Edith. Good Aunt Louisa will receive the sum of $50, which will please her. There will still be enough for the other gifts. It is as if the purse of a poor dying man had a double bottom. In the street an organ begins to grind out an old air that suddenly calls up the fragrance of his childhood, like a bouquet that has been placed suddenly under his nose. His illness has not obliterated Henry's sense of smell. What neither suffering nor a breach of faith nor a misunderstanding has ever been able to do this hackneyed air ground out by a street-organ accomplishes in an instant. He is torn asunder. All the old repressed tenderness, compelled to remain rigid for so long, makes wild leaps in his heart that has such a short time to beat, throws itself against the bars of its cage, tries to escape, poor thing, get out into the free air, before it is extinguished. Tears bead these eyes that have so rarely wept, save under the lash of the winter wind. "Give him some money! Give him some money!"

In a room where once it would have seemed pure madness to think of living permanently, a prisoner ends by discovering between four walls interests enough to create a very good imitation of existence. Insomnia is a nuisance, but he prefers it to the drugs that would have brought him sleep. When he slips off, his slumber is engarlanded with fantastic dreams, as if the doors of an unknown world were opening to enchant him, in compensation for all he has had to leave. When he was in good health, he had often enough had dreams at night, very strange ones, but now they load him with favours, lavish attentions upon him, as if they could not devise enough ways of amusing a prisoner. Kindly sleep hangs in curious festoons about the bed of a sick man who has at last dozed off. Now it is in his lungs that the railroad labourers are digging a trench, placing the ties and the rails; the train is going to pass; look out, you man down there, following the track on foot; don't be afraid to flatten yourself against the bank. It is Henry's lung; you can observe its curious little caverns and, if you keep a Journal, note them down. The prisoner tells his dreams to the people who come to see him, and that is one pleasure more. They remind him of a dream he used to have as a boy in which at one moment he was rebounding from a surface as hard as rock which hurt him frightfully and at the next was lying cosily in a feather bed.

Good dreams, coming so graciously to visit a condemned man, good dreams not coming with moral counsels but simply in friendship, with beautiful images for one who has dreamed so often wide-awake, coming when he is there all alone with his courage and his helplessness before the certain issue. To receive them more handsomely in his prosaic room, he asks Sophia to arrange the furniture in such a way that in the light of the night-lamp the shadows seen from his bed will create on the wall a kind of phantasmagoria. He would like to conform to the laws of this strange world which is so comforting to the sick; he wishes that his bed were in the form of a shell at the bottom of which he could roll himself up like a voluta, roll himself tighter, much tighter than a tired spaniel who curls up before the fire after a long winter's day of hunting. How much more pleasant to touch than the sheets would be a sheath of mother-of-pearl!

The daylight, far from interrupting the phantasmagoria, merely transforms it. Spring has come back, and as Henry can no longer go out for the first flowers their fragrance comes to him. Just now some cultivated flowers are addressing him in the name of the whole floral circle. They are the offering of the gardens of Concord to a gardener who cannot wield the spade. It is not merely his intimate friends who stop in and bring them; village people whom Henry does not know at all send him bouquets, sweetmeats and even game, which might tempt a man who hasn't much of an appetite. People whom, when he was well, he would have dumped into the same sack and powdered with the salt of his sarcasms return the sarcasms in advance changed into

flowers and delicacies. Henry is stirred as he had been
by the organ-grinder's tune. Isn't this bunch of hya-
cinths an almost terrible pleasure for a man who is so
soon to disappear and finds so many friends who cannot
be kind enough to him? One reason more for going; it
is a simple matter of decency. "I should be ashamed to
stay in this world after so much has been done to me. . ."
is the simple utterance of a stricken heart which even
now would bolt all its locks if certain sacred words that
are forbidden were pronounced before it. And there are
all the things of which he knows nothing. . . Can he
guess that in Michigan a workman who does not know
him at all except through his writings is making a beautiful walking-stick for him out of a rare wood, with a
silver head and an inscription, and that another man in
Indiana. . . But no, enough, enough; this would send
him under the earth at once. A wave of indulgence has
spread into the room with the spring and the flowers.
He must pardon a dear aunt who does not understand
the language of flowers when she asks him, with a very
confidential air that is full of responsibility, if he has
made his peace with God, and reply that this is impossible, dear aunt, since he has never quarreled with that
illustrious personage of antiquity. He must pardon
even that pious soul who speaks to him of another
world as familiarly as if he had been there, replying
mildly: "My friend, one world at a time . . ." He
who is about to dive into the black pond thinks rather
of the loon that dived in Walden, and like the latter he
has a mind to fling a mighty laugh of defiance into the
face of this honest soul.

From time to time Sophia writes a letter to his friends
at her brother's dictation, and she reads to him the
letters that arrive—from unknown persons sometimes.
He must not leave unanswered the letter from that

HENRY THOREAU

young man in Leedsville who has written such charming
things about the *Week on the Concord.* Juſt a word to
thank him and tell him that he is getting along well
enough, even if he has only a few months before him.
When he does not feel too feeble, Henry continues to
read, jots down a few notes, brushes up his manuscripts.
The illness that consumes him progresses ſteadily,
though he keeps his old calm. The explorer of Upper
Maine was never cooler on the rapids when he was
ſteering Joe's canoe. The eye and the hand have not
abandoned the direction on the current that is bearing
him on at this moment; if he capsizes, it will be because
the river is obſtructed by a whirlpool from one bank to
the other. Moſt of the time he is silent, like a good
pilot who does not wish to have his attention distracted.
But there is nothing morose in this silence; it is a sort of
self-communion, and so natural. His voice has become
so feeble, so feeble, that it cannot express very much.
And his mournful whisper might even becloud the end
of such a beautiful day.

Since seven o'clock in the morning, this Tuesday, the
sixth of May, 1862, a dying man has been turning and
turning, as if to free himself. . . Tender hands have
had to lift him on his pillow. . . One laſt time, juſt
after eight o'clock, an old mother, a siſter, a good aunt,
gathered about the little cot, raise the narrow frame of a
man who makes a sign for them to lift him ſtill higher,
upright, supporting with the pillows his laſt more and
more feeble breaths . . . liſtening, as they bend over, to
the vague murmur of words in which pass " moose ". . .
" Indian " . . . and the Wanderer is at the end of his
journey. Or perhaps he has departed for some faraway
hunt in the footſteps of the Indian, in the Happy Hunting Ground. . .

355

Three days later, a coffin passes, covered with wild May flowers, on the way to the church. If it contained Henry, it would almoſt have realized his wish to live in one of those tool-cheſts of the Irishmen who worked on the railroad. But it is so light that it can hardly contain the body of a man—unless it is his chrysalis. . . Perhaps on this splendid May morning, another Henry has emerged who has not needed to go out into the air, to raise the lid of the coffin, because he has praċtised so many of the tricks and fathomed the art of metamorphosis. Another Henry than the one who is there, as they say, under the flowers that his friends have brought —Henry as he was ten years ago, but quite new, though he wears his old corduroy trousers.

For one chap who knows him better than all the people in the procession has seen him, mingling with those who are looking on, seen him chuckling because they are carrying this body to the church. (Though, after all, if it gives them pleasure . . . it is all the same thing to a chrysalis. Those who once had the beſt of Henry by paying the tax for him can have the beſt of him ſtill. And besides, Waldo, who was a churchman, thinks so much of these things . . .) But why the devil didn't they make the coffin of good, dry driftwood? Isn't a man worth as much as all the sacred books of the Eaſt? Floating in a wooden shell, a vagabond might have gone on voyaging so comfortably. . . The dull souls! Then the same fellow has seen him resuming his grave air as he liſtens to the fine words pronounced over the coffin and filtering through the field flowers ſtrewn over it. And when the coffin finally comes out of the church, he has seen him resolutely follow it, as if it were journeying towards a familiar spot and one where he also wished to go.

About the grave it is not the spring daylight nor the

company nor the sad faces of these women that seem to ſtir this other brand-new Henry. What attracts him is this open earth, exposed by a fellow-digger. This beautiful earth. This good earth. It beckons to him. It surely has something to confide to him.

He wants to lie down in the earth, deep in the earth, so that it may clasp him and whisper in his ear its old secret. This muſt be something aſtonishing.

He is sure now that the earth alone can speak to him the words he has been waiting for. The earth alone can feel the fervour with which he thinks of the beautiful life that might open like this gaping soil—of the great rambles he would take, with a miraculous knapsack on his back, drunk with adventure—of the page that he would write on his return, a page too rich for any magazine to publish it—of the friends from whom no misunderſtanding would ever, ever, separate him any more (friendship, friendship, he would taſte it now, for the husk would be off at laſt!)—of the joy of unbosoming himself fully—and of all the men whom he has loved from afar without ever letting them know and who would know at laſt, at laſt. . . .

How beautiful it would all be! So beautiful that no notebook would ever be able to contain it, so beautiful that he would have to fling himself into this trench and carry it with him like a warm thought under the earth.